CONSIDER THESE OPTIONS . . .

_____

IN LOVE RELATIONSHIPS
- Each of us is responsible for his or her own unhappiness.
- If my lover does not do what I want, that says nothing about his loving me.

_____

IN PARENT–CHILD INTERACTION
- What my child does is not a statement about me.
- I do not cause my child's unhappiness; he does not cause mine.

_____

IN SELF-DISCOVERY
- There are no good or bad beliefs.
- Each of us is our own expert.

_____

TO LOVE IS TO BE HAPPY WITH shows you how to listen to the truth of your own nature for guidance and direction in all areas of your life. And you can do it because all you have to do is choose to do it.

There's no need to wait for happiness. From this page on it's yours whenever *you* want it.

About the Author

Barry Neil Kaufman, born and raised in New York City, teaches a uniquely loving lifestyle and vision called The Option Process®, which has both educational and therapeutic applications. He and his wife Suzi are mentors and teachers for individuals, couples, families and groups at The Option Institute and Fellowship (P.O. Box 1180, Sheffield, MA 01257). They also lecture in universities, hospitals, and have appeared in mass media throughout the country.

As a result of their innovative and successful "Option" program for their once-autistic child, the Kaufmans also counsel and instruct families wanting to create home-based teaching programs for their own special children. They teach professionals in this area as well.

Mr. Kaufman has written eight books, co-authored two screenplays with his wife (winning the coveted Christopher Award twice and also the Humanitas Prize), and has had articles featured in major publications. His first book, *Son-Rise*, which details his family's inspiring journey with their once autistic child was dramatized as an NBC-TV special network presentation.

His subsequent books include *Giant Steps*, which details intimate and uplifting portraits of young people he has worked with and touched during times of extreme crisis. *To Love Is To Be Happy With* shares the specific applications of their nonjudgmental living. *A Miracle to Believe In* recounts the emotional and oftentimes miraculous story of the Kaufmans' helping another family to love a little Mexican boy back to life. *The Book of Wows & Ughs* is a playful collection of sayings and insights. *A Land Beyond Tears*, co-authored with his wife Suzi, presents a liberating approach to death and dying. *A Sense of Warning*, shares life-changing psychic experiences that led the Kaufmans to their current work and teaching.

Barry Kaufman's eighth and latest book, *Happiness Is A Choice*, was published by Fawcett Columbine Hardcover Books in November, 1991. This extraordinary book distills the learnings of Barry's twenty years experience helping tens of thousands of people to achieve happiness into the most inspiring and hopeful statement of his work to date, a blueprint of simple, concrete methods to empower the decision to be happy.

For information on audio and video cassette tapes and books by the Kaufmans as well as program, workshop and lecture information, write: Option Indigo Press, P.O. Box 1180, Sheffield, MA 01257.

TO LOVE IS TO BE HAPPY WITH:

THE FIRST BOOK OF THE OPTION PROCESS

Barry Neil Kaufman

FAWCETT CREST • NEW YORK

Acknowledgments

To Suzi, always to Suzi, who wants to share the attitude as much as I do and who literally lived through each word and sentence of this book, helping me find the most lucid and loving expression of the Option Process.

To Marvin Beck, a loving mentor and fellow Option teacher, whose insights from his practice and from Option explorations with his students enriched the pages of this book. His input, clarity and caring were a gift.

To Jane Rotrosen, Forty Eighth Street's Wonder Woman, who was open yet unwavering, at once playing agent and devil's advocate...she sowed the seeds and planted the flower.

To Patricia Soliman, a very special and knowing person, who listens to the voice within. Her commitment and perceptive commentaries were invaluable.

To those who have made a real difference and who have, each in their own way, become part of this giving: Bryn, Thea, Raun, Nancy-Hands, Steve, Laurie, Judy, Roz, Elise, Jerry, Jeffrey, Laura, Cindy, Vikki, Marie, Harvey, Eileen, Sacha, Robert, Nancy, Rita, Irv, Lanie, Mandy, Sy, Ellen, Jesse, Suzi, Bill O. and...Abraham

And to my anonymous friend.

A Fawcett Crest Book
Published by Ballantine Books
Copyright © 1977 by Barry Neil Kaufman

ISBN 0-449-21119-3

This edition published by arrangement with Coward, McCann & Geoghegan, Inc.

Printed in Canada

First Fawcett Crest Edition: May 1978
First Ballantine Books Edition: February 1983

28 27 26 25 24 23 22 21

CONTENTS

Even in the silence,
before the words—
you knew.

To Suzi,
all light and love.

———————

The
difference
between
a flower
and
a weed
is a judgment.

prologue

These pages do not contain the words of a priest or a doctor, but the thoughts of one man becoming happier. As Option was given to me as a gift of love and I made it mine, absorbing, exploring and changing it, I give these ideas and this process to you. If it becomes yours, you too can pass it on!

This is a very private and personal book, although it might speak to a voice in each and every one of us. The words describe a journey . . . for me, a loving evolution out of the quicksand of unhappy beliefs.

The option process is not so much a tool or formula technique as it is an attitude and a developing process of seeing. There is only one truth, although there are many paths leading to it.

Then why the Option Process and why this book? There have been many renowned and lofty disciplines recorded through the ages. We have, more recently, been generously exposed to the beautiful and wondrous visions from the East. Yet, these avenues often appear foreign and unattainable to us.

Option, in contrast, takes the truths of Christ and Buddha, of Socrates, of Sartre and Kierkegaard, of contemporary psychology and philosophy, and puts them into the language of our everyday tongue. Ironically, there are those who would choose to dismiss it because it is not couched in elaborate jargon or cloaked in mystery. Perhaps, this is its distinctive beauty and virtue. There are others who want to define the Option Process as a therapy or education technique . . . to pin it down, compare, debate and squeeze it into an "acceptable" category. But somehow, Option is more cosmic than the sum of its parts . . . more than just a philosophy, a therapy, a method and a dialogue technique.

It is a vision for living, a powerful and effective alternative, born out of the attitude: *To love is to be happy with* . . . an accepting and loving embrace of ourselves and those around us. It is an evolving awareness that "I *love* you by being *happy* with you" (accepting and allowing of who you are and what you are) and "I *love* me by being *happy* with me" (accepting and allowing of who I am and what I am). Nevertheless, I might still want other things for both of us. Yet in loving you as you are, I would not *judge* you or *need* you to conform to my expectations or ideals.

For those of us who can or will just choose happiness and let it flow there is no method. But for me and perhaps others who have been or are currently burdened with discomforts, however large or small, the Option Process is an enlightening perspective from which to view our beliefs, so that a new calm and clarity unfolds . . . a new lucidity that enables us to make unprecedented choices for ourselves and to recreate our lives to whatever extent we want.

Each of us finds our own doorway. In that pursuit, each of us becomes capable of creating our own process. The mechanics are but the bare skeletons into which we breathe life. There is a designed procedure of questioning and a method for becoming happier outlined in this book, but its significance and effectiveness lies not simply in words or questions. Its meaning is derived from our tone and our attitude.

In many ways, the acquisition of the attitude is the method. From there, we can give birth to a new self and rechoose.

The real knowing lies only within each of us, not on the pages of a book.

If we give it time, the process becomes part of us. As we move toward knowing ourselves, we can more easily embrace our lives. Rather than remain strangers and caretakers of someone else's universe, we become creators of our own.

Our culture demands immediate gratification as it casually pollutes us and our environment. Its spokesmen scream for instant answers with precise and well-defined rules. This is not that kind of book . . . not that kind of process. Nor does it present "unfathomable enigmas" too difficult to penetrate, reserved only for the ears of experts. Option is a turning, a re-directing and a patient flow . . . in character it is possibly more of the East than the West. This book of the Option Process is meant as a companion for a very beautiful journey . . . not to be consumed in a one-night or two-night reading, but to be touched, embraced, explored and savored as we would a lover over an extended period of time.

Although I had found meditation and spiritual pursuits to be profound and couch-and-confrontation therapy to be helpful, Option provided me with the first clear and total vision of myself and my life—not from an alien and remote perspective, but in a voice I understood, a voice which was conspicuously my own.

And this was only a beginning, a blueprint that enabled me to allow my world to become a growing arena of endless possibilities . . . where loving and caring, healing and helping, and even psychic experiences are part of the landscape.

The words, the questions and the dialogues of the Process, which are at times exceedingly rational and precise, provide a pathway through our exceedingly rational and precise unhappiness. A dear friend once wrote: "I feel something in your presence or voice or perhaps the extraordinary work you've done with your son that goes far beyond Option. Whatever the tools by which you reached the place you inhabit, you, personally, have taken them far beyond what you've learned." Perhaps, yet it was those tools, the Option dialogues and Option questions, which provided me and continue to provide me with a basis from which I continually recreate and reform my style of living and loving.

As I became happier, as the confusion began to disappear

and as I dispensed with much of my unhappiness . . . a new energy developed. In permitting myself to pursue my wants and in being more accepting, more allowing and less judgmental, I found there was so much more for me to see and do for myself and those I loved.

Often when we look for what we expect or need to see, we miss all the other flowers in our garden. Does the loudest voice move us, or the clearest? It's our choice. The option process is a very personal evolution.

It is not a question of how much we don't know, but a discovery of how much we do know.

If someone makes a statement and I reply, "Wow, that's really so," that illumination is not the result of their profundity, but is my confirmation to myself of my own realization. The best someone else can do is tap my awareness of what I already know.

At first, aspects of the Option Process seemed as amazing and perplexing as the concept of "the sound of one hand clapping." Essentially, there was nothing to do to be happy . . . but to remove the unhappiness and let go of the self-defeating beliefs that short-circuited my flow. It almost appeared too easy, too permissive, too soft—not concrete enough. There was no one telling me what to do or adding to the already overwhelming mountain of "shoulds" and "have tos." I was at the throttle, giving myself new opportunities to unpack a lifetime of self-destructive beliefs. As I continued to explore and unearth them, I found many which I immediately and decisively chose to discard.

The concepts and ideas of Option came through to me with such clarity and substance that they required no support other than my own acknowledgment. There was no directing expert, who asserted his vision and authority by reasons of credentials, age or money. The meaning and truth transcends the voice and personality of the teacher who transmits it. Ultimately, the prominent voice we learn to respect is our own.

After all the years of confusion and distrust, I found myself learning to love the experience of my own music and to trust the direction of my own inclinations.

The lessons of the Option Process enabled me to change what appeared to be immovable and permanent . . . and

10

most specifically, to do as a matter of course and wanting many things others, most of whom were "experts," had claimed to be impossible.

In giving the gift of ourselves back to ourselves, in affirming and trusting who we are, we uncover a universe that can never be contained within the pages of a book. What can be communicated here is the path we can walk to get there as well as a taste of the beauty and excitement that awaits us.

As Option remains for me a most beautiful gift, I find myself wanting to share it with others . . . not as a panacea, not as a challenge, not as a life-style to flaunt, not as the way all of us "should" travel—but as a tool with which I and many others have been able to create personal worlds devoid of the expectations, conditions and judgments that create unhappiness. The result is a mellow and loving environment pregnant with enriching experiences. And even though, on occasion, I might make myself irritable or uncomfortable, I welcome that as a new opportunity to reexplore my beliefs and reaffirm the Option alternative.

* * *

One warm summer afternoon, as we strolled hand-in-hand, my nine-year-old daughter quite simply announced, "Daddy, I want to love everyone in the world who wants to be loved." And I want to write these words about the Option Process for everyone in the world who wants to read them. If this book reaches just one other person and really touches them, then it has helped to create new life and bears the fruit of love.

It is said that to have really loved one person is to have loved the whole world.

BARRY NEIL KAUFMAN

New York, 1977

11

1

the option process and me

Life appears as a beautifully-orchestrated symphony. The sun rises like a giant orange eye flaming above the horizon. A sea gull soars through the morning mist and then dives toward the water below. The seasons dance across windswept fields, their mellow cadence caught in the movement of their own melodies. And then there's the rhythm of me, natural and self-regulated . . . an easy motion flowing with my own nature.

But there were times in the past, times that seemed so frequent, when my movements were obstructed and blockaded by unhappiness. Sometimes for days, weeks and even years, I found myself tumbling over the cliffs of my discomforts . . . occasionally being ripped and torn by the jagged edges, cut and bruised by my own thoughts and emotions.

Before the Option Process, I lived in a stop-start atmosphere. My doubts, reflections and questions oftentimes became indictments. Like those around me, the not knowing, the worry and fear infected so many of my activities and pleasures. I wanted peace, but believed it was nowhere to be found. I loved people, but always feared losing them. I created fantasies that most often did not come to pass. The world appeared to be filled with joy and excitement, yet, at times so much of me seemed unlovable. I had friends, yet felt peculiarly alone. I was happy one moment, confused or frightened the next. Life was an up-and-down roller coaster that I couldn't seem to get off.

These were the dams inhibiting my flow. And when all else failed, I would rely on dramatic comparisons to soothe my personal trauma. I would instruct myself to review all those titanic catastrophes I had escaped by accident of birth . . . look at the wars, famine, disease, earthquakes and tidal waves. I even fed myself the age-old axiom: "I felt bad about having no shoes until I saw the man with no feet."

Adapting and coping was the order of the day . . . yet, somehow I knew these were half-measures. I persisted in searching for more.

In the mid-1960s, I scrambled through college as an aging adolescent infused with ideals and expectations. I lived with Sartre and Camus, burned midnight candles with Kant and Hegel, overturned stones with Aristotle and Aquinas. D. H. Lawrence, Faulkner, Fitzgerald, became my brothers as I pantomimed my life through their books.

Bouncing in and out of relationships, I tried to contain my energy while I explored new contacts and delved into new areas of learning. Yet, beneath the surface of all this activity, there were so many questions left unanswered, so many riddles impregnated with fear and discomfort.

But discomfort was fashionable in an era when classrooms were filled with youthful beggars being led into the maze rather than out of it. Freud was still king, which left many of us petrified in the face of our supposedly black and mysterious unconscious which could, without warning, crack through the thin veneer of our everyday sanity and reveal a ghastly prehistoric apparition of ourselves.

Days, months and years were spent doing gymnastics on intellectual and artistic high bars. Aloft, yet grounded. The exploring was intermingled with doubt and confusion. Graduation from college was capped with a degree in philosophy. Then, graduate work in psychology. I was lost in a world

14

where almost everyone saw themselves as victims. Like my peers, I distrusted myself and refused simply to act on my own inclinations.

Life, marriage and then the death of a loved one. At twenty-one, the fabric of my daily existence disintegrated, setting me adrift with only my ambivalence and discomfort as consolation. I turned to a Freudian psychoanalyst and danced my exterior dialogues on the carpet of his lonely Park Avenue office. The sessions continued for seven years. My chatter echoed against the walls of his silence. Almost drowning in painful associations, I waited for those few words which would dissolve the fog . . . interpretations for a lifetime served up by one who presumed he knew.

Restlessly, I plunged into a business venture in films and advertising that met with incredible success, yet the anger and self-doubt continued to flourish. Even when I terminated therapy with its half-measure concept of life, some of the discomforts still remained. A well-meaning psychiatrist left me with a popular slogan shared by many so-called mental health practitioners: "You will always have times when you are anxious, uncomfortable and fearful, but now you are better equipped to handle them, to cope." I had wanted a more affirmative resolution. I felt cheated and short-changed. And in that dissatisfaction, I knew my journey had still just begun.

In graduate school, the truth was reduced to complex plastic and paper replicas of reality . . . a theoretical masquerade supposed to represent flesh and blood. Motivated to move on, I continued the search.

With my wife Suzi who joined me in some of the explorations, I investigated and participated in numerous pursuits of awareness and understanding. Moving from conventional therapy and an academic vision of psychology, I researched altered states of consciousness through hypnosis and auto-hypnosis. Eventually I became skilled enough to put myself into a hypnotic state merely by touching my index finger to my forehead. Dramatic and fascinating, but incomplete.

As I embarked on what would become a seemingly endless pursuit, my thirst for evolving awareness and knowledge increased. The citadel of books was supplemented by experiments with a diverse series of theories and alternatives. Freud was tempered with Jung and Adler, retranslated and revised by

Horney and Sullivan. Touched base with the slapping hand of Gestalt, which was humanized by Perls, and with the fascinating exorcism of the primal scream, dramatized by Janov. Lived my existential love affair with Sartre and Kierkegaard. Came upon the soft and loving embrace of Carl Rogers just after having explored the trinity of Eric Berne. Passed through Skinner rather quickly, but lingered with Maslow.

Pieces of the puzzle. Each with its own beauty and wisdom, yet without the thread to weave the fragments together. Turned to the quiet wisdom of Buddha and Zen. On to Yoga and a lyrical version of Meditation. This was complemented by Taoism and the incisive lesson that "Life is not going anywhere, because it is already here." Then dipped into Confucius. "To know what you know and what you don't know is the characteristic of one who knows." Continued moving East with exposure to the philosophical base of acupuncture and reflexology. Faced West once again, viewing the collective consciousness of mankind and its genetic implications.

A beautiful and sometimes exhausting journey where philosophy, psychology, religion and mysticism merged. And yet, I knew to continue . . . to pursue that, as yet, elusive perspective which for me would ultimately illuminate the horizon.

Another evening. Another classroom. In a school that has since disappeared, I came upon a short, rotund monk-like Friar Tuck who sipped Coke and smoked one cigarette after another. He spoke of something called the Option Method . . . concrete, incisive and illuminating.

Although the initial words were not spectacular in content or presentation, I began immediately to crystallize a knowledge I had always had, but which had never been brought into awareness. As it materialized for me, I could feel the blood racing through my arteries. All my feelings and behavior did come from my beliefs and those beliefs could be investigated and changed by my own choosing. It seemed disarmingly simplistic. And then as I came to explore myself through this new perspective, Option became more than a philosophy . . . it developed into a vision that would become the spine of an evolving life-style we call the Option Process.

And all this was born out of a very special attitude: *To love is to be happy with.*

16

Unhappiness was finally taken out of the closet of mental health and put back into what the ancient Greeks called the arena of philosophy. Questions and dialogues were not indictments or judgments being made for diagnosis . . . they were merely catalysts to help clarify my beliefs and my thinking process. "Why am I unhappy?" and "What do I want for me?" became a profoundly moving perspective by which I could approach myself and precipitate new choices. I realized how I had used myself against myself because of what I had believed. What really dazzled me was my increasing awareness that *I had learned to be unhappy*.

The unhappiness mechanism had been internalized and operated with consistent regularity. Being uncomfortable was an unquestioned ingredient in my life as well as in the lives of all those around me. It was a way of dealing with myself and my environment.

I dreaded obesity and rejection in order to motivate myself to diet. I feared lung cancer so that I could stop smoking. I became anxious about unemployment as a way of pushing myself to be more conscientious and to work harder. I felt guilty to punish myself now in order to prevent myself from repeating a "bad" behavior in the future. I became melancholy when someone I loved was unhappy in order to show them I cared. I got angry at those in my employ to make them move faster.

When I surveyed the environment, I saw people punish in order to prevent, fear death in order to live, hate war in order to stay in touch with their desire for peace.

Signs of unhappiness were everywhere. I was taught that I "had to" be unhappy sometimes and that it was even "good" or productive to be unhappy. Our culture supported it. Unhappiness was the tattoo of a thinking, feeling man. It was the mark of sensitivity. It was also considered by many to be the only "reasonable" and "human" response to a difficult and problematic society. The expression "happy idiot" was not just a casual comment, but a suspicion that happiness and idiocy were synonymous. Like many before me, I adopted these beliefs and many others, never considering or testing their validity in my mind. I too became a living spokesman for unhappiness as I stumbled and dragged myself across the difficult landscape I believed life was supposed to be.

Unhappiness was used as a motivator to help me take care of myself and try to get more . . . all this so that eventually I would be happy or fulfilled. All these beliefs, taught to me so I might do the best for myself, had actually become a breeding ground for all sorts of fears, anxieties and discomforts.

Approaching myself with an Option attitude, I did not judge my unhappiness or tell myself that I could not be unhappy . . . or that I should not be unhappy. There was no implicit statement that I was "supposed to" be happy. After all, until this moment, unhappiness had brought its own rewards, keeping me and others motivated and in check. Yet, my unhappiness as well as the unhappiness of others was a very expensive commodity. It soured the wine. Fear, tension, discomfort and anxiety take their toll, literally short-circuiting our systems. The result is self-defeating consequences: loss of loved ones, unachieved goals, pain, ulcers, high blood pressure, violence, suicide and wars, among others. These by-products far exceed the effectiveness of the mechanism of unhappiness . . . and the underlying beliefs of unhappiness.

The Option Process helped me understand the nature of the underlying beliefs, my beliefs, which triggered my behavior and feelings. I became more able to freely choose with awareness what's best for me . . . to recreate myself as I wanted, to trade unhappiness for happiness. And in dissolving those consuming, troublesome and often painful beliefs (with their accompanying behavior and feelings) I grew happier, crystalized my energy and became more effective in getting what I wanted. In contrast to many of my previous misconceptions, being happier actually led me to getting more for myself.

As I processed the data of *me,* I found I could retain or discard information and beliefs as I saw fit. Nothing was bad for me . . . the more I knew, the better equipped I was in actualizing my wants. Perceptions and actions had no inherent good or bad, just the designation I gave them . . . the designation I chose to give them. My responses always followed from those choices. In discarding and adopting new beliefs, the knowledge, responsibility and expertise of my life was being turned over to me, where it always had been. And

18

that, too, was accomplished by my own decision, my own choice to do that.

There is only one expert on me and my world and that's me. Only one expert on you and your world and that's you!

There was no pretense that this was the only way to happiness . . . but the Option Process gave me a clarity and control that is always mine. Direct. Attainable. In unplugging my beliefs of unhappiness, I focused more easily on my wants and experienced myself *irrevocably under my control.*

No secret codes to master or initiations to endure. No mystery understood by a select few. No question of my being sick, maladjusted or disturbed. No judgments about what I do or who I am. No good or bad, should or should not. Even when I was unhappy and fed myself enormous doses of grief, I did so as a way of taking care of myself.

We all do the best we can, the best we know how based on our current beliefs.

Others who would label or condemn us do so for themselves, their assessments having nothing to do with who we are. Sickness, stupidity and inferiority are their judgments, having only as much power as we give them. Fight the devil and we make him stronger. Ignore him and he is likely to disappear. In changing my focus and allowing myself to be, I keenly experienced my own freedom.

Me investigating me became a joyful pursuit into myself. Like being my own Socrates, I uncovered my own beliefs and understood the whys of what I felt and did. In this adventure, there was no teacher, guru or knowing therapist with *the* right answer. I was the mover, the explorer and the discoverer. And the more I came to know, the more clearly I chose from happiness . . . instead of first becoming unhappy in order to move.

I was amazed to see how often I used unhappiness as a condition I promised myself if I did not get what I wanted or expected. If my lover did not care for me, I'd be miserable. If I didn't get the job, I'd be angry at the interviewer and myself. If I didn't get passing grades on an examination, I'd be resentful. Expecting and not getting . . . all just another way to motivate myself. It was believing that wanting was not enough.

19

If my happiness did not depend on it, I might not really work for it.

This was the dynamic of turning *wanting into needing*. When I want something, I focus on trying to get it. There is no fear of future unhappiness if I don't. In wanting, my happiness is not contingent on getting.

But in needing, I give my wanting extra importance by making my happiness dependent on getting. If I don't get what I say I need ((love, money, security), I say I will be unhappy. It's my self-fulfilling prophecy. I used to believe the worry and threats made me more diligent in pursuing my goals; but, in fact, it was often a painful and self-defeating distraction.

On some occasions, my needing actually led to extinguishing what I wanted. In fearing I would not get, I sometimes chose not to go after my goals to avoid the unhappiness. Why do that? There were many reasons, but the most prominent was the belief that if I tried and then did not get, I'd even be more unhappy than if I simply did not try at all. At least I might be able to console myself with "well, since I didn't try, I didn't lose anything . . . and if I really tried, I could have gotten it anyway." The pressure of needing created a short circuit and the result was immobility.

By contrast, when I began to consider what I wanted as "wants" and not "needs," then I moved toward goals without having my life or happiness dependent on them. I also did not have to live with the anxiety of worrying about missing my mark or "failing."

Unhappiness in my pre-Option days was also a gauge to measure the intensity of my desires and loving. The more miserable I became when I did not get what I wanted or when I lost something I loved, the more I believed I cared. If I was not unhappy about the threat or loss of something, maybe I did not want it enough. Even more plaguing was the belief that if I allowed myself to be happy under all circumstances, I might, thereafter, not want anything or care about anyone. If I was perfectly satisfied with present conditions, I might not move toward altering them or take advantage of new possibilities. I also remember believing it would be callous and inhuman if I were not unhappy in certain situations.

The insidious fear that happiness and inertia might be

20

synonymous was quickly dispelled. The more comfortable I became with myself, the easier it was to want more and dare to pursue more. In so many instances, my happiness was no longer at stake. Whether I secured what I wanted or not, I could still be comfortable.

Using the principles and the method of the Option Process, I had decided to change while the world around me seemed to remain the same. Yet, after a period of time, as I began to change, the environment around me also began to change.

In exploring the texture of my personal life, and in trying to neutralize the difficulties, I came to realize that going to work and earning a living was not a "must" or a "should," as I had always been taught, but an activity, in fact, that I really wanted to do. Yet, all this time I had acted as if I was being forced. I began to look beneath the unhappiness and understood that in believing work was a "should," I had never allowed myself either the comfort or the freedom to enjoy it. I touched on all my beliefs about stress being a necessary ingredient for success. In this considered evolution, I found myself discarding many self-defeating beliefs about needing things and about making myself unhappy if I didn't get them.

The unbilical cord was finally being severed. The old beliefs were being left behind as I redefined the cornerstones of my activities and involvements. Together, Suzi and I rejected much of the old unhappiness as we persistently explored our discomforts and our beliefs. Making new choices changed the very texture of our existence as we redesigned our lives and began teaching and counseling others.

The attitude, the methods, the dialogue techniques, the philosophy, evolved into a global concept of living. Our friends whom we exposed to the Option Process had found new meaning and direction in their lives, accompanied by a deep and abiding sense of peace. Private and group experiences were supplemented by working with and supervising other students, who evolved from their shells of discomfort and confusion to find a new freedom and clarity. Whether it began with a single conversation or involvement in a series of dialogues, when those who participated wanted, they underwent startling and beautiful transformations. In some instances, hate melted into love, sickness evolved into health,

21

aggression turned into acceptance, turmoil gave way to an almost mystical tranquility.

We were alive and planting more seeds.

Suzi and I no longer exchanged comments like "If you love me, you would do this or that." Each of us was happier with ourselves and with each other despite the reality that our first years of marriage had been difficult and stormy. We took our relationship and stripped away all the elaborate expectations and conditions, thereby eradicating many of the disappointments and conflicts. In accepting each other, we were more loving. And this flowed over to our children. Being more sensitized to the beliefs parents teach their children each and every day, we became increasingly more tolerant and respectful of the wants and individuality of the little people who shared our lives.

Nevertheless, if we ourselves and those we love still become unhappy and make choices away from each other, we do not view it as "bad" or unacceptable. For us, each unhappy moment is but another opportunity to discard a self-defeating belief as we walk the path toward becoming happier. These attitudes became the springboard for which we later approached a situation with one of our children that others had labeled as "horrifying" and a "disastrous tragedy." It was during this very special confrontation with the "impossible" that we fully realized what a beautiful and effective gift of living we had acquired. The story of our son is just one living example, among many, of the power, effectiveness and endless possibilities of the Option Process.

One brisk January 17, at 6:14 in the evening, Suzi and I joined together in patterns of breathing and loving to help facilitate the arrival of our third child. The method and the rhythms of natural childbirth filled the room with dazzling energy. A healthy, beautiful and blissful little boy peeked out into the universe and drew his first breath. His name was to be Raun Kahlil.

The joyful and ceremonious arrival of our son was immediately dampened by the events of the next four weeks. In the hospital nursery as well as at home, Raun cried day and night. Examination followed examination with no visible malfunctions revealed.

Three weeks later, a severe ear infection surfaced. The

22

...ibed antibiotics which, within twenty-four
... dehydration. His eyes clouded. His skin
... as the spark of life drained from our
...

...alization. Raun was placed in intensive
care... ...recariously between life and death. The
press... ...on caused both ear drums to puncture.
Our th... ...rgy were entirely devoted to wanting
our son to... ..., during his second week in the hospital, he beg... ...nd.

For all of us, ...d beginning. Now Raun seemed joyful . . . a peaceful and mellow harmony characterized the
remainder of his first year. He grew and developed with
beauty and strength. However when he was twelve months
old, we began to note a growing insensitivity to audio stimuli
as he became less responsive to his name and other sounds.

During the next four months, Raun's apparent audio deficit
was compounded by a tendency to stare and be passive. He
preferred solitary play rather than interaction with our
family. When he was held in our arms, his body would
dangle limply. More testing still produced no definite answers. Yet our son's behavior continued to change rapidly.
His delicate face and sparkling eyes turned toward another
dimension of experience.

By seventeen months of age, Raun had withdrawn completely from all human contact and slipped behind a seemingly impenetrable wall. He was diagnosed as autistic, which
has been traditionally labeled as a subcategory of childhood
schizophrenia . . . considered to be the most irreversible of
the profoundly disturbed and psychotic. "Incurable." "Hopeless." These were the underlying messages of the literature
and the professionals we consulted throughout the country.

A classic case of autism. Silent and aloof, Raun stared
through us as if we were transparent. And then there was
his incessant rocking back and forth to some internal symphony. The spinning, hour after hour, of every object in
sight. The self-stimulating smile and repetitious motion of his
fingers against his lips. The lack of language development
. . . no words, no sounds, no pointing gestures. No calling
or crying for food, no signals to be changed or taken out of
his crib. The loss of eye contact. The pushing away . . . the
deafening silence . . . the aloneness.

Yet, although Raun was lost to us, he remained beautiful and blissful in our eyes . . . like a dedicated monk contemplating his life force as he sat patiently before the altar of the universe.

Committing ourselves to an openness to see anyone, go anywhere for help, we consumed every book available on autism and journeyed to different cities to explore and observe. Patterning. Psychoanalysis. Sensory conditioning. Biochemical experiments. Megavitamin theories. And finally exposure to various applications of behavior modification, which is the concept currently in vogue.

What became increasingly clear was that most programs were little more than experiments. The ratio of children reached was dismal, perhaps only a few in each one hundred. And ironically, success often referred to the one or two children who learned to perform minimal functions on a very primitive level.

The more we viewed and understood the nature of these treatments, the more polarized we became. Raun was a beautiful human being with his own special qualities and dignity. His eyes were so intense, so bright and so alive. But who out there was willing to respect that?

Professionals, in the name of medicine and humanity and probably with the sincere belief they were helping, had little children strapped onto tables as one hundred and fifty volts were slammed into their brains during electric-shock treatments. Other boys and girls were tied to chairs to prevent them from rocking. Some were enclosed in portable black boxes or closets as a form of aversion therapy. One doctor, who used these techniques, stated quite casually that these children were not very human in their responses to his therapy. Incredible how insensitive he was to the obvious fact that if someone locked him in a closet, brutalized his system with electric shocks and tied his hands and feet, his inclination to relate to his therapists would be quickly extinguished . . . especially if he also had had extreme difficulty making sense out of his world in the first place.

How could anyone hope to reach and help a dysfunctioning child by disapproving and condemning him?

Refusing to relinquish our good feelings, refusing to extinguish the life of this delicate and different child by placing him behind the stone walls of some numb and faceless institution, we decided to trust ourselves . . . to design and create our own program without having any concepts of limitations. We would try to help Raun recreate and expand his world in the same way we had recreated and expanded ours through the Option Process.

Our guide was the Option Attitude: To love is to be happy with. In approaching our son, we decided there would be no conditions to which he had to conform . . . there would be no expectations which he had to fulfill . . . there would be no judgments which designated his behavior good or bad. Our movement would respect his dignity, instead of forcing him to adapt to our ideals or behavior. Working with Raun during his every waking hour (eighty hours each week), we met him on his own ground and entered his world. With love, with acceptance . . . always aware that for whatever reasons, Raun was doing the best he could.

We decided to do what was most apparent . . . if Raun was unable to be with us in our world, we would try to make contact by going to his world. The major thrust of our program was to be beside him and touch him in the most gentle and permissive ways. But the most important decision was to imitate him. Not a laboratory tactic performed from a distant or aloof perspective . . . we would actually join him with all our energy and enthusiasm. If he rocked, we would rock. If he spun or flapped his fingers, we would spin and flap our fingers. It was our way of learning, of saying hello, of trying to communicate our love and acceptance of him. Several doctors suggested that by imitating him, we were committing a tragic mistake of supporting "bad" behavior. For us, there was no bad or good . . . there was just a different little boy whom we wanted to contact.

We also lavished him with affection, loving and caring, fondling, music, smiles, gentle visual and auditory stimulation. We tried to present to him an environment he might find even more fascinating and more beautiful than the self-stimulating one he had created. And his motivation would have to exceed that of the rest of us. With his memory disability, which we had uncovered during our marathon observation periods, Raun's capacity to deal easily with us was severely handicapped.

At first, the movements were slow . . . almost imperceptible. We began to train others as teacher-therapists, using the concepts and methods of the Option Process as our tool.

Both our daughters, Bryn and Thea, were also teachers and loving mentors for their brother. The essential ingredient was the development of the Option Attitude . . . each and every day we had dialogues to explore beliefs and feelings so that we were more able to help ourselves help Raun. The specific tactics and techniques we established in working with our son were secondary to the tone and texture of our approach and contact.

Within eight months this dysfunctioning, totally withdrawn, self-stimulating, functionally retarded and "hopeless" little boy became a social, highly verbal, affectionate and loving human being displaying intellectual capabilities far beyond his years.

Had we given up our wanting and followed the advice of the "experts," our son today would perhaps be sitting in his own feces, alone and forgotten, drugged on Thorazine, spinning and rocking for endless hours on the cold floor of some nameless hospital.

Instead, at four years old, the child who they said would never speak or communicate sensibly, has become an exquisite and sophisticated conversationalist . . . filling our home with the music of his words every day. Affectionate, loving and vibrantly in touch, he continues to grow and learn by his own desire and statement.

Raun can already spell and read simple sentences. He loves numbers and does elementary addition and subtraction. With his chic and sparkling sense of humor, he imitates friends and members of our family in highly theatrical antics. His love of music has resulted in an intimate affair with the piano and in his now having created several tunes and melodies for himself. In a preschool playgroup for "normal" children, he exhibits a socialization and verbal aptitude which exceeds his peers, yet he nevertheless shows an inexhaustible ability to extract excitement and joy from his playmates and his environment.

We call Raun Kahlil the first Option child.

He has in many ways been a great teacher and mover of us all. Our dedication, which flowed easily and naturally from our attitude and wanting, facilitated the evolution and rebirth of an amazingly beautiful and creative human being. Had we not been comfortable, had we been overridden by fear and anxiety, perhaps we might have never even tried to *be* with Raun. And then the "experts" would point to the little lost boy dribbling into the soup of his own confusion and say: "See, an unfortunate and irreversible condition." But these words can never be anything more than the expression of a belief, which can become a self-fulfilling prophecy.

When we view something as difficult, terrible or hopeless, then we help make it difficult, terrible and hopeless. But when we decide not to see it as disastrous and difficult, by that decision alone, we begin to allow ourselves to see the beauty —and to find the answers.

The gift of living and teaching the Option alternative, the rebirth of Raun Kahlil, the happiness of being happy most of the time and the loving and caring shared with others has provided me with an exhilarating in-touch contact with the NOW of my life.

I guess I could have said that this person or that person has the power to make me better or happier. I could have continued to go outside myself with the promise of medication, libido analysis, religion, hypnosis, meditation, exercise or even the stars . . . all of which do provide certain comforts. But actually, we have only to go to our core to discover our own amazing humanity and power. We have only to allow ourselves to uncover our own knowing without fearing the results.

In presenting ourselves to ourselves without judgments, we found we knew it was really okay to be us . . . that, indeed, nothing is wrong with us and nothing ever was.

We all are, in our own ways, special and beautiful.

In most religions, disciplines and therapies, happiness is subordinated to the gods of sacrifice, adjustment, adaptation and endurance. Many even frankly state there will always be pain and unhappiness . . . and that's true, only as long as we believe it. If I believe I'll always be miserable, I will. If I believe I'll always be insecure, I will. But when I allow myself to suspend those beliefs and deal with them, I find myself discarding much of the network that enforces my self-defeating behavior. And as I change those beliefs through the Option Process, I change everything about me . . . my feelings, my behavior and my wants.

Not a treatment or miracle, Option is a perspective and

27

an evolution which maintains an infinite respect for the traveler moving along the path—a respect and learning environment in which each of us can become more of what we want to be.

And the implications are enormous. If Option applies to an autistic child, what about other children? What about all children? If it turned the impossible into the possible, what else can we do for ourselves and those we love? If we can fracture the spell of unhappiness and let our juices flow, there is no end. The Option Process is a meaningful, relevant and mind-expanding journey for all of us who have ever been confronted by a situation we've judged or others have labeled unhappy or tragic. The ramification of being able to hear the voice within us alters our approach to every life experience: the birth of a child, the death of a loved one, marriage, divorce, sex, illness, financial hardship, love relations . . . the list is endless.

We each have our own discomforts, but as we become happier, we will tend to see, touch and move our worlds in a more loving and caring way.

THE "THINK" PAGE (THE OPTION PROCESS AND ME)

QUESTIONS TO ASK YOURSELF:

Do you want to be happier?

Do you have to be unhappy now in order to be happy later?

Are you afraid of becoming too happy? If so, why? What are your beliefs about it?

Do you believe that "wanting" is enough to motivate you?

Do you turn "wants" into "needs"?

If you didn't get unhappy about losing something, does that mean you didn't care?

When you are fearful or anxious, do you find yourself confused and unclear?

OPTION CONCEPTS TO CONSIDER:

*THE OPTION ATTITUDE: TO LOVE IS TO BE HAPPY WITH.

*UNHAPPINESS IS A MOTIVATOR.

*YOU ARE YOUR OWN EXPERT.

*ONLY YOU KNOW WHAT'S GOOD FOR YOU.

*OTHERS WHO MIGHT LABEL OR CONDEMN US DO SO FOR THEMSELVES.

*NOTHING IS WRONG WITH US AND NOTHING EVER WAS.

*BECOMING HAPPIER IS A BEAUTIFUL (NOT PAINFUL) PROCESS.

*BELIEFS CAN BE SELF-FULFILLING PROPHECIES.

*WE ALL DO THE BEST WE CAN, THE BEST WE KNOW HOW, BASED ON OUR CURRENT BELIEFS.

*THE BY-PRODUCT OF HAPPINESS IS LUCIDITY AND CLEAR THINKING.

*HAPPY PEOPLE ARE MORE EFFECTIVE THAN UNHAPPY PEOPLE IN GETTING WHAT THEY WANT.

*YOU CAN BE EVERYTHING YOU EVER WANTED TO BE (read on).

BELIEFS TO CONSIDER CHANGING:

Unhappiness is the mark of an intelligent and sensitive person.

If my happiness is not at stake, then it can't be that important.

If I become perfectly happy, I will stop wanting things.

30

If I was happy all the time, I'd be an idiot.

Caring is measured by unhappiness.

If I'm not unhappy about my present situation, I won't try to improve it.

We are too old to change.

Change is painful.

2

the option method: on being your own expert

This chapter, in many ways, is *the last chapter* of the book. It is presented here to give a broad-based understanding of the method . . . now, as you begin this journey. A second reading, after completing the remainder of the book, will unfold a new richness and depth as well as reconfirming many insights and revealing new ones.

The accent here is on the nature of the Option dialogue, the series of questions and the probe into our system of beliefs. The form is simple and direct, a contemporary Socratic exploration. Each question is born from the content of the last statement made. Stripped of direction and judgments, we proceed naturally from ourselves.

But why begin with questions? To ask ourselves, to make an inquiry does not mean we are ignorant or that we do not understand. It's just a way of bringing knowledge and awareness to life.

Questions are not signs of doubt as much as opportunities to crystallize what we know.

On these following pages are notations on a layout, a design, a dialogue motif. It is a *bare skeleton* brought to life by each of us as we use it, *as we live it.* More than just an initiation, it is also the final service area in the journey through this book, which is, in reality, a journey through ourselves.

From the Attitude, "to love is to be happy with," comes the Method for helping myself to become happier in every way. In approaching myself, in accepting the model, I am accepting myself. There is no directed or designed piece of behavior. The unraveling and the discovery as well as the opportunity to change comes from opening myself to my beliefs.

In viewing them as they operate, I can decide whether I want to continue to believe them or not. Herein lies the crystallization of choosing or rechoosing, accepting or discarding. The only mysteries are the ones I make. References to emotional disturbance or mental illness are not applicable. Those are the judgments of others. An unhappy person is a person reacting to his *beliefs* of unhappiness. It's much more a question of learning and teaching myself with an open awareness of my own power, dignity and knowing.

There are no good or bad beliefs, no good or bad behaviors or feelings . . . We are what we are and in every way, we do the best we can, the best we know how, based on our present beliefs.

Unhappiness germinates when I see myself or events as being bad for me. The Option dialogue technique is for those of us who might want to live more happily and, thus, more effectively (without self-defeating results and painful by-products).

Great, it feels like I really want to do it, become happier and maybe even shoot for the sky—perfect happiness. I can certainly envision the benefits of ridding myself of unhappiness in my job, my love relationship, my sexual involvements . . . in almost everything. The ramifications are just incredible—moving comfortably, being in harmony with my body, expanding new horizons. But wait! What about the big, big immovable horrors . . . war, famine, poverty, disease? Shouldn't they still make me unhappy? Aren't they still

34

things to be legitimately depressed about?

Okay . . . let's talk about these realities. The focus of our attention has always been on *you* and *me*. Why? Because your unhappiness lives within you as my unhappiness lives within me. So what are we saying when we are angry and upset with the world's great problems? Aren't we saying that we really want them solved, the violence to cease, the poor to eat, the sick to be cured? That's what we want! But why are we unhappy about it? Because, as with other more limited personal dilemmas, we use the unhappiness (anger, frustration, fear) to help us stay in touch with what we want . . . to motivate and reinforce ourselves. To flip the switch. We're afraid that if we were not unhappy, we wouldn't try to do anything about "the great tragedies." Some of us might also be believing that if we didn't get upset, we would somehow be callous and "inhuman."

Initially, I use unhappiness to move myself to do something (join a protest march, volunteer for a benefit, send money to a charity). I feel so much better after doing something. The initial unhappiness also reconfirms that I care . . . that I am a sensitive and involved human being. "Yes, but I really do feel sad about those problems." Sure, if I believed that I would be a "bad" person if I didn't, then I would feel sad.

No one is here to argue with such feelings and reactions. But can't we still want to improve world conditions without being melancholy and anxious? Can't we find the motivation to help others from our loving and caring, rather than our outrage and anger?

Using misery (even our own personal depression) to fight misery just adds to the misery.

Good, that really helps. I could understand caring without being unhappy. Although I couldn't be happy about world conditions, maybe I could be neutral and attend to my other good feelings. Yet, another mountain suddenly appears. What about the big one . . . what about death? How could I help but be unhappy about dying? Those fears, like many others, come from my beliefs. If I were brought up in another culture, I might welcome death as the most beautiful part of living. No fear at all, just an embrace.

My anxiety about death and dying would have to come from my beliefs that it is bad for me. I might also have

35

many additional supportive beliefs about losing time to enjoy loved ones, being deprived of opportunities, etc. In this culture, most of us have acquired many fears (beliefs and superstitions) about our mortality. No one is suggesting they are silly or unfounded. If we believe them, they are real for us. So the question that could be asked is: What is the exact nature of my individual fears of death and why do I believe them? Although death seems inevitable, we each have our specific fears and anxieties. If it disturbs me, then perhaps I can include it as part of my exploration. "Would that mean if I didn't fear it, I would want it? Of course not . . . couldn't we not fear dying and still want to live? Isn't fearing dying really wanting to live? Hear this as it is said . . . we can look at what we want . . . the only thing we have to lose is our unhappiness.

I'm almost ready to go on . . . but, ah, just a minor case of the last-minute jitters. An old belief returns. I understand that the concept "if I were happy all the time, I'd be an idiot" is just not so. What stays with me is the concern that if I allow myself to be happy under all circumstances, how can I be sure I'll move. If I'm happy any place, it wouldn't make a difference where I was. Okay, let's look at that . . . the more we allow ourselves to deal with the questions, the more possibilities for becoming happier. When the happy skier stops on a ridge, does he stop moving (he's happy on the ridge) or does he continue going down the mountainside as he wants? When a musician is happily playing, does he get stuck endlessly on one piece or does he too move as his inclinations guide him? If I am happy swimming, won't I still stop when I am tired? If I am enjoying hiking, won't I still interrupt my walk in order to eat?

Happy people do not stop moving.

And doing something out of happiness does not cause lethargy. On the contrary, it usually increases our mobility and effectiveness because instead of fighting our fears and running from pain, we more clearly see our wants and move with ease toward them (or move simultaneously as we want).

In dismantling the beliefs of unhappiness, we free ourselves to allow our wanting and the undiluted energy flows within us. As we have seen, a fearful or anxious person often blocks data and has difficulty processing information since he is diverting his energies to deal with his discomforts. The happy

36

person would simply allow intake and digest, knowing that what he sees and understands can only make him better equipped and more effective. But this occurs concurrent to happiness . . . it is neither an end goal nor an intermediate goal. Other disciplines herald "self-awareness," "adaptation," "effectiveness" or "normalcy" as goals. And if you ask them why, they would probably say these goals are attained in order to be happy. Option cuts through it . . . we can be happy now . . . now while we are trying to change ourselves. Happiness is not a reward unless we withhold it from ourselves until we reach a desired goal. And would we withhold it if we knew we were going toward our goal anyway?

Stripped of all surface manipulation, there is only our wanting to be happier and our journey toward happier-ness. It does not matter how we define it or how we describe it or whether we agree upon what it is . . . we know when we are happy and feeling good . . . when we are there, we have no questions.

In using the Method, we become a *"therapon"* for ourselves, a second voice, a comrade in a common struggle. We could also be a facilitator for others . . . and let them be one for us.

For some of us, there is the Option teacher who can ask the questions, although each student still retains absolute control. But there is the alternate possibility of acting as our own *"therapon,"* serving ourselves by lifting the debris and allowing a more natural flow . . . helping ourselves to be happier.

Since the Option Process begins with the attitude, which is a way of life, a style of being and a perspective of seeing, let's review its nature. *"To love is to be happy with." No judgments. No conditions. No Expectations.* Allowing myself and others the freedom to be whoever they are, to do what they do or don't do. To be accepting without giving up my own wants or giving up trying to get what I want. Permitting my desires to be a function of wanting and not needing. A willingness to put aside my pretending because I am aware I do not need that protection from myself. Accepting responsibility for who I am, without indictment or recrimination. The "shoulds" and "should nots," the "have tos" and "musts" can be laid aside. If I know that nothing is wrong with me, then anything I come to uncover could only enrich me and help me in getting more of what I want. Being aware that others are also doing the best they can, the best they know how, based on their current beliefs . . . they're wanting to be happier, wanting to be more loving. |

In crystallizing my awareness and viewing the beliefs behind my unhappiness, I go with myself in no preset direction. Permitting myself to begin and end as I choose, with no accomplishment necessary in order to allow myself to feel good. To trust myself, knowing that I always take care of myself.

In exploring our behavior and feelings as it relates to our happiness and unhappiness, we begin the Option Process.

Most of us believe that we have to be unhappy now so that we can be happy later. In using unhappiness as a motivator, reinforcer and gauge (to measure our caring), we create a continual cycle of discomfort. In the present, we are unhappy or uncomfortable in anticipation of the uncertain future. And since there's always an uncertain future, in the present we are then always living with some unhappiness.

We break the cycle by helping ourselves to be happier by living in the *non-anticipating* now. In turning that corner, we also indirectly help others. Our increasing good feelings and acceptance is a loving and embracing way in which we come to allow others their own space and freedoms.

Unhappiness is based on a *logical system of beliefs*. Thus, we look within our own belief system since all the reasons are connected and activated there. Our perception and thoughts all filter through our belief system (resulting in our behaviors and feelings). Portions of this system form the apparatus to dissect and, perhaps, disconnect (as we want).|

Our endeavor is more akin to philosophy than psychology. It is a question of what we learned (and now believe) and what we want to do about what we learned (and still believe). In that process, *each of us is our own expert*, regardless of who asks the questions.

There is no one who knows more about who you are and what you believe than . . . you.

The design, mood and meaning of the exploration comes from you. If it doesn't, then it merely articulates the beliefs of another. And isn't that in part how we got here in the first place, when we began to ignore our own voice and put aside what we know.

If another's goal or interpretations supersede mine, then I am the recipient of an additional bombardment of beliefs, none of which helps me to uncover my own beliefs and accept or discard them as I choose. To know me and my wants is for me to do. "But how do I know if I'll tell myself the truth?" Just ask and then answer.

There is only one professional in my case and that's me . . . only one professional in your case and that's you.

The Option Method, coming from the Attitude, breaks down into three basic questions with one alternate question. Although each question has a diverse variety of forms and subquestions in order to clarify answers, the model is incredibly simple. *DO*

(1) _WHAT_ ARE YOU UNHAPPY ABOUT?
(2) _WHY_ ARE YOU UNHAPPY ABOUT THAT?
(3) _WHY_ DO YOU BELIEVE THAT? Or do you believe that?
(3) (Alternate) WHAT ARE YOU AFRAID WOULD HAPPEN IF YOU WEREN'T UNHAPPY ABOUT THAT?

What? That's impossible, you're thinking. It can't be any good; it's too simple and I'm so complex. It's too confining. Yes . . . and maybe, no. Yes, it is beautifully simple in terms of questions, but no, not in terms of its capacity to unravel and help us focus. Like happiness itself, the route to it is simple and uplifting.

The complexity is the journey through the unhappiness, through the maze of interrelating beliefs and short circuits. For some there is no method; they just decide to be happy. Period. Super-simple, yet attainable by a few. For the majority of us, our discomforts and fears are still strong enough and prevalent enough to short-circuit our flow and allowing. When

39

we consider the content of many of the following chapters: children, love relations, sex, health, guilt, money, the psychic experience and trusting ourselves . . . we will discover an "apparent" collage of conflicting ideas and beliefs. Some of it might appear perplexingly complex. Yet still, the discoveries are born out of only three elemental questions. There are no other tools required, except an awarenesss of wanting to be happier.

Let's begin with the first question, then explore variations as well as the subquestions. *What* are you unhappy about? Or *What* about that makes you unhappy? If you just lost a loved one or were demoted in your job, incurred a huge debt . . . if you are having problems with sex or money . . . the question at first might seem outrageous and ridiculous. How could anyone, for example, ask a person why they are unhappy about their lover dying? More than offensive, it's absurd. But is it?

It might seem silly because we each conjure up an immediate and emphatic answer that we are sure everyone has. Yet, the answers are not always what we expect nor are they beyond comprehension. Often, therapists, professionals and teachers believe they know the answer in advance (that's how they make diagnoses and predictions) . . . *but only you can know the answer.* Back to the question. What is it about your lover dying that makes you unhappy? No one is saying that we "should not" feel unhappy or, if we get unhappy, we should suppress it or not vent it . . . the probe is to identify the underlying belief. You'd probably be surprised how incredibly varied and different the answers are: "I am unhappy that she suffered so much." "I am unhappy about missing her." "I am unhappy about being left alone." "I am guilty because I didn't treat her right." "I am unhappy because I am so difficult to love, and will end up lonely without her." Each answer, following from our concept of *no direction,* leads us into different areas. "How will I know which one is my answer?" Ask yourself. A trail that begins in one place can move in many directions. We cannot assume there is an obvious answer or underlying fear, because there isn't. There is only my answer for me, your answer for you.

We each have our own reasons for being unhappy. And

since each of us is different, *only you can answer for yourself.*

The first question also has many variations. Often, we will say "I am not unhappy, I'm angry." So we deal with our own vocabulary and symbols. What am I angry about? What am I anxious about? What am I uncomfortable about or frightened about? Unhappiness is just a grab-bag word encompassing any feelings or thoughts we are uncomfortable with. The subquestion is for further clarification: what do you mean by that? Or again, what about that makes you unhappy? If I say I am unhappy about not having someone to take care of me . . . what does that mean? Physically, emotionally, sexually or materially? Each answer of *what* makes us unhappy can usually be refined by asking a clarifying question to further identify and pinpoint the unhappiness.

So we begin the cycle. What are you unhappy about? I am miserable that my lover died. What about that makes you miserable? I'll miss her. What do you mean? Well, there will be no one to share my life with; no one left to care. I'll be unloved. So being cared for or the possibility of being unloved now becomes the continuing focus of the questions and answers. Still at this point, we have not gone beyond the first question. Even when we ask the second question, often, we return to the first. There is no rigidity or predetermined logic, all of it comes from the last answer. Each and every time.

The Option Method is a way of being with ourselves . . . it is not pushing and pulling in directions, but allowing of our natural propensities.

The second question: *Why are you unhappy about that?* Again, there might be some of us who could react with annoyance and shout "What do you mean by *why?*" "Anyone would be unhappy if they lost a loved one." Sure, but your unhappiness is not being judged. The question is not an indictment or criticism, only a search for the reasons why. Often, when others have asked us why, their questions have had many overtones, such as the implicit statement that you should be doing it differently. This time the question is not loaded . . . there are no unstated judgments. It is just a vehicle to help us understand.

So if we had answered that we were unhappy about losing a loved one because we are then left alone, the next question would be: *Why are you unhappy about being alone?* Because I'll have no one to love me. Why would that make you unhappy? Because I want to be loved. The alternate question might be introduced at this juncture: *What are you afraid would happen if you weren't unhappy about being alone?* I would stay alone. I might not try to find someone else. Oh. Then what is being said is: "If I am not unhappy about it, I won't do anything to improve it." Here we see the exposure of a significant belief. In it, we can also see how, even with unhappiness, we are always taking care of ourselves, doing the best we believe possible for ourselves.

Now, the last question might be asked: *Why do you believe that?* Sometimes, we cannot find any reasons. In that case, we have the opportunity to review the dynamic and discard it if we want. "If I don't have a reason, then why am I still believing that?" On other occasions, we might have an answer. For example, I believe it because it's always been that way. The question that might take shape is: If it always has been that way in the past, does it mean it will always be that way in the future? That would be a clarification question. The answer might be: Well, I guess it doesn't have to be that way because it was in the past . . . but with my luck it will happen again. Okay, if it happens again, what would you be unhappy about? And here we are now back to the first question.

Since each belief is supported by other beliefs, the movement usually follows relevant lines. The *why do you believe that* question could be asked at any point, provided I am dealing with a statement about beliefs (I'm not talented, I'm unlovable, something is wrong with me, etc.). Underlying all the dialogues are usually some basic or global beliefs. When those are changed in an individual, entire spheres of behavior and feeling can change. Suppose, after investigation by the Method, I became aware that I had always believed that something was wrong with me. I choose now to discard that belief (as I come to know I am what I want and can always change as I wish). This would affect every concept of living and every area of my activity. The possibilities are endless when each question flows from the previous answer.

On some occasions, we might give ourselves circular responses. I loathe it because it bothers me because it makes me unhappy. Or I am unhappy because I am sad because I am depressed because I am uncomfortable. The substitution here is merely one descriptive word for another. A clarification question might be asked: What is it about being sad or depressed that particularly bothers you? There is no reason to refute or debate yourself. It is not "bad" to feel the way you do. Go with it, you'll do the best you can.

Another helpful note: Verbalize out loud, if possible. Why? So that you can hear it, you can give it solidity and more visibility. Your words make your ideas more reachable. We say it to know it better. Fears and beliefs alike are easier to grasp once articulated. It's also exciting to hear yourself say something you didn't know you believed.

A tight recap. There are three basic questions, each with a subquestion for purposes of identifying or clarifying unhappiness.

(1) *WHAT* ARE YOU UNHAPPY ABOUT? What do you mean by that or what about that makes you unhappy?

(2) *WHY* ARE YOU UNHAPPY ABOUT THAT? What do you mean by that?

(3) WHY DO YOU BELIEVE THAT? Or do you believe that?

(3) (alt.) WHAT ARE YOU AFRAID WOULD HAPPEN IF YOU WEREN'T UNHAPPY ABOUT IT?

Often the trail to the last question is some distance from the first, yet everything is always relevant to the place where we begin. Many times, when we are asked why we believe the beliefs we just uncovered, we have no answer. Often, we have accepted them without question. Nevertheless, that gives them no less power, but it does afford us an opportunity to decide whether or not we want to retain them.

There is one additional, highly useful question that we can incorporate as part of the Method or just use at random as an effective focusing device: *What do you want?* Often, we are so busy negotiating with our distress or confusion that we lose sight of our wanting. Just pausing and addressing ourselves with that question at any time can be a productive technique for centering ourselves. In the office, at home, on vacation; while eating, loving or running . . . if we find ourselves confused or doubting, we can stop momentarily and pose the question: What do I want? Frequently, you will have an immediate answer which will help you clairify your current actions and feelings as well as direct you more vividly toward your wants.

Perhaps, in review, we might gather together the most frequently encountered beliefs in our culture from which unhappiness often blossoms and is further supported. For some of us, their exposure as a dynamic on the pages of this book might have been just enough to dislodge them. If so, beautiful! If not, we can always assess what we feel about these beliefs and ask ourselves (if it applies), why do I believe it or what about it makes me uncomfortable or unhappy?

—THERE MUST BE SOMETHING WRONG WITH ME.

—IT IS NECESSARY TO BE UNHAPPY NOW IN ORDER TO BE HAPPY LATER.

—IF YOU LOVED ME, YOU WOULD . . .

—I MAKE OTHERS UNHAPPY.

—I CANNOT CHANGE; THIS IS THE WAY I AM.

—MY FEELINGS JUST COME UPON ME; I HAVE NO CONTROL.

—I AM UNLOVABLE.

—IF I JUST LET MYSELF GO, I WOULD BE BAD FOR MYSELF.

—I "NEED" LOVE, I "NEED" SEX, I "NEED" MONEY . . .

—IF I DIDN''T FEEL GUILTY, I'D DO IT AGAIN.

—UNHAPPINESS IS A SIGN OF SENSITIVITY AND INTELLIGENCE.

—IF MY HAPPINESS DOES NOT DEPEND ON IT, I MIGHT NOT WANT IT ENOUGH.

—WE "SHOULD" DO CERTAIN THINGS IN LIFE.

—LIFE HAS ITS UPS AND DOWNS; YOU HAVE TO TAKE THE "GOOD" WITH THE "BAD."

—IF I DIDN'T CRY, IT WOULD MEAN I DID NOT CARE.

—I HAVE TO GET WHAT I EXPECT: OTHERWISE I GET ANGRY OR UPSET.

—IF I WASN'T ANGRY, I'D BE A VICTIM.

—CONTINUAL HAPPINESS WOULD BE LIKE DEATH.

—I HAVE TO BE UNHAPPY IN ORDER TO KNOW WHEN I AM HAPPY.

—IF I WERE HAPPY ALL THE TIME, I'D BE AN IDIOT.

—YOU CAN'T LOOK AT LIFE THROUGH ROSE-COLORED GLASSES.

—LIFE IS NOT A BED OF ROSES.

—YOU CAN'T HAVE YOUR CAKE AND EAT IT TOO.

They look pretty wild strung out in a column. Although they just represent a tiny sampling of beliefs of unhappiness, they provide a well-integrated foundation for misery and despair. Maybe, before we move on to a dialogue of the method, we can pause. Take each of the stated beliefs on the list above and, one by one, ask yourself the question: Do you believe it? If your answer is no, then you just had the opportunity to reaffirm what you know. If you answer yes, then you might want to ask: Why? Whatever your ultimate conclusion, the questions are a way for each of us to help bring our own awareness to life.

THE "THINK" PAGE (The Option Method: On Being Your Own Expert)

QUESTIONS TO ASK YOURSELF:

Do you really want to be unhappy?

Are you afraid of giving up some or all of your unhappiness?

Do you believe that being perfectly happy would be boring?

Are you ready to be your own "therapon?"

OPTION CONCEPTS TO CONSIDER:

*QUESTIONS ARE NOT SIGNS OF DOUBT AS MUCH AS OPPORTUNITIES TO CRYSTALLIZE WHAT WE KNOW.

*WITH THE ATTITUDE, EACH OF US COULD CREATE HIS OWN METHOD.

*THERE ARE NO GOOD OR BAD BELIEFS.

*WE ARE ALWAYS DOING THE BEST WE CAN, THE BEST WE KNOW HOW.

*HAPPY PEOPLE DO NOT STOP MOVING.

*WHEN WE ARE HAPPY, WE HAVE NO QUESTIONS.

*THE ATTITUDE: TO LOVE IS TO BE HAPPY WITH. NO EXPECTATIONS. NO CONDITIONS. NO JUDGMENTS.

*ANYTHING WE UNCOVER OR COME TO KNOW CAN ONLY ENRICH US.

*UNHAPPINESS IS BASED ON A LOGICAL SYSTEM OF BELIEFS.

*EACH OF US IS OUR OWN EXPERT.

*ONLY YOU KNOW YOUR ANSWERS TO QUESTIONS.

*WE EACH HAVE OUR OWN REASONS FOR BEING UNHAPPY.

*OPTION METHOD IS A WAY OF BECOMING HAPPIER.

BELIEFS TO CONSIDER DISCARDING:

We must be unhappy in order to take care of ourselves.

To be happy all the time is to be an idiot.

Unhappiness is bad.

The following dialogue, and all those presented throughout the book, are compressed versions of explorations using the Method. Since they are focused on individual people and their answers, the function here is not to convince or convert. Nor are their conclusions necessarily capable of being generalized. Their revelations are theirs. They are presented merely as a more graphic representation of the questions as a technique and a style of inquiry. As onlookers, we can only

48

imagine the impact or meaning of self-discovery for another. It is only through ourselves that it becomes our experience.

Your becoming happier is for you to do. In exposing and exploring beliefs, in discarding old ones and choosing new ones . . . there is only one relevant subject area and that's you.

FIRST DIALOGUE

Q. *WHAT ARE YOU UNHAPPY ABOUT?*

A. I don't know whether I can make a simple statement about just what I'm unhappy about now because it seems to be many things. But, it all surrounds one particular event, which I hope, will come to pass.

Q. *What event is that?*

A. I decided I wanted to go back to work. I'm twenty-nine years old. I have two great little kids; Jackie is seven and Robby is four. My husband, Daniel, works for a pharmaceutical company. We have everything, at least it seems that way. All the material trappings . . . a nice apartment in the Murray Hill area, nice friends and a really comfortable living style. Yet, despite all of it, I'm bored.

Q. *What do you mean?*

A. Well, it has nothing to do with my husband or my children. Before I had Jackie, I was an art director. Women were becoming a significant force in the industry and all avenues were opening to me. When I became pregnant, I had decided to become Mrs. American Mother . . . that was really what I wanted then. It was so new and exciting for several years. Then, Robby was born. Somehow, with two children, my life style dwindled down to a very big hustle . . . from cleaning, to chauffering, to schools, to doctors' appointments, to shopping. In the evening or on weekends, when I'm all set to go out, Dan is perfectly happy to stay home . . . but that's where I've been all week. And besides, when we visit people, I have nothing to say. Dan has his stories and the others have their stories. But me, I feel as dull as my life.

Q. When you say dull, what do you mean?

A. I'm bright. I have a Master's degree in fine arts. I want to be involved in much more than just cleaning and doing chores. I love playing with the children, but day after day I want stimulation appropriate to my intellect. So I made a decision: I don't want to stay home and just pass the time. I want to feel useful and enjoy the challenges I used to have at work. So I approached Dan and explained to him what I wanted to do. He had many questions and comments. Since this was not the first time I'd brought the subject up, I knew he wasn't taking me seriously. Within two weeks, I had my first job offer. It was fantastic, but when I told Dan that I'd really got a job . . . the roof fell in.

Q. What do you mean?

A. In every way. He accused me of being selfish, inconsiderate, and a rotten mother for not wanting to be with the kids. Then, we got into a whole argument about our way of life. He felt I had every opportunity to do anything I wanted, every challenge . . . the museum, movies, plays, books. That's great, but that's not what I was talking about. We shouted at each other all night. I couldn't believe his reaction.

Q. Why not?

A. I felt like I was talking to a person from the dark ages. All the bull I've heard from him about how women should have the same right as men to choose, etc., etc. Boy, bring it home and he plays a different tune.

Q. WHAT ABOUT THAT MAKES YOU SO UPSET?

A. That he should be more understanding.

Q. WHY ARE YOU UNHAPPY IF HE ISN'T?

A. Because it raises all sorts of questions for me. Is this the man I thought I married? Does he really love me? Wouldn't he want me to be happy? The questions drive me crazy.

Q. What's so uncomfortable about those questions?

A. I guess I'm afraid that I might come to the conclusion that our marriage is a dream I don't want any part of and my charming husband is really a bigoted ass.

Q. If that was so, why would that be so frightening?

A. Because I really love my husband and my children,

because I'm not wanting to create some gigantic problem . . . I just want to go back to work.

Q. What's stopping you, if that's what you want?

A. Nothing, except the repercussions. I can hear it now. Suppose he absolutely says no, that he won't permit it?

Q. WHY WOULD THAT UPSET YOU?

A. Well, who the hell is he to permit or not to permit? It's absurd, why do I have to ask him in the first place? He never asked me whether he could take the job he has. When he decided he liked it, he said yes. I should be able to do the same thing, damn him.

Q. WHY DOES THAT MAKE YOU SO ANGRY?

A. I feel like I'm trapped. As soon as I want to do something for myself, I'm accused of being selfish and a terrible person.

Q. What makes that a trap?

A. If I stay home like a good housewife, I'll continue to be bored and moderately unhappy, which I've certainly had enough of. Now, as soon as I actually make the decision to go to work, all hell breaks loose.

Q. What do you mean?

A. My husband freaks, my mother-in-law calls me a witch, my sister accuses me of wanting to wear pants. All of which has nothing to do with me.

Q. Then why are you so upset?

A. I'm angry that they're judging me.

Q. Why does that make you angry?

A. Because I have the right to do anything I damn please (crying). It's not like I'm becoming a junkie or a prostitute; I just want to go back to work.

Q. What about their judging you makes you so furious?

A. Because they're going to decide I'm bad. My mother-in-law, for example, is thrilled to be a housewife, cook, and bottle-washer. She's happy and that's wonderful for her. But now she's going to take her values and lay them on me. Would you believe that even my sister, who is four years younger than me, asked me if I had a problem with my womanhood? Who are they to pass judgment on me?

Q. They would each have their reasons, your husband, your mother-in-law, your sister. Maybe the question we can

51

*deal with is: If they decided you were "bad," why
would that make you so unhappy?*

A. Because I'm not . . . it's that simple.

*Q. If you know you're not, why should you be so upset if
they say you are?*

A. I guess (long pause) I'm afraid I will start believing
them.

Q. WHY DOES THAT FRIGHTEN YOU?

A. Because I don't want to.

Q. Then why would you?

A. I don't know. Sometimes, once in a great while, I
think maybe they're right. The entire affair is for my
benefit, I really considered me FIRST . . . and let
me tell you, that doesn't happen often in my house.

Q. Then what is unsettling about thinking of yourself first?

A. I guess it does make me selfish.

Q. What does that mean?

A. Thinking of me first.

Q. And why would that be a source of unhappiness?

A. I don't know. I was always told that being selfish was
bad. You're supposed to be considerate of others. In
my family, when I was a child, the great heroes were
those who laid down their lives for others. "You can't
think of yourself," was my father's battle cry.

Q. DO YOU BELIEVE THAT?

A. Yes and no.

Q. What's the yes part of your answer?

A. Maybe it's bad. My kids and my husband are important and they should get proper consideration.

Q. What are you saying?

A. That, perhaps, in considering me, I'm really ignoring
them and they might suffer.

Q. DO YOU BELIEVE THAT?

A. No, not really. After all, take the kids . . . I'd be a
better mother seeing them when I'm happy rather than
feeling chained to them. It's not the time that counts,
but the *quality* of that time. I know that when I'm
happy, the way I am with the children is much better
than when I'm upset or bored. In fact, I already investigated special day schools for Robby and found a
magnificent one. Since Jackie is in school all day and
plays with friends in the afternoon, he's taken care of.

52

I really somehow know that what would be best for me would be best for them.

Q. Then WHY ARE YOU UPSET?

A. Because I want them to know that, but they won't believe it; they won't understand.

Q. WHY WOULD YOU BE UNHAPPY IF THEY DON'T UNDERSTAND?

A. Because I want them to.

Q. I know that is what you want, but why would you be unhappy if it didn't come to pass?

A. I don't know.

Q. WHAT ARE YOU AFRAID WOULD HAPPEN IF YOU WEREN'T UNHAPPY ABOUT THEM NOT UNDERSTANDING?

A. You mean if they were all miserable and upset and I would just be okay with that?

Q. Yes.

A. That would really prove I'm selfish and uncaring.

Q. DO YOU BELIEVE THAT?

A. I want to say I don't. It feels like I don't, because whether I was unhappy or not about their understanding me, I'd still love them. But they wouldn't know that.

Q. WHY WOULD THAT MAKE YOU UNHAPPY?

A. Because I want them to undersand, to know that I care and love them . . . this entire affair has nothing to do with them specifically, except of course, they have to adjust to a working wife and mother. But I've taken care of all the potential problems. I really think they believe my choosing to work means something about them. That in some way it shows that I don't care as much. No matter how much effort I put into explaining, it's like beating a dead horse.

Q. And if you did everything you could to help them understand, yet, they still didn't . . . WHAT WOULD YOU BE UNHAPPY ABOUT?

A. At that point, I guess I might not. I can't live my life for everyone to the exclusion of me. I don't want to.

Q. Then why do you believe you would?

A. I don't anymore. I feel really straight on going back to work. If they judge me, I can't help that.

Q. How are you feeling?

A. Better. Actually, I'm beginning to allow myself to be excited. Before I suppressed it under my anger. I'm feeling much better now. But somehow this still doesn't solve my problem with my husband.

Q. *What problem?*

A. Suppose he decided to make some sort of insane mandate that I can't go back to work?

Q. *And if he does, why would that upset you?*

A. Because I know I wouldn't listen. If I stayed home to please him, I'd just come to resent and maybe even hate him. I don't want to be forced into a living situation I don't want. So I guess I'm concerned he might get so upset, maybe he'll want a divorce or something.

Q. *I know this will sound like an outrageous question, but try to answer it if you want. WHY WOULD THAT MAKE YOU UNHAPPY?*

A. I really don't want to hurt my marriage, although I obviously do want some changes. I think they'll be better for everyone. Yet, sometimes I say to myself: if he really loved me, he would want this for me.

Q. *DO YOU BELIEVE THAT?*

A. I think so.

Q. *Okay, what do you mean?*

A. If he was not so damn angry, furious and feeling sorry for himself, he would know that it's best for me and in loving me, he would want it too.

Q. *And since he is angry and furious, you're saying he's not knowing what is best. If that's so, as you surmise, what would his not wanting you to work prove?*

A. I guess nothing. Forget what I said before, I know he really loves me. It's just so infuriating to try to deal with a very unhappy and accusing individual.

Q. *WHY IS IT INFURIATING?*

A. I really want him to be understanding . . . to really know it's good and to want it for me.

Q. *And if he doesn't?*

A. If he doesn't, he doesn't. I guess that would be okay. I can just do so much. I can't crawl into his head and change the signs—only he can do that.

Q. *What are you wanting?*

A. To go back to work, to be happy, to love my husband, my children and me . . . especially me. It's funny how when I really explore what I feel and why I feel that way in regard to work, I really understand that doing it for me is really okay. And not only good for me, but for everyone. A happy person is a much more contributing and loving member of a family than one who is bored and unhappy. I really feel good about my decision now.

Q. IS THERE ANYTHING YOU'RE STILL AFRAID WOULD HAPPEN?

A. Not for the moment . . . I'll do the best I can with my husband. If he reacts from his anger, I'll just keep trying. I can't help what he thinks, but maybe I can just kind of allow him to think what he wants.

Q. What do you mean?

A. We discussed this once before about being happy with someone. It's like I wanted him to say "wonderful, great, do whatever you want." Well, if I want him to allow me my choice, I certainly can allow him his reaction.

3

children are born happy

In an insulated world of liquid, the sounds are muted and every bodily need is cared for by the interconnected order of this universe. A regular melodic rhythm formed by the natural cadence of the heart fills the cavern with soft music created by the echoing of its percussion statement. The womb: a galaxy of life unto itself, the seat of creation and the genesis of man. It houses within its walls a growing embryo which develops each day in millions of ways until it begins to shape itself into the form of a person. The head, the arms, the feet and the hands begin to project from their own mass as if molded out of the very soup of the mother's energy. As it graduates into fetal form, it begins to ready itself for the great birth out of the universe.

Unlike visions of a clouded yesterday, man is not born so much into the universe, as if a stranger, but from the very fabric of the universe. The elements of which he is composed, the fertilization which begins his great thrust and generates new life within a woman are essential fibers of the world into which he will step. In birth, man moves from the enclosure of a gentle and controlled environment into a more random and unpredictable one. On a schedule determined by his biological and physiological formation, which is precisely inscribed into his genetic foundation, he creates a harmonious thrust with his mother and is propelled into the open air.

Each child thus becomes a pronouncement of nature . . . its movement and its beauty. After traveling through the tunnel of the uterus, the child greets his existence wide-eyed and draws his first breath. In this way, he becomes a living participant in our communal atmosphere and in taking that breath he makes the world his.

The child is simple, uncomplicated and uncluttered. His rather complex biological systems, involuntary reflexes and automatic processes seem to operate with their own ease. The new little man or woman seems to contemplate the universe without effort. Their wants are simple and in the fabric of society and family units, their biological needs are usually satisfied.

Communication on a primary level is often centered around the act of crying. When the child first cries, he is responding to the changes in his perception of his internal environment as his system moves from its own equilibrium. The shout or cry is merely the infant responding to himself, which we as adults interpret to mean "I am hungry" or "I am wet" or "I have a pain." It is our way of keeping in touch with the child's needs (biological) and monitoring his state of affairs. As we listen and react, the child also begins now to experience our pattern of responses to his gestures. So far, there is no such thing as unhappiness.

The child's cry now becomes his way of calling us within the confines of his present capability. We have taught him how to use his shouting as a means of communication to get what he wants. He is not making a statement about his unhappiness or indicting the world. It is when we say, "Ah, the poor child is hungry," that *we assign a judgment to the activity*. The cry is just a registration that the body is out of harmony and seeking to return (with food, relief from wetness, etc). By judging the child's hunger or wetness as bad, we are then projecting our beliefs onto the child, beliefs he has not as yet acquired. When we assume the crying child

58

is unhappy, we are really making a statement about our beliefs and saying nothing about the infant . . . for him there is no question of being unhappy, just the desire to reestablish his own homeostasis.

At this point, in a style consistent with his development, the child begins to create communication bridges with his mother and the outside environment. When his balance is reestablished, he moves with awe in his world . . . dazzled by a fascinating sensory collage of color and sound. His ears perk; his eyes dance in his head; his mouth tastes the flavors as his tiny hands explore the textures of himself and the things around him.

The child is continually and spontaneously curious. Searching. Open. Welcoming and happy. He moves unencumbered by judgments and reflection. His world simply just is. There are no decisions about what is good or bad, no lengthy consideration of wanting and not wanting. The child just finds himself moving in the direction of his desires and fancy. There are no questions, just the wondrous exploration. The movement of his arms, the impulses and enjoyment of food, the sucking at the breast of his mother or the nipple of a bottle, the voiding of his bladder are just a few movements in his natural propensity just to be.

These activities are not considered or judged by the child. Possibly they are not even contemplated. Perhaps they just follow.

What am I wanting to illustrate? That the child is born into this world happy. Isn't that always part of our fascination in watching an infant as he moves and explores?

The crying does not signal feeling bad, but is simply a biological response with sound to the changes in his balance. Crying only becomes "unhappy" when *we* give it that meaning.

The primary social interaction of the infant is with his mother and centers on food. Eating and the giving of nourishment begins the overture. The cries, the signs, the food offerings, the holding and the stroking are all aspects of this basic interaction. Excretory functions are also part of his world . . . another avenue of experience, another source of pleasure and satisfaction. Even when the child's face cringes and becomes red while he is defecating, he is not signaling discomfort or disapproval . . . but is summoning his system and concentrating on the activity at hand. Touching and being touched during these early months of life are also joyful experiences with no sexual overtones . . . no connotations; the array of physical and genital receptors are just aspects of his sensory encounter. For the child, there is merely the intake, the digestion and interaction with the universe.

His world is okay for him and he lives in it spontaneously, an awestruck sponge without judgments.

It sounds beautiful. . . . Incredible! What happens? Why and when do we stop being ourselves, hesitate and question who we are? There are many reasons, all of which relate to our experiences as infants and children and the beliefs we adopt.

Thus far, we have an organism who is adjusting to and absorbing his new surroundings by following his own impulses and desires. All natural movements to him. He realizes his natural self: Happy and loving. The child is grateful for being alive through his curiosity. Still no questions, just gliding from thing to thing . . . enjoying the people and the objects in his world. Enjoying himself.

There are no hesitations about whether or not he should stop playing with this object in order to start playing with another. Simply, when he finishes, he puts one toy down and picks up another. No activity is more valued than another . . . it is just what he finds himself doing at any given time. No thoughts of "should I?" or "shouldn't I?," just free-flowing movement toward wants. The infant is always acting from his own natural flow; he is not diverted by attending to his fears or unhappiness. In his world, he only finds himself wanting to crawl, wanting food, wanting to be dry, wanting to be warm. As he becomes more sophisticated through interaction during that primary stage, he develops a heightened sense of communication as a function of getting what he wants and moving others in his environment toward his own goals . . . like giving him food or a new diaper or a blanket.

If learning, enjoying, being tickled, playing with a ball are all equal and there aren't any "nos," what happens to change this idyllic process? *Since the child is an absorbing sponge . . . as he ingests his environment, he begins to ingest the beliefs of the people in that environment.*

He, too, becomes a believing animal and falls subject to all the ramifications and results of having those beliefs.

The feeding programs created by parents for their children are varied and have different consequences. Some feed their infants on a demand schedule, which the child creates and enforces. Others design scheduled eating programs more consistent with the eating and sleeping habits of the parents. For that child, wanting and communication are sporadically functional. He comprehends that, at times, there are definite responses to his shouts, while, at other times, there is no response at all. The inconsistency usually will stimulate him to cry even more in an effort to explore and test his communications effectiveness, never really knowing when to stop since he never knows whether this is the time he will get the response. If he generates a reaction after incessant screeching, it usually comes from an unwilling parent or one thrown off balance by the child's intensity. Thus, the ensuing feeding situation might be infected with anger or anxiety . . . communicated to the child in the form of altered skin odor, a changed heartbeat, and different patterns of touching and holding. The child senses the tension, experiences the dissonance and adjusts.

Later, in other areas, an exhausted and well-meaning parent might start to train the child through disapproval. "Don't cry. Be a good little boy and Mommy will feed you." Or the more implicit schooling that comes as a result of the parents reacting to their own discomfort while with the child. "Stop that right now—you're ruining Mommy's curtains; you're a bad boy." The child reacts to the scolding and disapproval with confusion and then begins to acquire the beliefs of the reprimanding adult. Herein begins the process of ME teaching unhappiness.

In the other arenas of his life, the infant is still just being himself, playing and exploring. Not specifically cognizant of the wishes or the values of his parents' world, he might play with his juice by spilling it and rubbing it into the living room rug. He might investigate his mother's school notebook by crumpling and ripping the pages, tearing them, fascinated by the sound. He mght examine his wooden blocks by throwing them to see them bounce and listen to their staccato

61

sounds . . . and, perhaps, watch them causally break a mirror or a window.

He's Columbus discovering his America . . . an astronaut exploring his moon. To him, what he does is just part of the beautiful and exciting journey of making contact with his world.

Given any of the above examples, parents, upon discovering their home in disarray, would probably be caught off guard and, perhaps, would respond with anger. Anger as a function of seeing their belongings ruined, anger as a function of trying to show the child disapproval so he knows not to do it again. They might also pull the child from the room, upset with the disorder or damages.

The parent is at that moment doing the best he or she can . . . trying to cope, to manage the home and to properly train the child. The anger or aggression toward the child would come as the result of the parents believing this type of response would be in the best interest of both the parent (i.e., it's healthy to vent anger) and the child (i.e., reprimanding is an effective teaching tool). In that regard, because of those judgments and those beliefs as well as others, this kind of reaction would be the very best response the parent would be capable of making. Like all of us, feelings and behaviors are generated from our beliefs about a situation. Although our actions may seem negative and even be clearly self-defeating, we behave in such a fashion precisely because we follow naturally from our beliefs . . . whatever they might be. Ask anyone, even those engaged in seemingly destructive acts toward children, and they will tell you they have the "best" of reasons. It is NOT a question of the character of our intentions as much as a question of the content of our judgments and beliefs.

But the child, unaware of the mores and regulations of the adult community, gets a very distinct message in the hostility being expressed toward him. When he is happy and just doing what he does, his parents get unhappy. In their disapproval, the child learns something is wrong with his loving and happiness. He is only exploring being himself and meaning no harm, when suddenly his world is invaded and he is explicitly or implicitly told he is being bad.

Most children do not comprehend their quandary. They do not understand the meaning of the anger and scolding.

62

The child is being shown what he does makes others unhappy. In effect, when he is being happy (throwing blocks, ripping paper, making a river on the floor with his juice), others become unhappy. He does not understand that the consequences of his actions are viewed by his parents with discomfort. The belief implicitly communicated to the youngster is: "He causes unhappiness" in others. The ultimate message: "There must be something wrong with me" or "I am bad for being me." The accusing finger is pointed.

There is an additional, implicit suggestion that the child is somehow not supposed to be happy. If the child cared, he would not have done an inconsiderate act . . . "If you loved me, you would listen to what Mommy tells you." There is the selling of another cardinal belief: "If you loved me, you would . . ."

The confusion heightens. Concluding that something is wrong with him and his happiness, the child develops the superstition that his happiness has unhappy repercussions. "Something is wrong with me if my being me is bad and makes others unhappy." And a further conclusion . . . "I must be something else and not be me in order to be acceptable." *Therein lies the teaching of acting, the acquisition of facades and learning not to be me.*

What seemed to be a simple effort to protect our property and properly train the child has many ramifications. In those very initial situations of judgments and disapproval, we teach our children many beliefs about themselves and about unhappiness. We continually reinforce them in further interaction as the years progress. Unhappiness becomes the lesson that is taught as a result of the "not-wants" of parents, also as a method of protecting the child from danger (believing that unhappiness will be an effective deterrent). In addition, the parent might expect that when he or she is unhappy, the child should be unhappy . . . as a gesture of the little person's sympathy and humanity. Thus, if we are upset and disapprove of the child's action, they should in turn be humbled and uncomfortable. If not, the child might not be a human being. Thus, the appropriate reaction is solicited, molded and highly regarded.

Didn't our parents show their unhappiness when we were hurt, when we cut ourselves or when we were unable to get what we really claimed we wanted? Initially, we are induced to imitate the response. Later, we are "supposed to" and "expected" to return the compliment. Be sympathetic and respond in a discernible way.

Unhappiness is shown to be highly valued. "If you feel sad when I feel sad, then I feel better." "If you feel good when I am feeling bad, then I feel worse." The staging is precise. The beliefs are illustrated repeatedly, and concretely translated to the child. He is being prepared to learn, absorb and conform to the values and mores of his culture and his community . . . and one of the primary ones is unhappiness. In effect, the child is a student in a conditioning situation in which he is being taught beliefs as a function of social interaction. Once he makes those beliefs his, he is no longer a recipient, but becomes a spokesman.

Wanting is now converted into a more trained and predictable response. Somehow, many of the child's untempered wants get bad vibes in reaction. As he moves into and through the years of his childhood, he gets the distinct feeling he is a bother. Questions of self-worth and self-image!

Highlighted in the series of beliefs little people are taught is the one "you make me unhappy." The concept is that they are directly responsible for another person's feeling bad . . . that others aren't responding to their own beliefs, but the child is by some means mystically manipulating the strings and making them unhappy . . . as if he could, as if he had the power!

Unhappiness in each of us is the product of our own beliefs. Parents unhappy about the broken dish or damaged rug or ripped wallpaper are unhappy for their own reasons. Maybe the child taps their concerns about failing as a parent. In the same circumstances, other parents might not even care. But whatever the reaction to the damage of their possessions, the unruliness of their child and the apparent not caring of their offspring . . . it is all a reflection of their own beliefs, judgments and conclusions. Am I suggesting that you sit passively by while a child rampages through the house and misuses your property? Of course not. What I am suggesting is if we are more aware of the genesis of our feelings and the consequences of our responses, we might want to find a way to curb the child's activity without seeming to say that we disapprove or dislike him as a person.

64

The drama continues. Beliefs about interlocking dependency (I cause your unhappiness and you cause mine) are repetitiously and graphically exemplified to the child. As a result, the little person becomes concerned with his power (as he adopts the belief) and does not allow his wants to flow freely . . . after all, just being himself makes his parents unhappy.

Again, reaffirmation of the concept that there must be something wrong with me . . . thus, "I am bad when I am me." Something also must be wrong with his wanting. Even the parent who becomes angry when the child keeps crying for things is implicitly saying to the child: "There is something wrong with you if you are lacking something or pressing me for your wants . . ." the message—"Suppress your wants and who you are. Be what I want and expect you to be and I'll love you."

How often have we heard a child scream in frustration: "Hey, I didn't ask to be born." He sees his very existence as the cause of pain and suffering . . . being loving causes problems. He now has to listen carefully and very cautiously so he will know what to do . . . because he now *believes* what he wants is bad.

The parent is working through his own dilemma. He somehow interprets his child's actions as being statements about not caring and lack of consideration. He sees the child as an unruly, untrained person in need of discipline. The parent often ties his self-worth to his child. "If my child is untrained or undisciplined, then I failed" . . . so they both find each other's existence as a possible cause of pain and certainly one of pressure. No one is saying that the parent wants this . . . that he is not loving the child in the best way he knows how. Only that there is a question: Is there a more effective way to be with our children, a more direct way to help them help themselves to be happier?

"If being me is bad, then I must learn to be not-me, which others say is good. Then, I have much self-doubt and insecurity about who I am. Since I want to be loved and since I want a peaceful environment, there must be something wrong with me if I generate dissonance in others."

Thus, living becomes a process of learning how to be as if the child did not know . . . always consulting his private

65

book on acceptable behaviors in order to move. Stop-start. The journey which at one time seemed easy and flowing, now becomes an obstacle course in which he tries to avoid making others unhappy while trying to determine what he wants.

Being human, the child uses others as a source of modeling. He imitates to learn and he copies for acceptance. The rules are laid before him at a very young age. Some children might scream at their parents . . . "Leave me alone" and then become petrified that being left alone might mean being left to die. So often, he contains the impulse. The dilemma is either go mad or grow up.

But in growing up where judgments, disapproval, conditions for loving and rejection are the order of the day, moving is often intermixed with suppression of wants and anger. Even anger at himself because there is something wrong with him . . . yet he remains furious that others want and continually ask him to be not-him.

Even the very question of loving is cast in doubt. "My parents tell me that they yell at me and punish me for my own good, because they love me." The child naturally becomes ambivalent about being loved. "If my parents' treating me badly and hitting me comes from their loving, then do I want to be loved? And would I want to love?" Loving, mixed with pain and anger, becomes a double-edged sword. Loving is injected with the serum of discomfort . . . perhaps the child might even come to fear being loved.

Our child's discomfort or unhappiness is his, but the beliefs he might have are most likely the ones we taught him.

What more could I ever want for myself than be loved without rules and conditions. What more could I give my children than the Option Attitude: "To love is to be happy with." In my loving my child, I would be accepting him and wanting him to be comfortable and joyful.

If I disapprove of my child, if I create conditions on his behavior in order to be loved, if I make judgments that his actions are a sign something is wrong with him, then I am pushing the child with hostility and aggression. Why wouldn't I simply be happy if my child was happy?

The immediate response is there are many things I might want for my child which seem to go against his apparent happiness . . . like suppose his way of being happy is destroying my house and I certainly don't want that. Okay, maybe there is a way to differentiate arenas of freedom. What is part of my child's world is for him to decide and what is part of my world is for me to decide. Implications. A parent often makes judgments about what's best for the child because the parent is believing that the child would not choose what's best for himself. Yet in doing that, I am saying to my child: "Something is wrong with you . . . you can't even be good for yourself." What would any of that matter if I were only in touch with wanting my child to be happy? His exploration, choosing and missing the mark and coming to bat again, is all part of his growth.

When he should eat or not eat, whether to play with this toy or that one, when to sleep and not to sleep are all arenas in which the child moves in his world. If he could choose more freely, without repercussions, if he could know that his inclinations and movements that come from him are okay, he would surely not come to doubt himself and believe something was wrong with him. He would not harbor fears about who he is and anxiety about his actions. In my loving him as he is and being accepting of his choices (even though they are not mine), I would be saying, "My loving you comes from my being happy with you . . . We both know that you're okay."

When the child spills into my world and breaks the windows of my house with a rock, then I might intercede if I wanted. That's my domain for which I have my own requirements. Yet, the tone and implicit commentary in my voice is all important. How I express my feelings is crucial.

If I communicated what I wanted without anger, without fear, without threats . . . just stating that I wanted my possessions respected, my child could not leave my presence believing he was rejectad or hated. It is only when I scream and call my child bad that I am telling him something global about himself.

Often a child who has been punished or hit still feels and remembers the trauma of the attack long after he remembers the reasons why and the lesson behind it. In fact, the aggression is usually so frightening in its implications (of rejection and loss of love) that the child hardly hears the message. What he retains is the anger, the disliking, the conclusion he is "bad."

There are Option alternatives which would grow naturally from the attitude of "to love is to be happy with."

One evening, Bryn, my ten-year-old feminine whirlwind, decided to use my typewriter without asking permission or guidance on how to operate it. When I returned home, she had managed somehow to short-circuit the electrical mechanism.

I guess I could have made myself upset (since I had intended to use the machine that very evening) and could have expressed my anger by yelling, "You don't care about anyone except yourself," and "You're thoughtless and disrespectful" or "You're a bad girl." But if we just briefly explore any of these judgments and accusations, trying to relate them to the situation and what we want, we might see why they would be unproductive and ineffective.

It is one thing to explain to children that you do not want them to do something; but that is altogether different from communicating disapproval of them as people by viewing and calling them insensitive, thoughtless or "bad." I would not want my daughter to believe or conclude she was bad or inept because she did something contrary to my wants or values. Screaming, verbal assaults and punishment provoked by anger only create resentment and a push against the parent's request (usually by the child's repeating the unwanted act).

During our discussion, Bryn and I tossed our feelings and thoughts back and forth. I clearly stated my preference always to have her consult me before using my things even though, at the time, she might feel she had the best of reasons. As I carefully noted my respect for her property, I asked her for the same courtesy. As a direct result of being accepted, my daughter was far more open to hearing my wants and honoring my requests than the child polarized and diverted by a barrage of anger and accusations. Bryn responded with caring and concern. Her focus was on helping me find another electric typewriter to replace mine while it was being repaired.

There was no guilt or lingering discomfort she had to feel or display as retribution for her trespasses or in order to "earn" my continued love. By heightening her awareness of my preferences and wishes, I had accomplished what I wanted. Bryn was attentive and sincere, responses not stimulated by fear and discomfort, but born out of an understanding and respect for herself as well as for me.

Why couldn't both my child and I allow each other freedom without the right of invasion? Each of us could maintain autonomy in our respective arenas, but negotiate with each other when we wanted to cross the line. In such an arrangement, each of us is saying that the other's wants and choices are okay and valued. And most important . . . respected.

An effective concept for negotiating with the child is *the trade*. In trading I neither bribe nor force, both of which have undercurrents of fear, punishment, anger and resentment. Instead, I use a barter system in which both parties are enriched by the transaction. It is the act in which I offer the child something he wants in return for what I want or vice versa. Some might want to insist this technique is still a form of bribery . . . but then all business transactions, deals with friends, and arrangements between lovers would also be bribery. In a trade, two respectful participants would deal with each other by allowing each to choose and suggest alternatives in a transaction without the threat of punishment or reprisal. The child would always have the freedom and the choice to reject (or accept) the offer . . . as I have the same opportunity.

The parent who has adopted the Option attitude would not be uncomfortable, angry or resentful with the child who decides to refuse the trade. Nor would that parent have reservations or misgivings about maintaining his own position.

I recall a very intense trading session with my son Raun. We were both jointly occupying our den. On this particular occasion, I wanted him to play with his toys in silence while I finished revising an artcle I had written. Initially, I had considered moving to my studio, but cancelled the impulse because I did not want to leave my son alone. Although he most often complies with my requests, as I do with his, this time he was intent on continuing his fantasy games, which included making a cacophony of loud noises . . . his vocal approximations of the sounds of speeding trucks, rescue helicopters and glossy red fire engines. For Raun, his games were certainly as important as my adult "game." And although I had a publishing deadline to meet and could even tie the delivery of the article to such essentials as buying food and supporting my family, I nevertheless chose to respect my son and what he viewed as the significance of his activities.

I opened negotiations with my first offer in trade: a tumbling session on the bed and an extended piggyback ride in exchange for some uninterrupted quiet. He smiled coyly and shook his head, clearly indicating his "no." My second offer was a quick swim in his small rubber pool. He seemed to meditate for several seconds and then rejected this second suggestion. His eyes glittered as he searched the room for ideas that might suggest other items for trade. Finally, he broke into a magnificent smile as he countered my offers with one of his own: two scoops of chocolate ice cream in a cone. I paused for several seconds and considered his counter proposal. I had little or no interest in driving to the store. I explained my lack of enthusiasm to Raun and then reiterated *my* best offer . . . a swim in the pool.

At first he didn't respond. But then, he turned and looked directly into my eyes, displaying great determination. He now proposed the tumbling session and the piggyback ride in addition to the swim—all in trade for his silence. Loving our interchange and delighted with the progress and equity of our trade, I told the little man we had a deal. For the next two hours, this free-flowing, three-and-a-half-year-old little boy continued to play elaborate fantasy games with his cars, trucks and little people. Never once did he make a noise . . . never once did he have to be reminded. Raun had only enthusiasm for carrying out his part of a bargain that he himself had helped formulate. It was an easy commitment since he was acutely aware of doing exactly what he wanted.

The essence of my behavior in *the trade* was dealing with my son as a peer, honoring him with respect and offering him the opportunity to choose.

The more skillful we each become in assessing each other's values and pleasures, the more effective we become as traders. And thus, whenever my child complies with my requests because he likes the activity offered him in the trade, he asserts his own will and gets what he wants. Ultimately, the child freely exploring his world is a happy and free-flowing individual . . . and isn't that what I was wanting for him in the first place?

Of course, there is no suggestion here that everything *must* be predicated on a one-for-one bargain. Often, we might choose to do things without asking or wanting anything in return. But when there is a question of differing interests or intentions between parents and children, the trade becomes an arrangement by which we can respectfully and lovingly motivate each other.

"It sounds like such a time-consuming process," some have suggested. Well, if I consider how often I have to tell and retell a child to do what he doesn't want, and then how often I have to reprimand him for doing it poorly or ineffectively, I can see how the "command" technique of child rearing is also very time-consuming. In addition, it creates negative by-products such as insecurity, hostility, discomfort, fear and resentment. The child who sees it in his best interest to do something as the result of a *trade* or understanding will require no enforcement or policing. In all probability, he will also perform his tasks and pursue his interests with a much greater degree of perfection than another child who sees himself as being forced. Ultimately, he will become the originator and initiator of his own trades.

When I see my child pushing, tumbling, throwing and making noise, I could know this is a child being happy with himself . . . sounds and visions of his being alive. If I allow him that freedom, that acceptance, I am allowing him to find in himself his wanting, his strength, his reasons to be. If not, then I am doing battle with him, cutting the juices of his flow and selling him beliefs that he is no good when he is himself. In setting up no conditions and no expectations, I am communicating to the child that he is okay and that I love him without judging, without requiring him to perform in a prescribed manner in order to maintain my affection and caring.

No child's behavior was bad until someone judged it so. His acts were not the cause of unhappiness, until someone believed them so. His existence was not a nuisance until someone made it so. In effect, from our wanting us and our

71

children to be happy, some of us have also utilized the tools of unhappiness.

How often have I heard, "When I hit my son, it hurts me more than it hurts him," "I punished my daughter for her own good" or "If I don't get angry, he'll just keep doing it." All these reasons, all the rationality, all the pushing in service to the belief that I must act or be a certain way to help guide my children in reaching their potential or at least, to help them become "good" individuals in the framework of the community.

I can have my children molded by my pressures and coercing, or I can pursue an alternative method of child rearing in which I foster an environment to allow my children the freedom to find their own reasons to be. Allow them to find their own wanting from within and their own avenues of expression as to what they feel and who they are. Encourage them to be and express themselves, even create avenues to help them draw water from their own wells.

Often, with children who are labeled as unruly and deviant, people use force and disapproval as a method of teaching and training them. The results are usually devastating because the child *pushes against being pushed*. Believing he "has to" or "must" or "should" in order to win approval, he rebels against that confinement of his choice and sometimes goes directly against it, even if it means hurting himself.

Take the child who is hungry and as he arrives at the dining room table, his father shouts, "Now sit down right there and eat . . . and you'd better eat every morsel of food." Either the child will shrink into the chair unhappily or go away from the table even though he is hungry. Pushing, no matter how good the intentions, usually creates the opposite resistance. On the other hand, if I could help the child come to know that the food is good for him, help him get in touch with his hunger and go with his wanting, he will probably do just what I want for him . . . he would take care of himself and as he chose to do so, he would do it happily.

Another liability of pushing is the apparent possibility of robotizing the child . . . having him perform out of the pressure to perform, having him react in a certain way to avoid disapproval or punishment, having him speak respectfully not out of love but out of fear of loss. What would I be

72

doing when I coerce my children to live in accordance with my expectations and accept my mores? The implicit statement is "be my way rather than your way." But if I love someone, then I am happy with them. I know they always do the best they can, the best they know how. If I accept them, if I do not judge the actions as having all sorts of meanings, if I love them without conditions, then they can be themselves and feel free to love themselves and me. In turn, they could listen and accept my wants and input. I would not want my son or daughter to be nice to me because they believe they "had to" (and probably as a result really didn't want to), but would rather have them love me because they wanted to.

In accepting the wants of loved ones, I am giving them the freedom to love me . . . the freedom to nurture and fertilize their wants. In such an environment, happiness blossoms because people are moving with themselves.

All the games the child learns to play are eventually used on the parents and experimented with during peer interaction. The child might now say to the parent, "If you loved me or want me to be happy, then you would buy me ice cream." He knows the beliefs of his parents and in turn, exploits them. Being taught that wanting is not enough, they fake needing (I'll be miserable if you don't get it for me) in order to motivate their parents to acquiesce. "I must have that ice cream or else I am going to be unhappy." This taps the parents' belief system and creates in the parents their own threat of unhappiness and guilt. This will possibly then motivate them to do the child's bidding, because the threat of the child's rejection might mean they are bad parents. Rather than face their own recrimination, they turn to a policy of appeasement, which reinforces the child's behavior.

In fact, this is the key to turning *wanting into needing*. Since wanting is not enough, it is the threat of unhappiness and the "must have" that is his way of moving his parent. In fact, it is his way of also pushing himself to pursue and nag his parents. A double-purpose function. In the end, if he does not get what he says he needs, he then fulfills his prophecy and becomes bitterly unhappy.

Thus, as the child grows, he also becomes an expert in using unhappiness, but what he does not know is that the

73

anger, fear, anxiety, threats and discomforts bring with them their own liabilities. All he is taught is that being happy or acting happy is not particularly rewarding. "If I act happy when asked if it is okay that I did not get a new bicycle, then my parents would not be motivated to spend their money on it. If my happiness was not at stake, they wouldn't bother. So, I show them that it is."

The incredibly beautiful phenomenon is that all children are aware their unhappiness is an act, a performance, a fabricated technique to help them get more of what they want. A favorite example in my life involves a specific inter-action one Sunday afternoon with my daughter, Thea, who was then just three years old. As my wife and I were in the midst of mounting a piece of sculpture, our impish little girl approached us asking for candy. Since this was certainly not a staple in our home and since the health food store was closed on Sunday, we could not satisfy her desire. My wife responded casually. She would buy Thea some candy the next time she went shopping for our supply of organic foods. The answer was unsatisfactory for our single-minded dynamo. As was consistent with the nature of her personality, she re-fused to give up so easily. Her polite initial request became a symphony of pleas. Her eyes narrowed as her voice became sharp and piercing. She even stamped her foot on the floor.

Escalating her approach, she supported what now had be-come demand with several fanciful arguments. We listened patiently and again explained the nature of our involvement. I redirected her back to her mother's willingness to buy candy for her during the week. For a moment, the clouds parted and Thea seemed satisfied. Then, her body tensed as she decided to use her most dramatic technique in a last-ditch effort to achieve her goal. Thea, quite suddenly, but with great intensity, began to cry. Her energy level was amazing as we watched the systematic escalation of her efforts.

Trying to counter her commitment and wanting to neutral-ize her "developed" unhappiness, I sat beside my daughter and tickled her belly. For a moment, she allowed herself to smile, but then quickly pulled her body away. As I persisted, she finally removed herself from my grasp and walked to the opposite side of the room. Again, she looked at me from beneath brooding eyebrows and flashed another quick smile through her tears. Turning away as if to purposely avoid my

74

gaze and concentrate on the activity at hand, she started to cry again. I could feel her sending me nonverbal cues: "Daddy, please go away and don't ruin my act. I'm just crying as a way to get you and Mommy to buy me candy now."

Fantastic. The unhappiness seemed to be controlled by a simple on-and-off mechanism—tears were easily traded for laughter and laughter easily replaced by tears. Our daughter was using unhappiness as a way to motivate us . . . as a way to get what she wanted.

The same evening, we engaged Thea in a discussion about the episode with the candy. It was awesome to listen to our little girl candidly explain to us her precise awareness of what she had been doing. Speaking without hesitation or misgiving, she said, "you know, before, when I was crying and everything . . . well, I was really just making believe so you would buy me candy."

In similar circumstances, another child might have been more successful using such a method. Pretending unhappiness would be the technique displayed each time she wanted something. And each time she achieved her goal, it would reinforce continued use of the tool. Resentment can also flourish in a child who sees herself motivating her parent because she is miserable rather than because she is loved. After innumerable occurrences of pretending unhappiness, the activity becomes so real that the child may actually no longer remember she is pretending . . . and at that moment, she graduates and becomes an adult.

The most effective means to successfully play a game—especially the unhappiness game—is to envision it as real. That commitment insures us of not becoming easily confused or forgetting the rules. And thus in establishing our unhappiness as real, it indeed becomes a significant and supercharged reality in the delicate and vulnerable chambers of our mind.

The child-rearing visions and techniques born from the Option Attitude, "To love is to be happy with," can also apply to later education and to more formal educational environments.

Teaching is not just a process of shoveling all the information we can into young people's heads; it is the art of drawing them out and helping them come to know what there *is* for them to know . . . and that varies from person to person. Teaching is not infusing another with data, but in stilling motivation. A teacher teaches by helping the child generate his own impetus to learn and satisfy his own natural curiosity . . . facilitating and allowing him to go with his interests and being with him as a guide and partner

If I accept a child without expectations, respecting his dignity and his capabilities, then there is no reason to judge his achievements in learning and absorbing. Whatever he accomplishes is the best he can do for this moment. Calling it poor or inadequate does little except intimidate and communicate disapproval.

Some professionals, in an effort to neutralize such adverse impact, use different labels that they believe are helpful in designating capabilities and functional in dealing with their classes and students. But they are also merely disguised judgments, to which are attached expectations and conditions . . . they are the beliefs which can often become self-fulfilling prophesies.

In a unique experiment performed in a midwestern school system, four classes of children diagnosed and tested as minimally "mentally retarded" were graduated to the next grade level. Two teachers were informed their students were retarded, while the other teachers were told nothing . . . they *believed* they each had a class of average students. At the end of two semesters, the teachers who believed they had average students had their classes performing almost on grade level and in some areas, performing on grade level. The two teachers who thought they had retarded children had very different results by year-end. Their classes had slipped behind dramatically and the children were functionally more retarded and behind their age level than before. There is a beautiful lesson here . . . in our haste and need to judge and categorize, we create unstated limits and adjust our in-put to conform to those limits. Call a child stupid, believe a child is stupid and we help create in him the appearance of stupidity.

People give accolades to the child at the head of his class and disapproval to the one at the bottom. But why is there a top and bottom? Probably because many professionals and parents believe by judging the child, they can best determine their progress and then use approval or disapproval to motivate him to continue to achieve or to do better. The major belief here is that disapproval or the threat of disapproval is an effective way "to move" our children. Even when that is not communicated directly, it is effectively stated with grades and comments on papers. The child, bombarded with these beliefs about good and bad students, tries to move through a potentially threatening environment where competition and comparison with peers is a basic tenet.

There is no difference between the child who learns slowly and the one who learns quickly except their rate of absorption and someone's *judgment*. The judgment is that one is better than the other. But such assessments have devastating effects. For the so-called slow or average learner, it is a commentary on his self-worth and does more to keep him where he is . . . first, because of the teacher's expectation that he had limited capabilities (which is subtly communicated to him and which he begins to believe about himself), and second, because of his own anxiety and fears of continued disapproval. Even the fast learner or honor student does not escape the pressures. He must continually maintain his "exceptionality" or otherwise face the repercussions of failing (getting a B instead of an A). In that game, he too is distracted by the anxiety of having continually to perform in order to be accepted and applauded. Unhappiness or the threat of unhappiness is used as a motivator by a system that believes its children "must" and "should" conform to ideals and expectations in education, rather than accepting the child with his talents, comforts, or discomforts and trying to help him, as an individual, to be the most he can for *himself*.

Even the unruly and disruptive child, whose attentiveness and learning is limited, does the best he can from his beliefs and unhappiness. Yet look at how we view him. Interesting that our culture is permissive with the mentally retarded child (who we say is doing the best he can) and not with the underachieving or unruly child (who we assume is *not* doing the best he can). But here again, is there really that difference? Many believe that because the unruly child has the aptitude intellectually to do better, the whip will straighten him out.

Just as the underachiever is trying or not trying in accordance with his beliefs and resulting feelings (perhaps he is trying to cope with fears of failure, anxiety about rejection, anger at being unloved, etc.) . . . so our disapproving and stern reactions come from our beliefs (unhappiness and harsh words motivate people, we have to teach him a lesson, etc.). Yet, in our severity, we are emphatically saying to the child that something is wrong with him . . . thus, pushing him away from us and learning, and motivating him to repeat his behavior as a function of not wanting our "conditional" approval.

Maybe, just like any of us, the unruly and different child is just wanting people to accept him for what he is. Maybe his cries for attention in the classroom, although apparently negative and negatively reinforced, are just his way of saying, "Can you please love me?" His actions are not an affront to us personally or a vicious statement against our mores. When a child or anyone is unhappy and self-defeating, they are saying many things about themselves and nothing about us. They can never be saying anything about us.

And thus in the process of becoming "educated," the mechanism of unhappiness becomes fortified by supportive experiences, by defenses and projections. The effort to disconnect them later is more difficult. Children, less sophisticated and still open, are more easily reached. Just as they learned to use unhappiness to motivate themselves and may have learned to fear their own wants in order to be cautious so they did not hurt themselves, they can change their beliefs, alter the system and learn to trust themselves again.

The place to begin with them and with ourselves is "to love is to be happy with," the Attitude of acceptance with no judgments and no conditions. The child could then try to learn and grow without limits or pressures. In allowing himself to go with his own curiosity and explore the world at his own pace, his contact with the environment is free and joyful . . . like the baby who laughed and giggled his way across the living room floor in search of his next adventure.

The Attitude "to love is to be happy with" cannot be simply portrayed as if on a stage nor can it even be effectively mimicked. Although I might have a surface response of "apparent" approval and acceptance, if I really disapprove, the negative judgment will ultimately be communicated.

Whether through tone, facial expression, body language or general tenseness, my point of view and feelings surface. These cues are easily recognized by the child who then becomes confused by the double messages. Overt gestures of acceptance are belied by underlying tones of rejection.

What's the question here? Can I learn child rearing techniques as a function of a memorized process? I don't think so. All the faddish courses on becoming an effective parent suggest changes through mechanics. They describe specific tactics and strategies which they call their method. In Option, if I have the Attitude, I create *my own method* of child rearing and develop my own style of interaction. There would be no need to learn or study "effectiveness" techniques (as if I didn't know them). My actions and responses would merely flow naturally from me as I loved and was happy with my children.

As a parent, the happier I become, the more effective and more loving I am with my children. The place to begin is with myself. As I change, the whole world changes. If I approach my children with the Option Attitude, I would allow them . . . want them to have their explorations and be accepting of the tone and content of their problems. My desire would be to help them come to their own awareness, rather than preach, scold, demand, or threaten them. I would want this, not as the result of some carefully planned tactic, but from my loving and caring for them. I also would come to know this is a beautifully effective way to deal with someone, as opposed to anger, fear, hostility and resentment that only create more of the same.

How casual we are about the words we use and yet how often they convey disapproval and unhappiness to our children. Our style of communication, which reflects our attitude, is so loaded with connotations of rejection and judgment that we seldom realize the tone and ultimate force of our comments.

If we consider some of the more typical parental statements, the underlying beliefs and disapproval are dramatically apparent:

—"Do what I say—NOW!"
—"By this time, you should know how to do it right!"

—"Who do you think you are talking to?"
—"Be quiet while I'm talking."
—"Clean up your room or else you will go to bed early."
—"Don't force me to say it again, or else."
—"You should act like a young lady, not an immature baby."
—"People will think you were brought up in a pigpen."
—"I know what's best for you . . . you're too young to understand."
—"Please leave the room, we're talking big people talk."
—"If you don't do your homework, I will cut your allowance."
—"For God's sake, you look awful! Why don't you get a haircut?"

Each of the above statements contains implicit or explicit disapproval. Even the "questions" are really only disguised accusations. There are other questions, some of which could have the appearance of neutrality, which are also criticisms: "Why are you acting like a child?" (behavior is judged inappropriate), "Why can't you work harder in school?" (implies that you're not working hard), "What is so important about a little party?" (belittles the activity as insignificant), "Who would put up with you besides your parents?" (suggests you are outrageous, difficult) and "How come you can't understand simple rules?" (a judgment made on intelligence and attention).

If I were feeling good about myself and my child (knowing both of us are doing the best we can, the best we know how, based on our current beliefs), there would be no reason to pass judgments. My desire would be to help him become happier and more effective in getting what he wants.

When I listen and hear children, I find them saying many wondrous things. When I respond as a loving and concerned person, I help them see themselves as okay and valued. Although I might want them (for my own reasons) to behave or choose differently, I could still show them that the expression of all feelings and thoughts (happy or unhappy) is okay. I can do this merely by listening without judging or reprimanding. As the child sees himself as more accepted, he becomes more willing to explore his wants and his problems. In that exploration, supported by my allowing,

80

he begins to find his own answers and unravel his own labyrinths.

If my daughter says she dislikes her homework and does not want to do it, instead of scolding or threatening her, I let her speak and vent her feelings. Then, I try to help her clarify her thoughts, but this is just a minimal first step. Afterwards I would ask her an Option question as I would with any person I was helping to be happier. In regard to her homework, my question would be "Why do you get upset (unhappy) when you have homework?" This is crucial in helping her uncover the "whys" or beliefs beneath her feelings. It also implicitly communicates I care and am interested . . . that my goal is to share and help, not to judge and disapprove.

In effect, when I am feeling good about my child, I am happy with her and want to help her. I know that only she can solve her own discomforts and find the answers that are correct for her . . . she is her own mover and teacher.

We only disapprove of those we love when we, ourselves, are unhappy.

Children are born from us, but they are not owned by us. They are not possessions. They can be a beautiful experience . . . doorways into our humanity. Children are free spirits for us to love and enjoy. We share the world with them . . . but their thoughts and wishes are theirs in the very same fashion in which our thoughts and wishes are ours.

81

THE "THINK" PAGE (CHILDREN ARE BORN HAPPY)

QUESTIONS TO ASK YOURSELF:

Can you cause unhappiness in others?

Are you afraid to be you?

Do you "get" things by being unhappy?

OPTION CONCEPTS TO CONSIDER:

* WE ARE BORN INTO THIS WORLD HAPPY.

* MY UNHAPPINESS IS A PRODUCT OF MY BE-LIEFS.

* TO LOVE IS TO BE HAPPY WITH.

* I DO NOT CAUSE MY CHILD'S UNHAPPINESS, HE DOES NOT CAUSE MINE.

* WHAT MY CHILD DOES IS NOT A STATEMENT ABOUT ME.

* I WILL ALLOW MY CHILD FREEDOM IN HIS OWN ARENAS (PLAYING, EATING, DRESSING).

* TRADING WITH MY CHILD HELPS HIM TO DE-
VELOP HIS CAPACITY TO CHOOSE, ASSERT HIS
WILL AND TRUST HIMSELF.

* I CAN GET WHAT I WANT WITHOUT NEEDING
IT.

* A CHILD PUSHES AGAINST BEING PUSHED.

* TEACHING IS HELPING A CHILD GENERATE
AND SATISFY HIS OR HER OWN NATURAL CU-
RIOSITY.

BELIEFS TO CONSIDER DISCARDING:

Newborn infants who cry are unhappy.

I cause unhappiness in others.

There is something wrong with me.

I hit and punished my daughter for her own good.

Unhappiness proves I'm sensitive and human.

SECOND DIALOGUE

Q. WHAT ARE YOU UNHAPPY ABOUT?
A. My kids, they drive me crazy.
Q. What do you mean?
A. When I'm trying to relax, to read or even chat with a
friend, in they come bouncing around with all their
demands. No matter how often I tell them to leave us
alone, they just keep coming back. Finally, I just
scream at them . . . and then they leave. And not
immediately. Sometimes, I have to keep yelling to get
any reaction. By that time, I'm usually so upset, I
can't enjoy myself any longer.

Q. WHY DO YOU GET SO UPSET?

A. They just don't listen and it makes me furious.

Q. Why, when they don't listen, does that make you furious?

A. Then I become a victim of my own children.

Q. What do you mean?

A. They just do what they damn please and make demands. I can't stand it.

Q. WHY DOES THAT MAKE YOU UNHAPPY?

A. Because I want my privacy . . . time for myself.

Q. Okay, that's what you want . . . but why are you unhappy if you don't get it?

A. Because I'm a waste (starts to cry). I just can't help it. I love my kids, but all I am is their cook and maid. Maybe that's all I am for my husband too. I want time for me.

Q. Could you clarify what you mean?

A. I want time so I can do things for my own enjoyment. Maybe take up the piano or learn to play tennis. Anything! I'm so busy all day, there's nothing left for me, except of course, screaming and acting like some sort of a witch. They make me be someone I don't want to be.

Q. How do they make you do that?

A. How? Well, by interrupting me so much, by nagging . . . they get me angry.

Q. But how do they GET you angry?

A. I get upset when they annoy me. (pause) I feel like I'm going in a circle.

Q. Okay, maybe if we go back to the question. If your children get you angry, if they somehow do it to you . . . how would you see it being done? How do they MAKE you angry?

A. Let me describe the scene. It's all there. My little "darlings" come skipping into the room, stand right in front of my face and just start talking. When I'm interrupted like that . . . I'm being abused, used, whatever. So naturally, I get furious.

Q. They did what they did, placed themselves in front of you and began speaking. But how did that "naturally" trigger your anger?

A. Well (very long pause), when I see myself as being

84

abused, I guess I get myself angry. I don't know any-more . . . sometimes I think it's the only way to defend myself. The trick is how can I not get angry when they make their demands.

Q. *How do you think you'd go about it?*

A. I wouldn't know where to begin. I'm back to feeling angry.

Q. *Okay then, what about their requests makes you angry?*

A. I don't want to be a ranting and raving mother. Even though I may be doing it to myself, I just can't seem to help it.

Q. *What do you mean?*

A. There's nothing else I can do . . . that's my only way to control them.

Q. *DO YOU BELIEVE THAT?*

A. I guess. If I just stated myself nicely and calmly, they would never listen.

Q. *And if they chose still to ignore you, WHY WOULD THAT MAKE YOU UNHAPPY?*

A. (Her face begins to cringe as she cries. A minute passes.) I guess it would prove they really don't give a damn.

Q. *WHY DO YOU BELIEVE THAT?*

A. If they loved me, they would respect my wishes and leave me alone.

Q. *Okay, but if they didn't . . . why do you believe that would mean they don't care?*

A. How could someone love you and drive you crazy at the same time?

Q. *What do you think?*

A. Okay. Can someone love you and care, yet still do things that upset you? I guess it's possible. Everytime I serve a T.V. dinner, Fred gets upset. But I love him . . . I'm just too busy that day to fuss over a meal. Yet, even though I know he doesn't like it, I still give it to him sometimes. The answer is yes.

Q. *Yes what?*

A. You can drive someone crazy and still love them.

Q. *Okay . . . so what you are saying is that if someone does things you don't like, that doesn't mean they don't love you or care.*

A. Yes, that's really clear now. I feel like I just got rid of a load. I guess I was believing my children were somehow saying they didn't love me. But that's just not so. They can drive me nuts and still love me.

Q. What do you mean "drive you nuts"?

A. Do things I don't want them to do.

Q. And how does that drive you nuts?

A. I guess we're back to the angry bit . . . they don't drive me nuts, that's my response. Understanding that really changes things. If I do it to myself, then I can undo it. I always saw people as MAKING me angry and unhappy, but that's simply not so. Let me just go over it for myself. (laughing) I feel better about my kids already. When they are playing their games and wanting me to do something, it really says nothing about their loving me . . . only that they want what they want. I guess I never stopped long enough to see that before. Somehow, that's a whole lot easier to live with. Great, but it still doesn't solve my problem.

Q. What problem?

A. Being the victim of all this nonsense. That's still the problem.

Q. What do you mean?

A. I'm still uncomfortable about being subject to my children's whims and demands.

Q. How are you "subject" to them?

A. I might be feeling better, but that's not going to stop them from intruding continually in my life. There's still something to be unhappy about.

Q. WHAT ARE YOU AFRAID WOULD HAPPEN IF YOU WEREN'T UNHAPPY ABOUT THEIR INTRUDING?

A. I'd love that. It would be great, just fantastic. But it's impossible.

Q. Why?

A. How can I be happy living with all that?

Q. What do you mean?

A. If I don't get unhappy, it'll go on forever . . . it won't change.

Q. Are you saying you're unhappy so that you can get the situation to change?

A. Yes, I guess so. But that's ridiculous.

Q. Could you change the situation without getting upset?

A. (laughs) Sure. I could change it without getting upset. It seems so obvious, yet I never realized that before. (pause) That's really nice. Really nice! Now I want to consider changing my responses to them, but somehow I just can't see speaking in a soft, pleasant voice.

Q. *Why not?*

A. Because they won't believe me. (more laughter) They don't believe me when I scream anyway, so why not try the alternative. I'm a little afraid to try.

Q. *Why are you afraid?*

A. If it doesn't work, I'll really be stuck.

Q. *What do you mean?*

A. Everytime I answer a question, I think I know what I'm saying. Then, when I consider "what do I mean," I find I'm not half as clear as I thought. (long pause) I think I've forgotten what we were talking about. Oh yes, I remember. I'll be stuck because there will be nothing left to try . . . but that's not true either. I can figure out another strategy. I can even just leave the house for a couple of hours. I'm sure they'll survive an afternoon without me waiting on them, hand and foot.

Q. *WHAT DO YOU WANT?*

A. I want to try. I want to let my children make all the requests and demands they want and just be accepting . . . but then I still want to give my answer even if it's "no." I just want to say it nicely, quietly . . . without anger and all that disapproval.

Q. *And do you think you'll do that?*

A. Yes, but . . .

Q. *What is the but?*

A. I was thinking if it doesn't work, what will I do?

Q. *What do you think?*

A. Maybe it doesn't matter. I can deal with that when and if it happens. I'm beginning to see there are other possibilities. In a way, my kids and I train each other. I'm just as much part of their nagging as they are . . . they know if they keep at me, I'll give in. (long silence) I feel better now. Before I felt like I had no choices . . . but I see I do. (another long pause and smile) You know, some of that anger is really at myself . . . for the compromise, for allowing myself to

87

be in this position. You know what I mean . . . being little more than cook and bottle washer.

Q. *What about that makes you angry?*

A. That I want more . . . for me. I love my family, I love helping everyone, but there's a limit. It's okay as long as I don't go over that limit. All I want to be is happy.

Q. *What's preventing you?*

A. Me. Me not doing what I want, which I'm going to start to correct. I guess there is also a part of me that disapproves of me being unhappy or angry.

Q. *Why?*

A. It shows I failed.

Q. *What do you mean "failed"?*

A. What kind of life do I lead if I'm always angry or upset all the time. I guess I call that pretty unsuccessful, wouldn't you?

Q. *Well, if I did, I would have my reasons just as you have yours. Why would you call it unsuccessful?*

A. I guess because it's not what I want and if I don't have what I want, how can I be happy?

Q. *Not having or getting what you want is one thing; being unhappy about it is another. Why are you unhappy if you don't get what you want?*

A. Because maybe I'll never get it.

Q. *What do you mean?*

A. If I wasn't unhappy, maybe I'd just live with it . . . and then it would never change.

Q. *DO YOU BELIEVE THAT?*

A. (laughing) No, not really. It always changes, whether I'm unhappy or happy. I guess being unhappy just hurts a lot more. I still feel boxed in . . . by my family. I can see Billy's face as clear as day. I can hear his voice: "Mom, please drive me to Richard's; Mommy, you promised to get me a new glove today; Mom, what's for dinner." He just keeps asking like some sort of machine. But I see it clearer now. He just asks and then I do the angry scene.

Q. *WHAT ARE YOU AFRAID WOULD HAPPEN IF YOU DIDN'T GET ANGRY?*

A. He might continue to ask from now to doomsday.

Q. *Are you saying you get angry in order to discourage him?*

A. Yes, in a way. There it is again. Trying to get what I want with anger . . . but the funny thing is it doesn't work. Sometimes I think I should say yes to them when I want to say no.

Q. *What do you mean?*

A. I'm talking about my good mother image. I believe I'm supposed to be responsive to my children. Maybe that's what gets me.

Q. *In what way?*

A. I really want to be a good mother, but not by sacrificing myself. I feel forced to put myself second all the time.

Q. *What do you mean forced?*

A. Good parents should be responsive to their kids.

Q. *Okay, that's what you believe . . . but how are you forced?*

A. I'm not. I'm just fulfilling my own personal expectation about being mother of the year. I love to do things for my family when I feel it's my choice. When it's not, that's when I feel forced.

Q. *You mean you're doing things you're not choosing to do?*

A. Yes, sort of.

Q. *Is someone forcing you to do it?*

A. No . . . but I wouldn't be living up to my image of a good mother. Then I guess since that's my image, it's also my choice to be or not to be that way. Maybe all I mean by forced is doing what I think I don't want to do.

Q. *How's that?*

A. Here we go again. As you asked me that, I felt so fogged. I say I do things that I don't want to do . . . but if I'm doing them, I guess I have a reason to. So, you know what that means?

Q. *What?*

A. That if I have a reason, then I must be deciding, choosing to do what I do. Essentially, I guess I'm doing what I want, although I don't usually see it that way. Even when I'm waiting on my children, I guess I do it because it seems easier for me than facing the alternative.

Q. *What alternative?*

A. Being a bad mother by not being responsive.

Q. *How does that make you a bad mother?*

A. I don't know. My friend Allison manages to do all sorts of activities for herself and yet, I think she's a great mother. Vivacious, happy . . . doing what she enjoys, but still attentive and loving to her children. Maybe if I was less available and giving myself more time for me, I'd be a better parent. Right now, I'm no joy for anyone . . . including me.

Q. *What do you mean?*

A. My angry and abrupt reactions . . . that's not the way I want to be.

Q. *DO YOU BELIEVE you would be that way?*

A. I really don't believe I would . . . but just suppose the very next time my children confront me I explode. That would really unnerve me.

Q. *Why?*

A. Then we've wasted all this time and I haven't gotten anywhere.

Q. *How do you know that?*

A. If I get upset, then nothing has changed. That's proof, isn't it?

Q. *DO YOU BELIEVE THAT?*

A. It's funny, but I really don't. Something has definitely changed. I feel released from my own bondage. I guess I'm afraid if I still was angry, it means there is more.

Q. *And if there were more reasons to be uncovered, why would you be unhappy about that?*

A. I wouldn't as long as I knew I could solve them.

Q. *And what do you know?*

A. If I solved some of my unhappiness today, here and now . . . even just a little, then I can solve tomorrow, tomorrow. You know, when I'm not feeling trapped or angry at my kids, I'm really aware of how much I love them (begins to cry). You don't have to ask me why I am unhappy. I feel really good.

THIRD DIALOGUE

Q. *WHAT ARE YOU UNHAPPY ABOUT?*

A. My son, I guess I wanted too much of him and nothing worked out. He just doesn't care about anything . . . except maybe his flute and sports.

Q. *Why does that upset you?*

A. He should be in college, trying to make something of himself. I keep telling him I'll pay for it. But no, not my son, he's gotta be a big shot . . . he's not interested.

Q. *What about his lack of interest makes you so uncomfortable?*

A. Because he'll be a nothing. Listen, when he gets out of the house and into the real world, it's not going to be so easy. He's in for some shock.

Q. *And WHY WOULD THAT DISTURB YOU?*

A. I want him to be happy, not miserable.

Q. *Are you saying you believe he will be miserable?*

A. Yes. Most definitely yes.

Q. *Okay. If your worst fears come to pass, why does that seem so painful?*

A. I was thinking maybe I did something wrong. If I had been a better father, maybe things would be different.

Q. *What do you mean?*

A. He'd be in school now, studying instead of wasting his time playing that dumb instrument. Maybe I could have done something else.

Q. *Even if you could have, why now are you unhappy about it?*

A. I guess to make sure I keep my eyes open and be more aware in the future. Whatever I did wrong, I don't want to do it again. That would really blow it for me!

Q. *WHY?*

A. Hey, the situation is bad enough.

Q. *What do you mean?*

A. I mean it's bad because everything I want for him, he dismisses.

Q. *Are you saying that it's bad because he did not do the things you expect of him?*

A. (long pause without a response)

Q. *What are you feeling?*

A. Confused.

Q. *About what?*

A. In my house, I'm all alone on this one. My wife thinks

our son ought to be free to do what he wants. My son . . . well, he's having a ball. Listen, he really doesn't have to be what I want him to be . . . all I want is for him to be all right. I don't think he's making the right choices.

Q. *Why not?*

A. Because every youngster today has to continue their schooling . . . otherwise, they're out of luck. (long pause) I guess I don't know anymore. Everytime I try to talk to him, he pushes me away. Sometimes, I think if I say do this, he'll do the opposite just for spite. I get this bad feeling deep inside when I think that maybe my kid dislikes me.

Q. *WHY WOULD YOU BE UNHAPPY IF HE DISLIKED YOU?*

A. Maybe that goes back to my making mistakes. What kind of father could I have been if my own flesh and blood despises me?

Q. *What are you saying?*

A. I guess I was a lousy father.

Q. *DO YOU BELIEVE THAT?*

A. Well, all the evidence points in that direction. My son is a vagabond musician who dislikes me.

Q. *If everything you believe about him was so—I'm not saying it's good or bad, true or false—if what you see as the worst has come to pass, WHY DOES THAT DISTURB YOU SO MUCH?*

A. It would make anyone unhappy!

Q. *But what are your reasons . . . WHY DOES IT MAKE YOU UNHAPPY?*

A. I want him to love and respect me.

Q. *That's what you want, but why should you be unhappy if he didn't?*

A. I just don't know anymore.

Q. *Okay, let's try it from the other side. WHAT ARE YOU AFRAID WOULD HAPPEN IF YOU WEREN'T UNHAPPY ABOUT HIS DISLIKING YOU?*

A. I'd just walk away. I'd let him do whatever the hell he pleased . . . I wouldn't bother with him. (long pause—a sigh) But I don't want to do that.

Q. *Then WHY DO YOU BELIEVE YOU WOULD?*

A. Well, I guess I wouldn't (laughs). It's such a foreign

92

thought—not being unhappy about what my son is doing and yet still disagreeing with him (more laughing).

Q. *Why are you laughing?*

A. I was just thinking that if I let my son be something I didn't want, doesn't that mean I didn't care?

Q. *What do you think?*

A. I don't know.

Q. *Maybe if we rephrase the question it will be easier to answer. DO YOU BELIEVE you could allow your son his wants, although they're different than yours, and still be a loving father.*

A. Yes, I do. I see that now. It's funny, like I always believed that the more unhappy you were about something, the more you cared. Like your unhappiness was proof.

Q. *DO YOU BELIEVE IT NOW?*

A. No. I really see the difference. Yet that was one of the rules I applied to my son. I could be miserable, yet it never seemed to bother him. I assumed that meant he didn't care.

Q. *And now?*

A. I don't think it necessarily means any such thing. Well that certainly changes my perspective.

Q. *How?*

A. I'm not going to start feeling bad every time he's feeling good. I'm off that seesaw. Okay, suppose I level off—it still doesn't change where he's headed.

Q. *What do you mean?*

A. He probably will not go back to school.

Q. *Okay, that takes us back to what we talked about before. Going to college, you said, was your expectation. If he still decides not to conform to it, WHY WOULD THAT MAKE YOU UNHAPPY?*

A. Oh Jesus . . . the only answer I can come up with is I want him to go.

Q. *I understand your desire is to have him back in school, but why would you be unhappy if he decided not to go?*

A. It comes back to me. I guess I see it as a comment on me and my wishes.

Q. *Do you believe that?*

A. I guess I do.

93

Q. WHY DO YOU BELIEVE THAT?
A. If he loved me and respected me, he would do what I wanted. But I guess that doesn't make too much sense. Plenty of times I don't want what my wife asks, but that has nothing to do with my loving her. I'm getting real confused. I'd like to stop for awhile.

Okay, I'm ready. We were getting close, weren't we?
Q. Close to what?
A. (laughing) Close to me seeing what I'm doing. While we stopped, I remembered this movie I had seen many years ago where a father, who had been a career officer in the Navy, wanted his son to join the service also. When the boy wouldn't, the father became furious and bitterly unhappy. But the boy loved his father, he was just too frightened to join. Maybe that's the same for my son. I want what's best for him, but he could see that as awful, I guess. So, he sets different goals—big deal! Maybe it doesn't mean anything about his loving and respecting me. I don't know . . . I'm not sure.
Q. What don't you know?
A. What THE answer is.
Q. Perhaps if we explored it, we might uncover more, if you want.
A. Great . . . let's go.
Q. What are you confused about?
A. What is my son saying when he rejects what I want for him? Maybe nothing . . . I really see that! All I ever wanted was for him to be happy. Yet though he seems to be doing what he wants, I suspect sometimes he's just reacting AGAINST me.
Q. And if he were, how would you feel about it?
A. If I thought it meant he didn't like me, then I'd be uncomfortable.
Q. Why?
A. I'm back to what I said before, I want him to like me.
Q. Okay, that's what you want . . . but why would you be unhappy if he didn't?
A. I guess I'm worried it's my fault!
Q. Do you mean you failed?
A. Yes and no.
Q. Let's take the yes. Why do you believe you failed if

your son's choices differ from what you wanted for him?

A. Somehow, I'm beginning to hear the questions. All right, I see how his choice is not a comment about his loving me and I can understand that HE believes he is doing the best for himself . . . that leaves me without any reasons to believe I failed.

Q. Then, DO YOU BELIEVE IT?

A. I don't know. It seems ridiculous to believe something without any reasons. It's hard to let go.

Q. WHY?

A. (his voice breaking) You beat yourself up all these years because you believe something . . . then one day you have a discussion, like this one, and you decide you no longer believe it. Look what that says about me . . . what I've been doing all these years.

Q. What do you think it says?

A. I kept pushing my son because I thought if I could get him to do what I wanted, it meant he respected and loved me. And in fact, he's done the opposite . . . probably, in part, just to get away from my pushing.

Q. If that was so, WHY WOULD YOU BE UNHAPPY TO KNOW IT?

A. I hear you. I'm not. I'm thankful to know it. Maybe I can change what I've been doing, stop nagging my son and politely suggesting he's a bum. Maybe he would even start to hear me once in awhile. Funny how you have expectations for your children because you think that's really a good thing. But now I see how it backfires. It's his life, I can at least try to respect that and keep my hands off. But if he wants my opinion, I'll tell him the truth. (pause) Well, I can't say I'm happy about his flute and his not wanting to go to school, but I can say it's okay now. (smiling) I guess what I mean is I'm okay now. I think I'm even ready to listen to him play his music.

4

moving the mountain of beliefs

Each and every day I am making hundreds of choices, although it often doesn't feel like it. I seem to want to be happy and comfortable, but I do not feel that way. I look at myself confused . . . wanting more as I tramp into doctors' offices looking for "ups" and "downs" to release me from my depressions. I turn to religions for the grace of peace and to mystics for a glimpse of Nirvana. Or, I just cling to my scotch-and-sodas seeking a lift.

I even deify my unhappiness by calling it mental health and abdicate my responsibility by classifying it as an "emotional disease" or "malfunction" of my unconscious which is beyond my control. I search for half-measures, coping techniques and meditative bliss to soften my pain. I continually look to others for what has always been within my power . . . *I have the freedom to choose and change.*

So what do I really want? The Freudian might call for adaptation and adjustment. The Gestaltist signals for awareness and being in touch. The Humanist urges self-actualization. The cultist shouts for sacrifice and worship. But why? What is it that I chase with such haste and fascination? It is my wanting to be happy . . . to feel good with myself and those around me. All my quests for possessions, respect, lovers, health, and just items I believe I need in order to be happy. The focus of the Option Process is finding and experiencing happiness now, while I still pursue my goals and interests.

Not only have I believed that getting things would make me happy, but I have also believed that current unhappiness is a necessary part of getting there. "Grin and bear it," I used to tell myself. In essence, I had the basic belief that I had to be or should be unhappy now in order to be happy later. "Pay your dues." "You can't be happy all the time." "You have to take the good with the bad." "Life has its ups and downs."

Each of my beliefs lies atop a mountain of beliefs. And unhappiness, which is the experience of certain kinds of beliefs, is based on a logical system of reasoning.

If I unveil my system of beliefs, I create for myself the opportunity to disconnect the short circuits of unhappiness. If I pull the plugs on my self-defeating concepts, the Option Attitude will evolve naturally.

Buddha once said, "Remove the suffering and you get happiness."

It is what remains when I have dispelled the misery, the discomforts and the fears. It is what I find beneath the debris of my bad feelings and unsettling visions.

And what is a belief? It is a judgment, which is really a question and an answer. Most often, beliefs are presented as statements. The buliding is tall (the question: is it short or tall?). The temperature is hot (the question: what is the temperature according to my variables so I will know how to dress?). A car uses gas to operate (the question: what makes the car run?). These are beliefs about my environment.

But the beliefs I deal with in regard to my happiness are ones that involve *judgments of good and bad*. Is it good for me and what I want? Or, is it bad for me? From the questions of good and bad develop all the judgments (answers) that crystalize my wants, my feelings and my behavior.

The fact that I believe the sky is blue usually seems a

simple statement of observation. But when the sky is blue means no rain during a severe drought and I'm a farmer, then another judgment or belief comes into operation. The sky is blue means no rain which is "bad" for my business . . . and the reaction might then be unhappiness.

Seems rather simple, but what about those "spontaneous" actions that do not seem to rely on judgments or beliefs. What about automatic responses . . . like my jumping out of the way when being attacked with a knife? Is that reaction really so automatic? If someone lunged toward a two-year-old child with a knife, he would probably not even flinch or move out of the way. But attack me, and wow, watch me move.

Although my response occurs in such a split-second fashion, I am still acting from my beliefs and fears (ones the child has not yet acquired). I know about the properties of a knife. I might be terrified of being cut and fear the possible consequence of dying, of which I might have additional fearful beliefs. Also, I have beliefs about people running at other people with knives. They're dangerous, crazy and moving out of their way is in one's best interest. And so on.

Each statement above expresses beliefs . . . all different kinds about knives, pain, people, violence, death, action, etc. Even though I act swiftly, this is merely an example of the amazing speed with which my brain waves and thought patterns are processed. Since they are neurologically and electrically formed and triggered, the speed of their messages is so great that I can actually have hundreds of thoughts (beliefs) operate within a fraction of a second. Therefore, the ensuing movement out of danger appears automatic. Actually, it is the result of a complex series of judgments and beliefs.

The significance here is that all of us are a bundle of beliefs. *We are believing animals.*

How do I acquire beliefs? Most of my basic beliefs were taught to me . . . by parents, peer groups, teachers, religions, institutions, governments, cultures, etc. Then, as a student of life and recipient of those beliefs, I became a participant insofar as I adopted those beliefs as my own. Often, I carry them with me through the years, forgetting where and when I acquired them.

I follow from my beliefs (the ones I chose to acquire)

and each of us can have different beliefs about the very same things. Perhaps the following illustrates in gross simplification how diverse our beliefs can be about even the very same occurrence and how crucial they are in affecting our reactions and feelings.

About to leave for college, a young woman is poised to enter a train that will take her away from home for the very first time. Her family stands on the platform, awaiting the last good-bye. Her father is filled with pride and is genuinely excited for his daughter whom he sees as having grown into being an alert, intelligent and independent young lady. Nevertheless, he is somewhat distressed and disoriented, believing he will be lonely and miss his "little" girl. His wife, crying softly into a plaid scarf, is overwhelmed by her personal sense of loss and by the swift passage of time. The little sister is filled with joy, elated by her older sister's exit. She anticipates inheriting her sister's room and becoming the pampered "only" child. During this quiet drama, a stranger passes and casually observes the entire situation. He registers no feelings whatsoever about the matter.

Although participants in one experience, each person reacts based on his or her own beliefs. The father believes the situation to be both good and bad, the mother envisions it as negative while the younger sister assesses it as beneficial to her. The stranger made no judgments. He did not tap a belief about the circumstances. Thus, he developed no feelings about the event.

What I feel and how I act depends on my beliefs which are freely chosen or acquired by my acceptance of them. No act, event or person is intrinsically good or bad . . . I call it what I will. I define it, love it, hate it, embrace it, reject it and become happy or unhappy according to what I believe about it. Therefore, the beliefs I acquired in childhood or the ones I just adopted yesterday exist right now for me if I still believe them today . . . because *today is all I ever have.*

And in the dynamic of adopting and rejecting my beliefs, I am confronted by choice. And if I can choose or rechoose old beliefs, the beliefs of others or establish new ones, then I am what I choose to be and I can recreate myself as I wish! And when I am wanting to do that, the process is beautiful . . . not painful.

If we were taught as children that going out in the rain was bad, that we would get sick, then we might not go out in wet weather if we adopted that belief. Later, as our ideas or experiences with rain change, so might our beliefs and judgments. Rain could now be seen as a beautiful and joyful experience . . . we might now venture out into it often and with great comfort.

Generations of Catholics did not eat meat on Friday because they believed it to be bad . . . against the laws and tenets of their religion. Now with the change of certain laws and rules, eating meat on Friday is perfectly acceptable. People who, for thirty years, would never have touched meat on that day almost instantly altered their beliefs when they thought they had permission to do so. Thus they dramatically changed their feelings about meat eating on Friday and also changed their behavior.

Not so many years ago, medical reports stated that it was healthy to jog; so a lot of us went jogging and felt really good about it. Then, as some joggers collapsed and died with their sneakers on, we learned that jogging could be extremely stressful and taxing to the heart. Immediately, we altered our belief, stopped jogging and frowned on those who continued. Later, after still more research and reports, we were informed that with proper medical supervision, jogging was healthy again. We read all the material until we decided that we had enough "evidence" to change our belief back to "jogging is good" and then we jogged again. Others, who did not accept the new evidence, might have continued to hold onto the belief "jogging is bad."

My beliefs are judgments, freely made and maintained . . . yet changeable.

Even if I seem to give up or abdicate the apparent choosing to others, I have still chosen. I am still connected. I say: "Let the President decide" or "Let the doctor decide" . . . and each time I put myself in their hands, I do so from my beliefs that they might be better equipped to make the "best" choice, which I judged would be my best choice. Beliefs about governments, learning, parents, sex, self-image and self-worth, children, future, death and potential are just some of the basic bricks of my personality.

They can be investigated for a clear understanding of my own system and then changed. The old cardinal concepts of "I do not choose my feelings; they just come upon me" and "I am a victim of what happened to me in the past" and "I can't help it, that's just the way I am" are all open to question.

The inference is, if I choose my beliefs, then I am responsible. But perhaps that is not what we believe or want to believe. Why not? Responsibility is only threatening if I want to protect myself from the past (with beliefs like "I couldn't help how I acted—that's just the way I am") or protect myself from the future (with beliefs like "If I make the wrong choice and it has 'bad' consequences, it'll be my fault and then what?"). There is no past or future . . . there is only me now for this moment. Me now from moment to moment. My beliefs about past and future were simply my tactic of trying to take care of myself and justify my actions.

Responsibility in the NOW is only a problem if I believe I would choose against myself, hurt myself out of some mystical failing. Then, indeed, I might not want to know my own power. Yet, by contrast, if I know I always do the best I can for myself based on my beliefs and available information, then increased awareness can be an opportunity to become more effective, to experience my own freedom and to take more assertions in finding my own happiness.

I am the ruler over my kingdom of beliefs. Just as I could say that life is good today, I could judge it bad for me tomorrow if I were suddenly crippled or overcome by some dread terminal disease. I could have once believed that certain types of people were bad, until I had contrary exposure and changed my belief.

As long as changing a belief is possible, then changing the resulting feelings and behaviors is also possible. I am *free* to become anything and everything I want to become . . . even to remain exactly the same. And so, in a fashion, at this very moment, I am everything I want to be, based on my current beliefs.

If I rid myself of those beliefs I do not want, those I consider self-defeating and which result in unhappiness, then I open my life up to every conceivable direction.

THE "THINK" PAGE (MOVING THE MOUNTAIN OF BELIEFS)

QUESTIONS TO ASK YOURSELF:

Have you recently experienced changing a belief (just one)?

Do you have to be a "victim" of your past?

If you really wanted, do you believe you can change?

OPTION CONCEPTS TO CONSIDER:

* "REMOVE THE SUFFERING AND YOU GET HAPPINESS."

*MAN IS A BELIEVING ANIMAL.

*NOW IS ALL WE EVER HAVE.

*BELIEFS ARE JUDGMENTS, FREELY CHOSEN AND MAINTAINED.

*I AM WHAT I CHOOSE TO BE AND CAN RECREATE MYSELF AS I WISH.

*IN CHOOSING BELIEFS, I AM RESPONSIBLE FOR WHO I AM.

"CHANGE BELIEFS AND YOU CHANGE FEELINGS AND BEHAVIOR."

BELIEFS TO CONSIDER DISCARDING:

I have to be unhappy now in order to be happy later.

Everyone has to pay his dues.

I can't be happy all the time.

We have to take the good with the bad.

Life always has to have its ups and downs.

I do not choose my feelings; they just come upon me.

I am a victim of what happened to me in the past.

I couldn't help the way I acted; it's just the way I am.

FOURTH DIALOGUE

Q. WHAT ARE YOU UNHAPPY ABOUT?
A. I'm out of control . . . as if my emotions have over-taken me and there's nothing I can do about it. I get angry even before I know I'm angry. And although I say to myself, I don't want to be here, I'm still burning.

Q. What is it about being overwhelmed by your fury that disturbs you most?
A. That I'm a victim of something inside me.

Q. What do you mean?
A. Well, just today, I was in a taxicab and it was very important for me to get downtown on time for an appointment. The cab driver was moving leisurely down Seventh Avenue as if he had all the time in the world. I asked him to go faster . . . he said, okay. Two minutes later, he was casually sitting behind a bus when the entire left side of the road was clear. Then, I don't know what happened to me. Suddenly,

I was screaming and cursing at him. Later I apologized, of course, but I felt embarrassed . . . it was like I was some kind of a maniac. It must be from my unconscious . . . some crazy seeds planted there when I was a kid.

Q. *Can you explain why you say that . . . what do you believe is occurring?*

A. My reaction in the taxi was crazy . . . unrealistic. It seemed to have nothing to do with me. My emotions felt separate. You know, for a couple of seconds, while I was in the middle of screaming, it was like I was outside my body and observing myself. I couldn't believe it!

Q. *When you were "outside" yourself, looking at the you who was angry, how did you feel?*

A. Even more upset . . . I was angry about being angry.

Q. *Why?*

A. All I wanted was for the driver to move the damn cab faster and he was doing the opposite.

Q. *What about that was so upsetting?*

A. Wouldn't it be upsetting to you?

Q. *Perhaps, but if I got upset, I would for my own reasons. And you would have yours.*

A. I know what you're saying, but I had no choice. It's better that I screamed at him than if I steamed in silence. I don't want to get an ulcer.

Q. *If you feel angry and expressing it is a way to get it out . . . to neutralize it, then you are doing the best you can to take care of yourself. Suppressing anger or venting it is your decision and obviously you've made it for yourself. What I asked was WHY . . . what were the reasons you were so angry?*

A. If I didn't get to my client on time, I might have lost a substantial order.

Q. *And WHY WOULD THAT MAKE YOU UNHAPPY?*

A. Because I wanted that damn order and I was going to lose it because of some dumb cabbie.

Q. *And if what you feared came to pass—you did lose it . . . WHY WOULD YOU BE UNHAPPY?*

A. Because I wanted it . . . that's how I make my living.

Q. *Of course. You wanted the order, but why would you be unhappy if you didn't get it?*

A. (exhaling a long sigh) Listen, I don't have to get every

order I go after. In this instance, I guess I really didn't allow myself enough time to get downtown. If I'd had my wits about me, I would have given myself at least ten more minutes. It would be okay not to get an order . . . unless, of course, it's my fault.

Q. *What do you mean?*

A. I don't mind not writing business, except if the reason relates to something I did or should have done . . . then, it's definitely not okay.

Q. *Why not?*

A. Because it means I couldn't cut it. Period. I failed.

Q. *What do you mean by failed?*

A. That means I'm responsible. You know (laughing), I can't blame it on an act of God, like they say in insurance policies. It was "an act of Robert" tripping over himself. If I had just relaxed, given the appointment two more seconds consideration, I probably would have allowed myself more time. Then a slow cab ride would have been fine, but I didn't do that. I ended up sitting in traffic, furious.

Q. *WHAT ARE YOU AFRAID WOULD HAPPEN IF YOU DIDN'T GET FURIOUS?*

A. Then I wouldn't do anything and the cabbie would just take his sweet-ass time.

Q. *DO YOU BELIEVE THAT?*

A. (sighing) I know I just said that, but suddenly I'm not sure I believe it any longer. Even if I didn't get angry, I would do something . . . I know I would.

Q. *Are you saying that you were angry so that you would do something?*

A. Yes, that's exactly so. I never really saw it so clearly before. (grinning) Funny, but when I left the cab I kept thinking how my ranting and raving didn't move the driver. In fact, the result was the opposite of what I wanted. The driver stopped the car, turned around and proceeded to give me a big argument. Even more time was wasted. That's definitely an eye-opener . . . to see me making myself angry so I would do something. Okay, that's part of it . . . but there's more underneath.

Q. *What do you mean?*

A. It's the way I react to the whole business of failing.

Q. *Could you explain what you mean?*

A. Yes. I become angry in response to seeing myself mess things up.

Q. *When we began, you said your anger came from nowhere and just seemed to take control . . . as if it were separate from you. Are you now saying your anger comes from your awareness and judgment that you've failed?*

A. (a soft smile) Yes, I guess so. My anger IS, in a very real way, my specific reaction to failing. Wow . . . look at what I just said; the opposite of what I believed just a few minutes ago. Funny place to come to . . . the full circle. It really knocks me out. (long pause) My feelings are not half as automatic as I thought. I guess I DO have reasons. You know, even though I know that and it's really a great discovery, I still feel off balance.

Q. *What do you mean when you say "off-balance"?*

A. I still sense a discomfort. My anger comes from my belief that I've failed, but I don't know why failing upsets me. Can we go on?

Q. *Sure. Why does failing upset you?*

A. Well, maybe you can tell me why it triggers anger in me.

Q. *If I answered the question, I could only give you MY reasons. And only you would know your reasons. Do you want to take a swing at it?*

A. For me, failure is more than just not getting. It's trying and missing that hurts. Oh, it's crazy all right . . . being locked into seeing everything that doesn't go your way as a personal defeat. I even start to believe I purposely don't do the best I can for myself.

Q. *WHY DO YOU BELIEVE THAT?*

A. I don't know why I believe anything any more.

Q. *If you guessed at an answer, why would you believe you would purposely go against doing what's best for yourself?*

A. Maybe there's no why. Maybe this is all just my game.

Q. *How's that?*

A. It's only when I'm under pressure that I make those kinds of judgments about being off or purposely being a poor performer. It's during those time I accuse mysef of being inadequate. I wonder if that relates to what we were talking about before.

Q. *What do you mean?*

A. The bit about being angry to do something. Maybe I accuse myself of being inadequate so that I won't be inadequate.

Q. *Are you saying that without the accusation you might be bad for yourself and not do the best you can?*

A. Yes. And I just started to realize it as I was talking before. When you asked me if I believed I would purposely hurt myself . . . well, I immediately knew deep down it wasn't so. In a way, I was afraid not to get angry.

Q. *WHY?*

A. Because that would confirm I didn't care about myself. The anger was proof that it really mattered.

Q. *Okay. Do you still require such proof now?*

A. (his face softens . . . smiling) No . . . certainly not that kind of proof. I guess it's a question of believing in myself. When I get down to it, I do. Now the trick is just to remember this fantastic bit of information for the next time. Knowing me, I'll probably just get furious again.

Q. *Although you've always reacted angrily in the past and perhaps for the same reasons you've mentioned today, why now DO YOU BELIEVE you would still continue to react that way?*

A. Why? I don't know. Isn't that crazy. I don't know.

Q. *WHAT ARE YOU AFRAID WOULD HAPPEN IF YOU DIDN'T GET ANGRY?*

A. It goes back to the same thing . . . maybe I won't take care of the situation.

Q. *DO YOU BELIEVE THAT?*

A. No, not any more. It's coming clearer and clearer. I see what I've been believing and what I've been doing. No, I don't have to be crazy to take care of myself. And I don't want to be. And let me tell you, that sounds great to my ears.

Q. *What do you want?*

A. I want to know more. Now that I see it's explainable, I know I can change.

108

loving is the experience of
feeling good . . . being loved
in return is the bonus. When
I cut myself off from loving,
I am actually cutting myself
off from feeling good.

5

love relationships and the option alternative

I crawled on the hardwood floors of my childhood and built rainbows across the horizon. On a painted landscape of pinks, yellow and powder blues, the letters grew ten stories high . . . L-O-V-E. My expectations formed a hot sun in the sky as I became infatuated with my dream.

The culmination of it all! To love and be loved! To find that person who had waited silently around the corner of my fantasy. They told me about the bells I would hear during each embrace. I couldn't help but be dazzled by the lovers reunited in red-rosy-cheeked romances displayed on the silver screen. From hairspray commercials to billboard cigarette advertisements, I was tempted and invited by the promise of arms that enfolded and mouths that beckoned.

"I'm ready . . . I can't wait," I said to myself despite my ambivalence at the loving in my family with its mixed metaphor of pain and punishment. Standing on the sidewalk of my youth, just past puberty. Slinking past the bookstores of my dreams, waiting. Designing scenes of romance and cotton-candy love behind the walls of my eyes.

And finally it came to me or me to it. The first time my eyes lit up for another human being. Zap . . . it grabbed me in the quick and I was flying. I was dazzled by that quiet, pretty girl with long eyelashes sitting in the third seat of the first row, a contemporary June Allyson scrubbed so clean and innocent. Later, it was the vivacious dancer whose body moved with such hypnotic ease, her smile suggesting all the fun and warmth I had ever imagined.

And I never limited those fantasy figures to members of my immediate peer group. There was the teacher who caught my fancy and sent me into dreamlike states right in front of the chalk and erasers. The Jane Fonda figures who raced like veiled apparitions through my most intimate daydreams. The neighbor's wife three doors down. I even constructed the perfect lover out of the components of everyone I ever knew, fitting different bodies to different faces, changing personalities and interests to suit my whims.

I could feel the high. Then, I graduated into closer, more binding love relationships. Slowly, I dared and finally allowed myself to take the distance out of my crushes . . . touching the hands of my fantasies. Suddenly, I was let loose on the roller coaster of a love relationship. I grew old so quickly. Adjusting and readjusting.

"What's happening?" I said to myself. "This isn't the trip that I had imagined." "Hey, this isn't what I wanted at all!" A thousand years of protest bellowed from between the sheets. "Where's the magic when she touches me?" "How come it seems so damned ordinary?"

I've known some who gave up at this juncture, deciding to accept less than they wanted. Others kept pushing, pursuing and hunting for the magic. But for most, there was at least one honeymoon . . . certainly, for me. We were two people flowing together, who gave and shared ourselves in harmony, who loved and were loved in return. Heart-shaped bathtubs, midnight boat rides, sunsets holding hands on the beach, wine sipped by candlelight, hands exploring so gently and eyes that said it all. Beautiful! Yet, it disappeared. Was the honeymoon over after only one day or was it one week or perhaps even a year? Why couldn't we sustain it? What happened in the daylight of our time; why did it change the morning after?

I had wanted the love and the loving, the soft tender

112

touches, the caresses, the sharing and even the images from the silver screen. I was willing to ride Hollywood right out the window. Yet, why did I get burned?

In wanting my fantasy, everything seemed dreary and colorless in comparison. What was I really telling myself as I lay alone under the quilted cover of night and whispered, "I need love!" I am "supposed to" have it. I "must" have it. In effect, I was saying I would be miserable, dejected and depressed without it. I created impossible mental models with which I continued to compare my reality and watch it suffer. I tried to manipulate my partners to conform to my own preconceived notions. I subjected my love relationships to elaborate conditions, all sorts of judgments and a manifold of expectations. I didn't know any other way.

Somehow, my fantasies became a breeding ground for all the questions and an incubator for unhappiness.

I remember sweating through so many relationships. Disjointed. Confused. And yet, at the same time, I guess I was unwilling to explore them . . . even to ask myself any questions. I thought, if I'm uncomfortable now, I don't want to increase my distress by really finding out what is wrong. I believed I might walk through a doorway to greater unhappiness, never suspecting that in confronting my beliefs I could dispel them and change them.

I thought I needed a chisel when all I had to do was give myself permission to explore.

The first question was the most difficult . . . no, not the question as much as daring to ask it, to begin. "What am I unhappy about?" Suddenly, my mind went blank. "I don't know," I answered myself. "I'm just unhappy." But then my lips betrayed a growing smile. I knew I had more reason than there were minutes in a day. As I relaxed, a flood of beliefs filled my head.

The most prominent realization was "I am not getting what I want or think I want." Ironically, I was not ever aware of that thought until I asked the question. *When we are busy "working" at our relationships or worrying about losing them, we seldom allot time to explore and investigate them.*

Is the nature of our love relationships right now all that we are wanting? Or are we fearing the next one as we remember the bittersweet quality of the one before? The only

113

question that surfaces: Is there more we want from our relationships? If the answer is a no, we can pass. But if not, we can try to uncover some of our difficulties in an attempt to allow our current relationships to flow more easily . . . or, perhaps, to free ourselves to make new ones.

Although it seems petty now, there was one particular event in an earlier involvement which would annoy me greatly. Whenever I would see my friend, I always anticipated her greeting me with a great ceremonious hug . . . a gesture that I believed made our coming together special and valued. I even told her that was my particular joy. Yet, often she would just greet me casually with a flat Monday morning hello and I would become furious. Why did I get so upset? I guess I believed it was a sign she did not care enough. Her loving and affection was overshadowed by my distrust and anger. Accusations short-circuited the flow. "She couldn't love me, otherwise she would do the things I want." But how could that be true? How clear it seems now, but how ungraspable then. I was actually creating my own dissatisfactions by setting up specific images and activities to which my partner was "supposed to" conform. When she didn't, I made a truckload of assessments about what I believed her actions meant.

It was my game with my own expectation. My misery was mine. And if I had made all those judgments about a greeting, there must have been so many other areas in which I did the same thing. Once I tipped the iceberg, I wanted to understand more. Okay, if there were ways I could make myself unhappy, then maybe I could unmake myself . . . free myself from the bind. At least I could try. Ultimately, each exploration became a beautiful awakening . . . seemingly complex at first, yet so transparent in the end.

Although there are many different binds of unhappiness in love relationships, as vast and varied as there are people and beliefs, some are more prominent than others and occur with great frequency.

THE "AM I A SUCKER" BIND—My relationship is fairly new and still growing, but I'm beginning to notice that I seem to love you more than you love me. After all, I'm always so attentive to your interest in literature, your job and the people you meet. You, on the other hand, never ask me about my day or how I feel when I'm unhappy. If I keep loving you more than you love me, I begin to become afraid I'm going to be a sucker. So, to minimize my risk, I decide to withhold some of my love so I won't be in that position and won't get hurt. Perhaps I even believe this might stimulate you to try harder in our relationship. But instead, as you see me withhold my love, you withhold yours. Because of all the witholding, we conclude we do not love one another even though that may not be true. Finally, we either split or remain together while having bad feelings about each other.

THE "WE HAVE NOTHING IN COMMON" BIND— Although we love each other and that's why we were married in the first place, we don't really seem to have much in common. I'm into politics and he's into music. I like tennis and water-skiing and he always wants to play basketball with the "boys." So I tried. After all, marriage is a sacrifice of sorts (I believe) . . . I was always told you should put aside your own interests in order to share those of your mate. If you don't, the marriage will never work. So I gave up politics and attended concerts, traded my tennis racket for a seat in the bleachers as he played ball. I don't know exactly when it began, but I became angry. Why do I have to give up what I want? Why can't he just love me the way I am? If he loved me, he wouldn't do this to me. I resent all the compromises and not being able to do my thing. We really have nothing in common. And how could I allow myself to be put in this position? It's no use, I decide, we're a classic case of incompatibility.

"THE BRICKS OF SILENCE" BIND—Every time I bring up certain subjects, you get unhappy . . . so we just can't talk about it. If we do, we'll have an argument. Everyone always told me that a good relationship is one in which the parties don't fight, since disagreements can lead to evidence of incompatibility and separation. So I become afraid to talk about one or two subjects. These become our first "bricks of silence" as we begin to build a wall between us. Soon other subjects we disagree on fall into the category of what we can't talk about. As the wall becomes higher and the items increase dramatically in number, I become more and more afraid of a split . . . there are so many things to be careful about.

115

The fear of separating becomes stronger. Soon the discomfort becomes extremely uncomfortable for both of us (after all, we can't talk to each other about it since it might create "heavier" problems). One of us decides that it's best to break up the relationship in order to relieve ourselves of fearing we might split up. Later, I realize that the silence which was our way of protecting our relationship, in fact, resulted in ruining it. We did what we feared most . . . ended the love relationship.

As I allow myself to look, it becomes clearer to me. I really can trip over my beliefs and judgments. It's incredible how I could end up going down paths I never intended to walk. I always thought I had to be careful and weigh everything . . . make elaborate judgments so I would know what to do and be able to take care of myself. Yet, it is the very same judgments that seem to cause the problems and confuse the issues.

Judgments. Judgments are beliefs. In the *"Am I a sucker?"* bind, I am saying I am unhappy because I believe I am not getting enough of what I should get from my lover (she doesn't love me as much as I love her). Or in the *"We have nothing in common"* example, she decides that she is not getting enough since the bulk of the interaction is composed of her sacrificing her own interests for him, with little in return. In the *"bricks of silence"* dilemma many judgments were made. Perhaps, the most significant was that I am not giving enough . . . otherwise there would not have been so many taboo areas and I would have made the difference. All these judgments are either about material issues or about the quality of loving and feelings.

As I look at it, it's amazing how material assessments come so fast and furiously. The woman who feels she is not living the life-style her mate had promised. I've met her. The individual not satisfied with the creature comforts, from clothing to cars. The man who thinks his partner should do more for the household. These are *material* judgments about *not getting enough.* In contrast, there are *material* judgments about *not giving enough.* The person who sees herself as not contributing enough to her lover's comfort or material support. The man who feels diminished because his gifts are small or inexpensive.

Then there are judgments about *not getting enough* in the

area of *feelings* and *loving*. The man who sees his partner as cold, aloof and sexually abstract. The woman whose concept of a loving mate is soft, tender and caring . . . and who finds a rather cold, disapproving and abrasive man next to her in bed each morning. In contrast, here too, there are also judgments about *not giving enough*. The person who sees himself as not exciting or interesting enough to keep his lover happy. The man and woman who see themselves as impotent, unfaithful or incapable.

I have often noted a very specific quality about the nature of the initial judgment about not getting enough. It gets twisted into another assumption . . . that I must not be giving enough. I assume I "should" have been able to motivate my lovers to give me all I want and believe I deserve. If they don't, it must be my shortcoming. And then I conclude: "There must be something wrong with me!" When I have believed such a self-indictment was unalterable, I have terminated relationships just to escape the pain and self-doubt.

How did it go from being so beautiful to being so difficult in such a short time? I guess as I ask that question, I'm not really sure it was ever beautiful except in my mind. Well, that's not accurate either. There were times that were almost euphoric. Why then did the loving sour? Why did I decide to make those judgments about not getting and not giving in the first place?

They are based on my *expectations* and *the cardinal belief of love* (If you loved me, you would . . .), which are the two major causes (beliefs) of happiness in relationships.

In having expectations, I am needing my lover or friends to do or be what I expect in order to be comfortable and happy. If I don't get what I expect, I become unhappy. Yet, for me, it is this phenomenon in my relationships that creates friction, discomfort, and, at times, separation.

My fantasies are created in a vacuum. They often have no real connection to the reality of who I am and who my lover is.

Thus, I create an improbable, if not impossible, task for myself—trying to match my everyday experiences to the content of my dreams. The result: I set myself up for disappointments. Creating fixed images to which my partner or friends must conform has its liabilities. In effect, we are

117

asking others to fulfill our dreams of what we believe they "should" be or do, which is very different from allowing them to be or act in accordance with their own wants. Although expectations might appear to help me concretize my wants and seem to create motivation (the carrot in front of the donkey), they often backfire!

This leads me directly to the *cardinal belief* of love, which was taught to me and heavily reinforced very early in childhood. *"If you loved me, you would . . ."* It was the *standard of proof* for my parents, my friends and for me. If he or she does that thing or activity I want, then they love me. If they don't, I take it as a sign they don't love me or care.

The restatement of this belief echoes throughout the hallways of most homes. If Robert loved me, he would be more caring. If Jane loved me, she would put more effort into our business. If Harry loved me, he would want to satisfy me more in sex. If Tina cared, she would support me. If Judy really loved me, she would be nice to my parents. If Ted loved me, he wouldn't be unfaithful. If Laura cared, she would write more often. If Mark trusted me, he would tell me more. Endless in content, but the classic form is still: "If you loved me, you would . . ."

But since my wants and expectations are my own and not necessarily my lover's (who may have his own separate wants), he often does not conform to mine. Then I make a judgment based on my cardinal belief and assume I have many proofs that show me I am unloved and unlovable.

Suppose I arrived home to an empty house for the hundredth time. My wife is out with her friends shopping and dinner isn't even prepared. I look through the emptiness and the silence, saying to myself, "If she loved me, she would be here when I get home. She would not be out with her friends. She would have prepared my dinner." Since she did not conform to my expectations of a good and loving wife, I conclude that she does not love me, or at the very least, she does not love me enough.

My relationship, I deduce, is lopsided. This initial disillusionment turns into a more meditative depression. "Maybe, there is something wrong with me . . . I should be able to motivate her to care more, to love me more, to be more considerate and attentive. I should be able to make her love me."

But since I haven't been able to do it in the past, I believe

I won't be able to do it in the future. I get angry and I use this distress to push my wife into loving me more . . . ironically, it secures the opposite result, with her pleading, "Leave me alone." Pervaded by a sense of powerlessness, I contemplate leaving the marriage to escape the discomfort. Later, as I review my actions, I see how my expectations, judgments and unhappiness had reaped a self-defeating harvest. My first want was to be loved and to love. Now, I might be cutting myself off from both.

Can we see the progression? First, I judged that I was not getting enough. This was based on my expectation that a good wife is home every night, cooks dinner and is attentive. I then used my cardinal belief as a standard of proof. If she loved me, she would do all the things I wanted. Since she didn't, she did not love me. And because I see that as bad, I become unhappy, which in turn I try to use to motivate my wife to be more attentive. But *that* results in me getting even less of what I want. Ultimately, as the pain increases, I want to leave the relationship . . . which was the opposite of my original concern and attention.

Maybe another view of the same situation will help. Although I assumed that my wife did not love me because she was out of the house, my wife, at that very moment, could have been doing many things for herself . . . none of which was a comment on our marriage or her love. She might have been exploring her own self-worth and moving toward a more liberated life-style. She might have been feeling confined and was seeking an outlet. But nothing she did said, "I don't love you." She did what she did for her own reasons and from her own beliefs. My using the cardinal belief as proof was arbitrary . . . *my assumptions come from my own judgments and fears*. It proves nothing if someone else does not perform to my expectations.

Some real questions arise. Do I want to have expectations? If they set up conditions and judgments for *me making me* unhappy (I feel bad because I did not get what I expected), could I do without them? I could still want and try to get, but allow the future. If I don't make happiness the reward of getting, I could perhaps be happy now while I try for what I want. Expectations are not productive . . . not if what I want is to love and be loved.

119

And the cardinal belief also has its fallacies and resulting unhappiness. Since my lover does many things from his or her own beliefs and resulting feelings, then my belief that "If she loved me, she would . . ." is certainly never conclusive. She could still love me and not do what I want or ask, just as I have loved her while doing things she disagreed with.

How often have we loved a parent and yet did the exact opposite of what was requested. When we were attending to our wants, we were simply attending to our wants . . . not saying "I don't love you or care." Yet, how often did they tell us "You don't love me."

I can remember experiences of being annoyed at a meeting or situation during the day and then dragging my moodiness into the evening . . . and perhaps being coarse and easily angered. Yet, that was just a statement about my own discomfort and unhappiness, not a comment about the person I loved. Nevertheless, it might have appeared as if I did not care. So, again, the cardinal belief is, in fact, *not* a standard of proof. It is really just another judgmental way of using unhappiness to take care of myself. Can I discard that belief if I want to? Sure . . . if I know discarding it would be a better way of taking care of myself. But if I am not sure, I can hold it where I am. I don't have to push . . . just allow it.

This leads me to question another fundamental belief which is active for most of us in viewing love relationships. The belief is I am responsible for the unhappiness of others and they are responsible for my unhappiness.

If I believe that I have the power to control others, then I might think I have the power to determine their desires and behavior. Yet, if I create my own feelings and behavior from my own beliefs, the only person I can possibly control is myself. What I decide to do is my decision. And what others decide to do is their decision.

In effect, *each of us is responsible for ourselves.*

If I do not like or approve of what you do, I decide that for my reasons. If I become unhappy about it, I do because I believe it's bad for me. My unhappiness comes from my judgments or beliefs about a situation. I could also reserve my judgment about what you did and not become unhappy. There are endless options. My unhappiness is mine. The myth that others make me unhappy or I make them unhappy is just another belief I had been taught from day one.

There is more to get from all this discussion and the examples, more to learn from being angry if my wife isn't home, more to know about the couple who feared arguing, more to extract from the man unhappy that he might be a sucker, more to absorb from the woman resenting being pushed away from her interests. *While we are unhappy and attending to our fears, we are not loving.*

People love in direct proportion to which they are happy.
If I loved flying and I love someone who is frightened of flying, their not wanting to be in an airplane with me does not suggest they don't care. If I loved someone who was fearful of the dark, their refusing to go into a dark room with me does not mean they are not loving. If my partner is jealous because he or she fears being left alone, that does not prove their lack of love.

If my wife, husband, lover or friend is uncomfortable, insecure, fearful, anxious, they will do many things that might suggest they are inconsiderate and unloving. Yet, the only thing their actions really say is that they are unhappy about something and trying to take care of themselves. Even if they seem cold, inconsiderate and self-defeating, they are doing the best they can in accordance with their current beliefs. What I say about the actions of others is my trip. My labels are my labels. The only conclusion I can draw is that while people are unhappy, they are distracted from loving in order to attend to their fears . . . which, in effect, could never be a comment on their loving, but only an example of their unhappiness.

My judgments can lead me to strange and erroneous conclusions. I could say to someone who is claustrophobic . . . if you loved me, you would overcome your fear of elevators. But your fear might be more immediate than your loving (we are walking toward the elevator in a high-rise apartment). Out of self-protection (as you see it), you run from me and the building to avoid danger. Ironically, I could interpret your fleeing or your apparent unhappiness as a criterion for judging that you don't love me enough. I could have the belief that when someone loves me they would not fear anything when they are with me. But that would

121

not be a proof about their loving me, just an exercise in passing judgment.

The claustrophobic person on the other side of the interaction, if he shared my beliefs, might make his own judgments. He might resent me for needing him to be or perform in a certain way to "prove" his love. And if he chooses to go in the elevator and be terrified, he might have just opted to attend to his stronger fear of losing me. So the gesture still revolves around fear. Again, another exercise in expectations and judgments . . . not a proof of loving or lack of loving.

Let's even take it further. If the claustrophobic does my bidding, he might come to resent me. Finally, he would resent himself for being so manipulated (he should love me for me and not for what I do). Herein lie the germs that feed self-hate and inner-directed anger. I don't like myself for letting *me* be put in such a situation. I believe I am not loved for me, but for my performance. But is that really so? A person who asks me to do this or that as proof of my love is just trying (in that request) to cope with their own fears.

The plea is "please love me no matter what I do, no matter how I appear." *Accept me . . . be happy with me.* And if I were able to get in touch with wanting that for myself, I would want it for my loved ones too. I would know my fears and expectations have everything to do with my unhappiness and nothing to do with my loving. When I really understand the process, I can discard many of the beliefs and conditions of unhappiness.

It's intense, complex and yet very simple. There's so much to see yet there isn't. Unhappiness takes so many forms, it appears endless . . . but the dynamic always follows from beliefs and judgments. If all this just helps us to understand that "to love is to be happy with," then we've heard all there is to hear. *No conditions, no expectations and no judgments* can become not only guideposts for our relationships, but also a very pragmatic, non-idealistic approach to getting more of what we want.

Allowing my lover her wants (even though I might not share them or participate in making them happen), permitting my lover her good feelings as well as her unhappiness, is really a beautiful way of giving her space and loving her.

122

There are those who would say the Option Attitude is selfless. On the contrary, clearly seeing, understanding and accepting the dilemmas of those I love is the most effective step toward helping them become happier and deal with themselves. In their increased happiness, they become more loving, and isn't that really what I want for myself and for them?

Okay, we've made it to this point. Why not take a break . . . have a cup of coffee. I know you feel you've been bombarded with ideas. Don't worry about what you can't remember . . . you'll retain what's useful for you and the rest doesn't matter. And if you feel it does, you'll know to reread this section.

Okay, I'm ready to go on. Are you? Come, be with me.

When I use unhappiness as a motivator in love relationships, it usually backfires!

When my lover's unhappiness meets up with my unhappiness (when I get unhappy about her being unhappy), it results in my either *bribing her, ignoring her or attacking her.* Ultimately it could lead to *leaving her.* I do this not out of maliciousness, but to improve my relationships. My behavior is performed in the name of love. Often, I am aware that I use unhappiness as a tool, but am I always aware that it usually backfires?

Since my lover is unhappy because I play cards every Thursday night, I will stop playing cards so she won't be unhappy. This is my way of bribing her not to be unhappy with me. Later, I begin to resent depriving myself. "If she loved me, she would not make me sacrifice my enjoyments for her." I believe that I "must" do this or that in order for her to love and be happy with me. And if I "must" sacrifice, I can easily begin to believe it's not worth it. Backfire!

What I originally wanted was to increase my good feelings . . . what I succeeded in doing was generating more unhappiness and extinguishing my own good feelings.

Ignoring our lovers or *depriving* them is another way of using unhappiness to fight unhappiness. Since my lover is always unhappy when I am not home, I will continue to stay away as often as possible as a way of "training" her not to need me to be home as a condition of her feeling good. I do not want to be confined or responsible. I will deprive her of what she "needs" so that she won't "need" it anymore. But, in fact, she then becomes even more unhappy. Backfire! I wanted to help her feel better, but now she feels worse since she also believes that I am being malicious and unloving by not being home.

The *attack* is another way, via unhappiness, to solve my interpersonal problems. If I confront the person with anger and disapproval, they'll see how much it means to me and will stop doing what I don't want them to do. I am saying, "If you continue to be this way, I will be harsh or angry with you in return." But in doing that, I am really showing my disapproval of the other person. My actions, which I believe will be an effective deterrent, just become a wall to push against and even if the person is willing to change, they probably don't want to be shoved and condemned into moving. Their reaction is to fight me. Backfire! I wanted to put the fire out; instead I fueled it.

Unhappiness as a tool to motivate doesn't really work. It generates more problems than it solves. Even though it appears to work for the moment, the underlying resentment and anger it creates ultimately undermines any "apparent" success. What I initially wanted was to love and be loved. What I achieved was the opposite . . . I was less loving and less loved. To the extent I am unhappy, I am not loving. This is not to say what I did was wrong . . . it was the best I could do based on my beliefs at that time. When I was depriving, bribing, or attacking my lover, I did so because I believed it would ultimately be beneficial to our relationship. So there is no need to kick myself around the block. If I know these beliefs are self-defeating, I can now discard them and be more allowing in my relationships.

This is the last step . . . the recap and what it could mean standing on the diving board at the end of this chapter. Unhappiness in my love relationships inevitably comes from my beliefs. What has been isolated are the two major causes of unhappiness in this arena: expectations and the belief "if you love me, you would . . ."

When I am hurt, anxious, or angry, I am doing the best I can in relation to my present beliefs. But as I come to see these beliefs as self-defeating and changeable, I can discard them and decide to be more accepting and less judgmental because I really know it gets me more of what I want. I can use this exploration as an opportunity to be happier, although awareness does not force change—it only presents me with additional opportunities. Change comes from our choosing to change. We can always stay where we are, if we want.

In seeing I am not responsible for another's fears or their loving, I can be free from their recrimination and allow them to be free of mine. In understanding how unhappiness when used as a motivator often backfires, I can decide to give up using it as a tool. In knowing that others move directly against my "musts," "have tos" and "shoulds," I can discard those demands as ineffective and try to help my lover be motivated for his or her own reasons. With each new conclusion (belief), I see new options.

Tests and conditions never prove love; they just prove we are all capable of tapping someone else's fears. The unhappiness of others and their attending to their discomforts has all to do with them and nothing to do with me. I see that when my lover comes from her fears, she is not in touch with her loving. It is not a proof that she doesn't love me or want to love me more.

Even if my relationship crumbles, I could know that *nothing is wrong with me. I do the best I can, the best I know how, based on my current beliefs.* And so does my lover. But as I give up my self-defeating beliefs, I can function more effectively for myself, as can my lover.

I can know in my individual journey toward becoming happier, I am always trying to love others more as others are trying to love me more. The happier I become, the more I notice that I approach others with the Option Attitude: *To love is to be happy with.*

Sometimes, I stop my flow with the belief that if I am not uptight or unhappy about the possible demise of my relationships, I will not attend to them. But that belief is true if I make it so. I do not need to be unhappy to take care of myself and try to be more loving. I have everything to gain by becoming happier and nothing to lose . . . except my fears and anxieties.

My unhappiness can have many different underlying beliefs, but I have found as I clear myself of expectations and discard my cardinal belief of love, my whole world changes. I live the Option alternative by adopting the Option Attitude. As I become less judgmental, I become more accepting and loving. For me, as I have altered my beliefs through the Option Process, I have noticed I get so much more of what I want in my love relationships and the evolution spills over into every aspect of my life.

There is nothing to do to be happy, except shed my unhappy beliefs. What I choose to explore and change is my decision. Option does away with the rules, the promises, the shoulds and should nots. This book is not going to add to the collection of self-defeating beliefs, it will present an opportunity to clear them away. There is no doctor or priest advising with great authority how we ought to live our lives. No one is going to hold our hand or tell us what to do. We don't need it nor do we really want it. We each know what is best for ourselves. Option is only a tool, which changes from hand to hand. It can be as effective as we want it to be.

In love relationships, or any area, I can begin getting more of what I want by accepting and seeing exactly what I do and the harvest of my unhappiness. Then, I can use the Option dialogue to uncover and alter beliefs. Or, if I have witnessed in this chapter many of my own beliefs in action, I can *decide* right now (if I want) to discard some of them.

There is more than an attitude and a vision of living presented here . . . more than a method and dialogue technique . . . allowing ourselves to be more loving is a most beautiful journey.

THE "THINK" PAGE (LOVE RELATION-SHIPS AND THE OPTION ALTERNATIVE)

QUESTIONS TO ASK YOURSELF:

Are you more loving when you are happy or when you are unhappy?

Do you expect your loved ones to conform to your wants?

Is your loving someone conditional on their loving you? If so, why?

Are you afraid of being hurt in relationships?

Do you have preset rules for your love relationships? If so, why?

Do you find yourself often saying "he should" or "she should"?

When you love someone, do you accept them for what they are or do you judge them?

OPTION CONCEPTS TO CONSIDER:

*EXPECTATIONS ARE A MAJOR CAUSE OF UNHAP-PINESS IN LOVE RELATIONSHIPS.

*"IF YOU LOVED ME, YOU WOULD . . ." IS NOT A STANDARD OF PROOF.

*IF MY LOVER DOES NOT DO WHAT I WANT, IT SAYS NOTHING ABOUT HIS LOVING ME.

*PEOPLE LOVE TO THE EXTENT THEY ARE HAPPY.

*THE HAPPIER I AM, THE MORE LOVING I AM.

*WE CANNOT MAKE OTHERS UNHAPPY, ONLY THEY CAN DO THAT FOR THEMSELVES.

*EACH OF US IS RESPONSIBLE FOR OUR OWN UN-HAPPINESS.

*TO LOVE IS TO BE HAPPY WITH.

*I DO THE BEST I CAN AND SO DOES MY LOVER, THE BEST WE BOTH KNOW HOW BASED ON OUR BELIEFS.

BELIEFS TO CONSIDER DISCARDING:

If you loved me, you would . . .

Her unhappiness is proof she doesn't love me.

My lover makes me unhappy and I make him unhappy.

If I can't motivate my lover to love me more or to be happy, then something must be wrong with me.

I should be able to make others love me more.

FIFTH DIALOGUE

Q. *WHAT ARE YOU UNHAPPY ABOUT?*
A. I'm not really unhappy, I'm depressed.
Q. *WHAT ARE YOU DEPRESSED ABOUT?*
A. About being melancholy, lifeless, no energy . . . you know.
Q. *What is it about being lifeless that bothers you most?*
A. That I'm not doing anything.
Q. *WHY DOES THAT MAKE YOU UNHAPPY?*
A. Maybe I should backtrack . . . what do you think?
Q. *Why do you ask?*
A. I guess I'm not sure which is the best way to proceed.
Q. *What do you mean?*
A. It's the same problem I feel about not doing anything. Since I just feel confused, admittedly I can say I don't know, so I ask others to tell me. To guide me.
Q. *WHAT ARE YOU AFRAID WOULD HAPPEN IF YOU GUIDED YOU?*
A. I'd screw everything up.
Q. *What do you mean?*
A. About six months ago, the guy I was living with for over three years split. And we had almost gotten married two times. Quietly, on Saturday afternoon, he announced he had had enough and walked. Shit.
Q. *Why do you say "shit"?*
A. Because I really loved him. (crying) This is all I did for two months. Cried my eyes out . . . I did the whole "poor me" trip. Thought of slitting my wrists. But now I don't even know anymore. I really loved him, our relationship really mattered to me. But we were just incompatible. Different people from different worlds right from the beginning.
Q. *What do you mean?*
A. I mean I used to lay it on our incompatibility, but maybe that wasn't it. He always had to do what he wanted to do and I was supposed to follow. Whatever it was . . . where to go on holidays, what restaurant to eat at, who to invite over for the weekend. It was

129

like I never really mattered and I knew it. So, I fought him all the time.

Q. *Why did you fight?*

A. Because I wanted him to think of me, to appreciate and consider me. After all, if he loved me, he would have been a helluva lot more considerate.

Q. *DO YOU BELIEVE THAT?*

A. Well, when I'm loving him, I was always considerate.

Q. *And when you weren't?*

A. Then I could be a real bitch.

Q. *When you were a "bitch," would you say you loved him less or didn't love him at all?*

A. That didn't matter. If I was in a lousy mood, then I just acted nuts and difficult . . . but I still loved him just the same.

Q. *Okay, before you said that "If he loved me, he would be more considerate." Do you believe that?*

A. Oh . . . you mean maybe all those times he acted angry and pissed was because he was feeling angry and pissed, but he still loved me? Funny how I was always sure it meant he didn't love me. I never thought of that before. When I'm unhappy, I don't have the patience or interest in being loving or sweet . . . but that doesn't mean I don't care. And you know, to make matters worse, when he would get that way, I would withdraw from him and become really angry.

Q. *WHY WERE YOU ANGRY?*

A. I don't really know any more. I wanted him to love me more.

Q. *WHAT WERE YOU AFRAID WOULD HAPPEN IF YOU WEREN'T ANGRY?*

A. That he wouldn't care . . . but that doesn't make sense. Half the time, my yelling alone sent him running from our apartment. I know it sounds silly, but part of my screaming was to get him to love me . . . and it really got me the opposite. Another part of my screaming was because I was really furious at myself.

Q. *WHY WERE YOU FURIOUS WITH YOURSELF?*

A. I had expected so much more from that relationship. I really misjudged it.

Q. *What do you mean?*

A. It wasn't what I had expected. It's like making a plan,

thinking about it in your head, how it would be and what you would feel . . . and then nothing fits. Nothing works out; it's horrible how it all crumbles.

Q. WHY WOULD THAT MAKE YOU UNHAPPY?

A. Because I had my heart set on it; everything was going to be so beautiful. You know, this wasn't the first guy I've lived with. I was so upset when it wasn't working.

Q. WHY?

A. Because I wanted it; I needed to be loved.

Q. I know that you wanted love, but why were you unhappy when you didn't get it?

A. Why was I unhappy . . . because I didn't get it. I mean, when you care about something and it doesn't work out, of course you get unhappy.

Q. WHY DO YOU BELIEVE THAT?

A. Well, look around, because you do.

Q. I understand that's what you do . . . when you care about something you don't get, you then become unhappy. THE QUESTION IS WHY?

A. I don't know. Maybe because it's natural.

Q. WHAT ARE YOU AFRAID WOULD HAPPEN IF YOU DIDN'T GET UNHAPPY ABOUT NOT BEING LOVED?

A. Then it would mean I didn't care enough, I'd be cold and unfeeling, and then maybe I'd never be loved.

Q. DO YOU BELIEVE THAT?

A. What? Is the question: "Do I believe if I didn't care, I wouldn't be loved?" or is the question, "If I don't get unhappy, then it's a sign I don't care?"

Q. Which question do you want to answer?

A. I don't believe I have to be unhappy in order to care. I really don't, although I guess I've acted like I do. It was my way of making it important. I guess if I didn't get unhappy, I was afraid I would stop trying. Funny, somehow I'm back to the beginning . . . about being melancholy and not doing anything.

Q. How?

A. I saw trying again with another guy as so painful, that I stopped wanting it. That's why I'm so lethargic. I use myself up being afraid of the pain and then I don't feel anything.

Q. Why do you believe it'll be so painful?

131

A. It's not that I mind working at a relationship; it's just all the heartache and disappointment when it doesn't work out.

Q. Why is there heartache and disappointment?

A. I guess you feel used and old.

Q. What do you mean?

A. You're not fresh any more. It's like being worn out by all the guys you've tried to make it with. Energy expended and lost. There is nothing left to feel but exhaustion.

Q. Why is that?

A. Just thinking about trying again knocks me out.

Q. What about trying again or thinking about trying again does that to you?

A. I guess I see a long struggle, and zero as the ultimate reward.

Q. Why do you see it that way?

A. Because it's always been that way.

Q. Why if it has always been that way, do you believe it will always be that way?

A. I guess it doesn't have to be a struggle. Maybe I see it that way to protect myself.

Q. Against what?

A. Against getting sucked in again. Against wasting time and energy on some slob, instead of finding some really gentle, mellow man who really cares.

Q. WHAT ARE YOU AFRAID WOULD HAPPEN IF YOU DIDN'T SEE IT AS A STRUGGLE?

A. I might get involved too easily, too casually. I'll get tied to another unlikely prospect for a peaceful home.

Q. Are you saying you see it as a struggle so that you will be very careful choosing next time?

A. Yes. Isn't that silly? I never quite realized that before. I guess I could not make that judgment and still choose carefully. (smiles) Sometimes, though, I think I see it as a struggle so I'll be smart enough not to bother to try again. Hands off.

Q. Why would you do that?

A. It's not really what I would want to do. I guess that's the ultimate way to protect myself, to stop me from getting involved again and getting hurt again.

Q. WHY DO YOU BELIEVE YOU'D GET HURT?

132

A. I'm suddenly finding I don't really believe it any more. In a way, my uptightness would probably contribute to making it happen.

Q. *What are you wanting?*

A. To try again . . . Lo and behold, I said it and I really mean it. This time, I'd want a simple, sane and loving relationship.

Q. *Do you still believe in any way that you have to be unhappy in order to take care of yourself in choosing your relationships?*

A. No . . . definitely not. Whether I was unhappy or not, I'd still try to choose the best. I wouldn't have to be unhappy first. (laughing) I could see myself even having much more energy since I wouldn't be busy beating myself up. I'd just be me. Do you know how wonderful that sounds? Just being me.

6

kiss your guilt good-bye

The sunlight bathed the room in an almost surreal mist. He sat listlessly on the couch as he watched her move ever so slowly. Each gesture came after seemingly enormous effort. The edges of her lips were cracked from age. Her skin was deeply lined and resistant to the movements of her mouth. However, her eyes, deeply set into a still attractive face, sparkled when she talked. This was a joyful morning for her . . . always a joyful morning to be in the company of one of her grandchildren.

Once an active participant in her environment, she had been forced by her arthritis to take a more passive role as viewer and recipient of news rather than its creator. In fact, she always had difficulty making her days and weeks appear interesting to others, since she envisioned their lives as filled with great designs and activities. For her, the little things had now become distinctly significant . . . a book of light poetry, an amusing television program, the little dog who was her constant companion, the unexpected smile of a child or her daughter's voice echoing in a telephone receiver. Each of

135

these small events was a gift.

Somehow, he knew all this . . . sensed all this as he sat with the woman whom he had come to view from a distance, a separation generated by his own unresolved questions. He wondered whether he would, indeed, want to live so long, especially if he was ill or disabled.

These visits had become a way of dispensing with an obligation . . . more to pacify his insistent mother than to engage his grandmother. Almost three months had elapsed since his last visit, during which time his parents had accused him of being insensitive, inconsiderate and callous. It was the word "callous" that tapped something very disturbing inside and flooded him with guilt. He didn't want to be ungrateful and cool to those who loved him. The more uncomfortable he felt, the more he pushed himself to see his grandmother. Although he knew he loved and respected this very mild-mannered lady, it was his guilt and self-consciousness that dominated him.

Somehow, even though he sat opposite her, he was too distracted by his own inner currents to become involved. As he watched her sip tea and smile at him, he couldn't help but smile back. For a moment, some of those old, warm, very warm, feelings caressed him. Still, he could not seem to concentrate. Her words fell on deaf ears. He found himself drifting, daydreaming about the white-water canoe trip he planned for the following weekend. He could see the sleek, slender boat cutting through the turbulent water and polished rocks. He could feel the sense of off-balance he always experienced on the river . . . the very same kind of uncentered sensation that possessed him now.

The fantasy abruptly ended when he was startled by his grandmother's hand gently tapping his shoulder. Her head rocked back and forth, in a cadence as even and calculated as a pendulum. She smiled as she suggested perhaps there was somewhere he might be wanting to go. Her manner was easy and accepting.

Immediately, he froze—feeling exposed, transparent. He believed she knew his underlying feelings. His lack of interest was apparent. Uncomfortable and embarrassed, he felt even more guilty than before. He could not believe how ridiculous and insensitive he had been to ignore her conversation while sitting only five feet away.

Somehow, had she been angry or accusing, he might have quickly come to his own defense. He was tired; it had been a long night—the excuses would have been endless. But it was the softness of her gaze, the patient understanding that really unnerved him. He kept telling himself he should pay attention, should be responsive . . . after all, what else does she have but these infrequent encounters. And yet, at the very same moment, he resented feeling so obligated.

The more uncomfortable he became, the less able he was to listen to her words. Even her smiles made him self-conscious. Finally, the feelings of guilt became so unbearable, he decided to leave, excusing himself with an obviously invented appointment. Nevertheless, she insisted she understood and kissed him affectionately on the cheek.

As he waited for the elevator, he felt even more peculiar . . . for he really valued this woman, alone and almost captive in a cold, cement high-rise world. But somehow, he knew his good feelings had been buried beneath the debris of his guilt and his discomfort had soured a formerly fun-filled event of warmth and sharing. He turned awkwardly to say good-bye as he slunk sheepishly into the elevator.

Another day. Another city. Another Option student, a young executive for a textile company, decided to stay late with his secretary in order to review and catch up on paperwork. Robert knew his prime motive was other than work, but he persisted in telling himself he was not thinking about what he was thinking. After all, he considered, work was an excellent reason for coming home later. It was the excuse he had presented quite innocently to himself as well as the girl he lived with. Within a half hour, the office was completely empty except for the two overachievers. Robert suggested they work in his office, where they could be more comfortable. After carefully locking his door, he began to mix his dictation with some light touching and body brushing techniques. She continued to write, obviously open to his advances.

Within minutes, the two were on the floor between the file cabinets. The pencil and pad rested on the deep pile rug just beside their bodies. After finishing their encounter, they left the office together hand in hand. In the lobby, they parted in a perfectly businesslike manner. As Robert began to walk toward the entranceway, he was intercepted by the woman he lived with. Visibly upset, she confronted him, her eyes filled with disappointment and anger. She explained to him how she decided to surprise him with a visit to his office and had heard his entire performance on the office floor.

Trapped and feeling transparent, Robert began to apologize. "Logistics are crucial," he thought to himself. "I have to convince her that I feel bad about this . . . and yet I do and don't." His excitement about his adventure was dissipated by his intense feelings of discomfort. He saw himself as having "caused" his lover agony. Guilt pervaded him as he began to realize he had jeopardized something he valued. The worse he felt, the more he assured himself and his mate that he would never do it again.

Guilt is what a "good" person feels when he has done something "bad."

Doing something bad can also include not doing what we believe we should have done. If our training was classic, as soon as we realize our trespasses, we immediately feel bad. This great internal whip is a system of checks and balances that supposedly helps us stay within the rules.

There is the person who regrets having an affair and calls it bad so he will make sure not to do it again. The young man who feels guilty of participating in making his girlfriend pregnant and is willing to buy the Empire State Building to help her (and to neutralize his guilt). The executive who begins to feel very bad about slacking off and suddenly has a burst of energy.

These people are feeling guilty and are acting out of their guilt. They are functioning within the first goal area of guilt: *To help themselves do what they believe they should do or stop themselves from doing what they believe they shouldn't do.* In effect, like other unhappiness, guilt is used to motivate or unmotivate as the case may be.

When I feel guilty about neglecting to help a friend or about being angry with my lover, I am saying if I did not become unhappy about what I "should" have done or "should" not have done, I just might not correct my undesirable behavior. The self-inflicted psychic pain acts as a deterrent or an incentive. Here again is the emergence of the word "should." When I believe I "should" have behaved in a cer-

138

tain fashion, I am articulating an expectation (I must always be ready to help my friends or I must be loving all the time with my lover). These "shoulds" are then further compounded and supported by guilt.

The second goal of guilt serves a different, well-accepted function. *Guilt is the way I show my "humaneness" to myself and others* by feeling appropriately bad in certain circumstances now so that I can feel good later. In this way, I am paying my dues. We are also much more willing to forgive the remorseful wrongdoer than the one who exhibits no repentance because we believe the person who feels guilty about an action is less likely to repeat it in the future.

This is more than just a question of taking responsibility. It is labeling (judging) my actions as bad and feeling as well as displaying anguish. It is a form of penance, self-judged and self-executed, in which unhappiness becomes a cleansing vehicle. Although often displayed to others in order to earn a pardon, at times, guilt can be suffered in silence and secrecy as we attempt to satisfy our severest critic . . . ourselves.

The third goal area of guilt is using the *threat* of guilt as an enforcer of a promise, whether it be implicit or explicit. Instead of wanting to be successful at a job or love affair, a marriage or a competition, we turn it into a need by creating a promise. I promise to make a lot of money. I promise to make you happier and be gentle. I promise to be a great husband or father. I promise to love you forever and ever. These promises are commitments to perform, whether they be said to others or to ourselves. We also have our "not to" promises. I promise not to be unfaithful. I promise not to steal or cheat. I promise not to lie.

Why do I make promises? Ultimately, it is a tool to motivate. It heightens my concern, energizes my commitment and creates an obligation. I say to myself or another that I must do this or that, otherwise I will suffer unhappiness (wanting becomes needing).

If I fail to deliver what I promiesd, I hold myself responsible and feel guilty for "breaking" my promise. This is again my way of letting myself know that I missed and punishing myself so I won't do it again. This is also an example of *me punishing me*, as if I believe I would not do what I want unless I promise . . . and hold the threat of guilt over my head.

An essential fueling belief for guilt is that I am responsible for another's unhappiness. If someone gets unhappy or upset because I did not perform or deliver, I often believe I did it . . . I made them unhappy, "caused" or "created" their unhappiness. Yet, if each of us creates our own happiness and unhappiness in accordance with our own beliefs, I could not be responsible for someone else's disappointment and despair. Another person's anger or sadness is theirs, which they choose for their own reasons. If doing the best I could at any moment was not enough for them and their expectations, they make their own judgments for their own purposes. If a young boy has performed poorly in school, the scolding and angry parent was not made unhappy by the child. Their discomforts say nothing about their son, but everything about themselves and their own disappointments.

It's fantastic that guilt is not limited to any one area or subject. I can feel guilty about anything: too much sex or too little, love, money, marriage, business, infidelity, social injustice, etc.

Yet, guilt has its own self-defeating qualities. Reinforcing my behavior with doses of self-inflicted pain and anguish often brings very distracting side effects. As a result of my guilt, I feel trapped to do "this" or "that" in order to absolve and avoid my uncomfortable feelings. And although I might, indeed, want to alter my actions, I tend to resist being pushed . . . even if it's my own pressure.

In more extreme cases, guilt might actually push me away from the very thing I want. If I was rude and abrupt to a friend, I might feel guilty so that I will be sure not to do it again. What I really want is to be warm and cordial. But as the embarrassment and pain of my guilt grows, I choose to avoid my friend. The less I see him, the less opportunity I have in achieving my desire to be warm and helpful, which is what I was trying to enforce in the first place. In effect, the mechanism has backfired!

This is the stop-start of unhappiness. My original goal in using guilt or the threat of guilt is to intensify my wants . . . so I would try harder. The irony is by passing judgments on myself and in not permitting myself to miss the mark, I sometimes extinguish the original desire by creating tension that inhibits my free movement.

Why the short circuit? Guilt is moving away from what I don't want, rather than clearly moving toward what I do want. *It is a negative movement away from pain.* I am afraid if I do not feel guilty I might continue to do this bad thing or not do the things I should. The implications are dramatic. The implicit statement is "I do not trust myself." I am suspecting I might purposely go against myself . . . and do what is bad for me. Therefore, I feel guilty to insure I don't. Touchdown with a prime belief: if I would be bad for myself, then there must be something wrong with me.

Is there an alternative? Yes, I can question my beliefs about guilt like any other unhappiness. When I am aware of feeling guilty, I can ask myself . . . Why am I guilty? and what am I believing right now that makes me guilty? By tracking through the beliefs, I can uncover the "why" of my feelings and herein lies the opportunity to discard or change the underlying belief.

If I could want without needing to get or making promises, I could want almost anything I fancy. *If my happiness was not dependent on getting, I could go after everything I want without anxiety or fear.* In fact, I would increase my clarity and energy effectiveness in getting what I want because I would not simultaneously be battling with my fears and anxieties.

In eliminating the judgments of "bad" and the pressure of promises, I eliminate the usefulness of guilt and the threat of guilt. I do not have to worry about delivery if I never said I "had to" or if I didn't judge it bad to have not delivered. I could try. If I miss, I could accept it and still be motivated to improve my aim for the next occasion.

If I know I am not bad for myself or others, I would not feel guilty. I do the best I can according to my current beliefs. The results of my actions are lessons, not indictments. And the lessons I learn from unproductive actions can help me focus on what I really want for myself. Being in touch with such an awareness would make guilt indispensable and unnecessary.

No matter what anyone judges as the "appropriate" guilty response, we could know that we celebrate our humanity not in our unhappiness, but in our loving and caring.

THE "THINK" PAGE (KISS YOUR GUILT GOOD-BYE)

QUESTIONS TO ASK YOURSELF:

Do you often feel guilty about your thoughts and actions?

When you are feeling guilty, do you let others know how you feel? If so, why?

If you didn't feel guilty about doing something you believe is wrong, are you afraid you would do it again?

Do you expect others to feel "bad" when they do not deliver what they promised?

Do you make promises? If so, why? What are you afraid would happen if you no longer made promises?

OPTION CONCEPTS TO CONSIDER:

*GUILT IS UNHAPPINESS USED TO MOTIVATE, UN-MOTIVATE AND TO PAY DUES.

*NOT TRUSTING OURSELVES IS OFTEN SYMBOL-IZED BY GUILT.

*A PROMISE IS OUR WAY OF MAKING SURE WE

DO SOMETHING WE ARE NOT SURE WE WANT
TO DO OR TRUST WE WILL DO.

*IF OUR HAPPINESS WAS NOT DEPENDENT ON
GETTING, WE WOULD GO AFTER EVERYTHING
WE WANTED WITHOUT ANY FEAR.

*THE RESULTS OF OUR ACTIONS ARE LESSONS,
NOT INDICTMENTS.

*OUR HUMANITY CAN BE CELEBRATED BY OUR
LOVING AND OUR CARING.

BELIEFS TO CONSIDER DISCARDING:

Guilt is what "good" people feel when they have done
something "bad."

Guilt is necessary to keep people honest.

If I don't feel guilty, I might do it again.

The only way to count on someone is to make him promise.

When I let someone down, I'm responsible for his unhappiness.

―――――

SIXTH DIALOGUE

Q. WHAT ARE YOU UNHAPPY ABOUT?
A. About what I did.
Q. What did you do?
A. When my husband Tom was away at a convention,
Gary dropped by. He wasn't aware that Tom wouldn't
be home. In fact, he had just come specifically to see
him. You know how good friends don't have to make
appointments. And then I was alone with nothing to
do and he was really free for the evening, having
planned to spend it with Tom and me. So . . . so, I

suggested he stay. That seemed harmless enough. Maybe it was the drinks?

Q. *The drinks?*

A. Yes, I poured some sherry for both of us and one glass led to another. Then, I guess, it just happened. I mean it wasn't planned or anything. I'm not even sure I even really wanted it. I just can't believe I would do that . . . it's just not me. I feel so cheap.

Q. *What do you mean by "cheap?"*

A. My husband is out breaking his neck while I'm home in bed with another man . . . and not just another man, a dear friend. Sounds like some silly daytime soap opera. (crying) But it isn't, you know; it's me.

Q. *WHAT ABOUT THAT MAKES YOU SO UNHAPPY?*

A. That I slipped, that I was out of control.

Q. *WHY IS THAT SO DISTURBING?*

A. I guess it shows me when I let loose, play it by ear, I'm really terrible. I'm not that classic dissatisfied woman looking to shack up. I really have a reasonably decent relationship with my husband . . . it's not perfect, but certainly not bad enough to warrant cheating behind his back. (sobbing softly) I mean for just one lousy night over three months ago, all this . . . I've been paying ever since.

Q. *What do you mean?*

A. I mean I feel terrible, I can't stand myself. If I could only take it all back, I would.

Q. *Why?*

A. Because I shouldn't have done it. I didn't set out to cheat on my marriage and I certainly don't want my life filled with lies.

Q. *I understand that's not what you are now wanting, but why do you feel bad about what you did three months ago?*

A. Why do I feel bad about what I did? (long pause) When you do something wrong, you naturally feel bad.

Q. *Possibly . . . but why do YOU "naturally" feel bad?*

A. (smiling) You know, I really don't know why. That sounds silly. I was going to say it's automatic, but that doesn't seem right. I guess feeling bad is another way to say I feel guilty.

Q. Okay, fine. If you define your feelings as guilty, why do you feel guilty?

A. Why? Wouldn't anyone feel just a bit guilty after cheating on their husband in his own bed with, no less, a family friend.

Q. Maybe, but each of us would have our own reasons for feeling guilty. What are yours?

A. Well, I guess I see it as betraying a trust. If Tom and I had decided to have an open marriage, with each of us going our own way from time to time, then it would be okay. It's the undercover part that I feel guilty about.

Q. What do you mean?

A. I think I'd feel better if he knew. It would be in the open. I guess, in a way, that's also what I'm most afraid will happen. I don't really know how he'd react . . . especially since the man was Gary. Damn, I don't know why I let myself get into this. I was so incredibly stupid. First, I blamed Gary; but he didn't drag me into the bedroom. We both went hand in hand. Two very consenting adults. Why the hell did I do it? I'm furious with myself.

Q. WHY ARE YOU ANGRY WITH YOURSELF?

A. I shouldn't have done it; it says something about my character. I wouldn't want Tom doing the same thing. Everything is upside-down. Mostly, I'm unhappy and feeling so guilty that I ever did it in the first place.

Q. WHAT ARE YOU AFRAID WOULD HAPPEN IF YOU DIDN'T FEEL GUILTY ABOUT HAVING THE AFFAIR?

A. That I might do it again and again. (startled expression) Wow, did I say that? I never realized I believed that before.

Q. Are you saying that by being guilty about having an affair, it will prevent you from entering into other ones?

A. Yes, that's exactly what I mean. If I weren't remorseful about it, I might do it again . . . wouldn't I?

Q. Well, maybe we can explore it. Do you want to have another affair?

A. No, really and truly no.

Q. DO YOU BELIEVE IF YOU WERE NOT UNHAPPY OR GUILTY THAT YOU WOULD?

A. As I think about it, it doesn't make any sense. Even if

I don't feel guilty, I still know that I don't want to hop in bed with anyone other than Tom. That seems so clear now. I guess I was afraid that if I wasn't guilty, it meant I wanted to do it again or I just might slip again. (smiling) That's beautiful. I see why I've been feeling so guilty. But . . . but isn't it normal to feel bad when you've done something wrong?

Q. *What do you think?*

A. I don't know any more. I guess I'm believing if I don't feel guilty, maybe it means I'm callous . . . that I don't care.

Q. *WHY DO YOU BELIEVE THAT?*

A. Because . . . just maybe that's what I've been taught. If you do something wrong or bad, you're supposed to feel bad.

Q. *Why?*

A. I thought I answered that . . . you are supposed to.

Q. *Sure, but WHY are you supposed to feel bad when you do something "wrong"?*

A. I guess to punish yourself. Retribution. It's a crazy learning process that I've done for years.

Q. *Do you need the punishment of feeling bad or unhappy in order to learn?*

A. No. Of course not. I see that now. It's strange. I don't feel at all guilty right now and for the first time in three months, I'm absolutely clear. I don't want to go outside my marriage and I'm not afraid that I will. Before, I felt so guilty I couldn't even get to what I wanted. I just kept beating myself up.

Q. *And now?*

A. Well, I guess, whether I feel guilty or not, it doesn't change what I did. I guess hating myself was my way of making it all right. You know the old story . . . after you pay for your transgressions, everything is okay again.

Q. *WHAT DO YOU WANT?*

A. (visibly drifting . . . after several minutes, no answer)

Q. *What are you feeling?*

A. You know what popped into my head. I thought I'd like to tell Tom everything, but for the life of me, I couldn't come up with a reason. I guess I also think if I tell him without being totally broken-up, tearful and

146

frightened, he would think I was terrible.

Q. *What are you saying?*

A. That I'd like to tell him, but I'm afraid if I don't seem guilt-ridden and miserable, he wouldn't accept it. Look, I sure don't want to ruin my marriage over anything like this.

Q. *Do you believe you would?*

A. I wouldn't. (smiling) In many ways this whole thing has just reaffirmed what I want . . . which is my husband. I guess my marriage does have some real problems . . . especially communication problems. Maybe that's what this was all for . . . bringing things into the open. Without guilt, I even feel freer to really try to understand. I guess before I was too afraid.

Q. *What do you want?*

A. To feel good, which is exactly what I'm beginning to do right now for the first time in three months. It never occurred to me that I didn't have to feel guilty . . . that, in fact, I made myself guilty. Strange, how my response felt so automatic.

Q. *And now?*

A. I see how I used the guilt. I guess I can feel good about myself and be a loving, caring wife without punishing myself. Funny . . . now that I'm no longer unhappy about what I did, I'm much more willing to look at it.

7

trusting ourselves

The young woman stood frozen on the worn steps of her apartment building. Misty rays of sunshine peeked between two faceless glass structures and caressed the auburn hair falling over her shoulders. An excitement danced through her body as she tasted her womanhood; she had just blossomed into her nineteenth year. Decked in faded denims topped by a patchwork leather jacket, she looked at once casual and chic. Three or four more minutes passed. Lost within herself, she still had not moved. It was as if she was cast in stone, cemented to the very steps upon which she lingered.

Slowly she surveyed the sleeping street, catching and holding the rare freshness of a weekend morning. The mellow music. The slow-paced motion. Her immediate inclination was to spend this lazy Saturday enjoying the city. She had originally planned to spend the time with her parents, whom she had not visited for over a month. Yet, that decision was reached without contemplating the possibility that this day might be warm and clear, after weeks of rain and overcast skies. Feeling ambivalent and hesitant, she questioned herself. Should she go to her parents or shouldn't she? Did she want to go? Did she want to trade the beauty of this day for a dingy ride on the subway and bus for two confining hours and then face the possibility of an unpleasant encounter with her parents? Her fingers rubbed her palms as she again absorbed the feeling of the city street. Her decision was to withhold making a decision until she had a chance to walk.

Around the corner at Thirteenth Street, she headed down toward the park. Even the buildings that hung over the sidewalk casting heavy shadows, seemed alive. An old man walking his little dog smiled a lecherous smile at her. She laughed. Two children holding hands skipped by her. She tapped one little girl on the head.

"What a glorious day," she thought to herself. What a contrast to graffiti on cold subway cars rocking and pitching in their tunnel world. She could even hear her mother's questions echo back and forth in her mind: "How come we never see this boy you're living with?" "Why don't you visit us more often?" "You're so thin and always in those dungarees. You're such a pretty girl, why don't you take more care of yourself?" These intrusive images created their own distracting drum beat. She shook her head as if to dispel her thoughts. A little boy jumped rope past her, but this time she failed to register his vivacious body and eager smile.

"That's it," she considered, "I just don't want to go . . . ah, but maybe I should." Three more blocks and now she remembered that her father had bought her some new brushes and canvas. She definitely wanted the supplies, but couldn't she get them another day? "Why am I doing this," she thought to herself. "Damn it, either go or don't go!" She could feel the anger mounting as she walked quickly to a telephone booth. "Okay, just relax," she coaxed herself. She deposited a coin in the slot, dialed a number and waited. No connection. In fact, no tone at all. Pushing the lever up and down, she realized the phone had swallowed her money without delivering. "Just like this city," she sneered. Back on the sidewalk, she continued walking. "Maybe it was a sign." "But of what?" Stopping on a corner, she concentrated on voiding her mind by using a technique she had once learned in meditation. Once again, she began to ingest the music of the city.

150

Yes, it was a peaceful, mellow morning—the air and the tone of light were truly rare.

As she passed an art store, thoughts of her father returned. She did need those brushes and she was almost out of canvas. If she went now, she knew by the time she returned it would be dusk. She could feel the tension building. "What's the matter with me. Just make a decision and do something." As the beads of sweat broke out on her forehead, she could feel the rising and falling of her chest. Entering the park, she sat down on an old wooden bench.

A little boy with giant freckles, two fluffy old English sheep dogs, a young man playing his guitar, a baby asleep in his mother's arms and an old couple out of an Andrew Wyeth painting were part of the endless parade of humanity that passed her by. She saw nothing. She heard nothing. She played out an interior dialogue as she contemplated generating energy to visit her parents. As the hands on the clock methodically consumed the minutes, she slowly traded her vibrancy for anger. Almost an hour elapsed. Still undecided, she felt trapped between her two choices. It was as if she did not know what to do or even how to decide.

The original question disappeared as she became immersed in her own dilemma: Why was she such an indecisive person and so angry? Floating uncomfortably in her own unhappy limbo she sat there, neither enjoying her day in the city nor visiting her parents and getting the supplies she wanted. Confused and frustrated by her own thoughts and beliefs, she never moved from the faded park bench.

Why the confusion . . . the not knowing what to do? As the young woman envisioned her visit as something she was "supposed to" do, she found herself pushing in the opposite direction. She resisted being told she "had to" or "should" do something, even though she was the one telling it to herself.

She also attended to her not-wants and her contemplated unhappiness (subway ride, bus ride, questions from her mother). In the process, she lost focus on her wants (to enjoy herself and the day). Rather than trust her initial inclination to take a walk in the sunshine, she short-circuited her momentum with unresolved questions. Perhaps other beliefs about her abilities and self-worth came to bear. Ulti-

151

mately her incapability to answer became the center of her attention—all of which had nothing to do with her original plans or desires.

If I look to my own wanting, there is much to observe. When I disapprove of what I want, it is because I believe I want something else or because I fear the consequences of what I want. I would disapprove of my desire to eat if I wanted to be thin or if I feared being fat.

The most fascinating observation is *I continually pass judgments on my wanting.*

I am either busy finding evidence so I can do what I want or finding justification to suppress what I want. Sometimes, like the girl on the park bench, I have found myself frozen in confusion. In those instances, my questions and doubting were not vehicles to help me get in touch with my wanting, but statements of not trusting myself.

There is no implication here that thinking and weighing evidence is incorrect, but there is a learning experience in understanding why we do it.

What I choose to believe and what I know are very different things. *Beliefs are acquired, deduced or created during the act of thinking. Knowing comes directly from my nature— it is not a product of logic and reason.* But then, how do I come to know.

The answer goes back to understanding first how I came *not to know.* As we have seen in a previous chapter, the child is taught to believe being himself creates unhappiness in others and when he is being himself, it is often judged bad . . . thus, something is wrong with him. To protect himself from himself (he believes he does "bad" things like *make* his parents unhappy and angry), he suppresses his own natural desires. Carefully, he watches cues and rapidly acquires the beliefs of others so that he will know what to do. In the process, he loses touch with his own inclination and natural tendencies.

This is later compounded by the teaching of additional beliefs. I remember how often I was instructed to slow down . . . to pause . . . to act only after careful consideration and judgment. I was taught to stop and gather as much evidence as possible before making my choices. Yet, the quantity and quality of evidence required to make a decision varies greatly from person to person. One scientist asserts there is definite evidence life exists on other planets; another expert claims the opposite. They might even disagree about what evidence is evidence.

How many people have argued over the validity of conclusions from cancer research? Numerous scientists have a primary belief that the more people smoke, the more likely they are to get cancer. They cite a mountain of statistics as proof. Yet in showing more smokers have cancer than non-smokers, have they taken this correlation and called it a cause? Perhaps people who are going to get cancer also choose to smoke. The causes of cancer and smoking might be the same, not that one causes the other. I am not suggesting this is so, although some doctors would argue the point.

There are numerous ways to interpret evidence. For example, certain statistics can demonstrate that in larger fires where more people die there are always more fire engines. One might conclude fire engines are a hazard to people's health.

The absurdity here is to heighten a point. I have taken a correlation and called is causal. *All evidence is self-serving to the beliefs* of the person interpreting it. In a previous chapter, the example of jogging illustrates how professionals, with identical backgrounds, will view the exact same data and arrive at dramatically different conclusions. Not only is the evidence judged, but it is discarded or used in accordance with other judgments. And it goes on and on. But making judgments is different from KNOWING.

My lover has blond hair, blue eyes, weighs 110 pounds, loves ice cream and music. But when I say I really *know* her, is that what I mean by knowing? Surely these particulars are aspects of her, but my knowing transcends this data. They are the facts I can ascertain about the person. But there have been occasions when I have had a wealth of information about someone, yet I still say I do not know them. Or the converse, upon just meeting someone about whom I have very little information, I feel that I really know this person. There is a substantial difference between knowing (having facts) *about* someone and *knowing* someone.

When I see a painting I like, hear a song that catches my fancy or touch a texture that's delightful . . . do I really have

153

reasons to like them or just natural inclinations in certain directions? If I decide to buy that painting and come up with reasons for purchasing it, the mental gymnastics would take place after the fact of my enjoying it and wanting it.

Are my actions based on reasons or do I create reasons to justify my actions?

We want and then we find the reasons.

We create reasons (beliefs) so that we can give a rational basis to our choices. Otherwise, we believe we would just be acting on our ungrounded desires, which we don't trust.

No matter how definite and accurate I try to be, none of my conclusions in the realm of reasons and belief are ever absolute. They are just choices I make.

Everything I do represents a choice. And in essence, *my choosing is either consenting to my wants or deciding to go against them.* In choosing beliefs and activities, I either move in harmony with myself or not. And this is a highly creative process; I choose to trust myself; I choose to hate myself; I choose to be happy and unhappy about a situation; I choose to eat and sleep, to work and play. In choosing to allow, I permit my wants to surface naturally from me as I move about in the universe.

How will I know when I am moving with myself or against myself? There is a simple test we can do when in doubt. We can ask ourselves a question: Am I moving away or toward? The differences are quite distinct. Concentrating on my fear of being sick is very different from moving toward my wanting to be healthy. Hating my job is attending to my unhappiness and motivating myself away while the alternative of clearly seeking new employment is moving toward what I want. To expend energy worrying about divorce is the opposite of trying to find new ways to make my life and my relationship work. If I move away or against myself, I am acting from my discomforts and unhappiness. If I move toward my wants, I am moving with my flow. Although I certainly might be going in the same direction while attending to my not-wants, my unhappiness would most probably short-circuit me along the way . . . as my vision would be clouded by anger and fear and my energy would be diverted away from focusing on getting what I want. When I become aware of unhappiness motivating me, I can ask first: "What do I

want?" and then: "Why am I unhappy?" These questions can
be useful tools to help me change my focus and my direction.

Knowing is moving in harmony with myself and my
wants, without first requiring evidence or justification.

In effect, there is nothing I have to do except stop stopping
myself . . . allow and trust my wants as a beautiful alternative to drowning in the quicksand of self-defeating beliefs.
Wow . . . sounds dangerous! But it's not. If I believe there is
something dangerous about such a movement, then I must
be believing there is something elementally wrong with me.
If so, I can explore that belief and my reasons for maintaining
it.

A beautiful example of knowing can be seen in a classic
experiment performed with young infants. They were placed
in a situation under special conditions to determine their
capabilities in choosing their own diets. A vast variety of
foods of both animal and vegetable origin was placed within
easy access of each child. In combination, they provided all
the food elements, amino acids, fats, carbohydrates, vitamins
and minerals considered necessary for human nutrition. Each
child was given unguided freedom to select his own diet.

During the first few days, the infants experimented and
tasted the foods. They ate at random with no specific patterns.
Each morsel of food consumed was diligently recorded by
observers. Over the period of the experiment, which in some
cases lasted several months, an astonishing pattern emerged.
The infants, having absolutely no concept or knowledge of
food content or nutritional value, had eaten a combination of
foods sufficient to maintain themselves with optimal digestive
and nutritional results. Even when they ate excessively of one
food product in a day, they adjusted their intake over the
next several days.

A possible conclusion: If we allowed, we all would be able
to take care of ourselves. Without training or specific knowledge, these children were able literally to "know" how to
balance their diets and how to eat healthfully for themselves.
Their own inclination and their bodies were their guide.

A knowing person is a happy person in touch with his
wants. Knowing and wanting draw from the same well. And

what each person would want, would be right for him.

Although it is attractive and mellow to move in harmony with myself, I once had doubts that such evenness might turn my life-style into a mindless and thoughtless utopia. But that too is just another judgment . . . it would be mindless only if that's what I decided.

We can do an experiment with ourselves. We could get in touch with our good feelings and allow ourselves three minutes a day to come from ourselves without interfering with judgments . . . just act on our wants during that time. We could do it ten minutes or two hours a day if we choose. Since we are the experts for ourselves, we then could evaluate and decide the merits of such freedom.

Uncluttered by doubts and fears, I find myself a far more effective human being. My focus is more directed, my energies more crystalized. I take care of myself better and get more of what I want. I don't even have to control my experiences to want and enjoy them. A beautiful sunset, the smile of a newborn infant, the sight of a horse gliding through the tall grass are all outside my control. Yet, I could be happy and want those experiences, needing no reasons to substantiate my good feelings and desires.

There is nothing to rehearse . . . nothing to practice or memorize. I have only to unload the weights and drop the beliefs. And that decision is for each of us to make for ourselves.

For me to say to myself "I'll go with what I know" or "I'll move with what feels right to me instead of going where the evidence leads" is an *act of trust* and an *affirmation of self.*

THE "THINK" PAGE (TRUSTING OUR-SELVES)

QUESTIONS TO ASK YOURSELF:

Do you like to do the things you believe you "have to," "should" or "ought to" do?

Are you afraid to go with your own inclinations or hunches? If so, why?

When you say "you really know someone," what exactly do you mean?

Do you always need reasons before you allow yourself to do something? If so, why?

Are you afraid if you were just "you," it would not be in your best interest? If so, what are you believing about being yourself?

Are you uncertain about your wants?

Are you uncertain about your wants when you are happy?

OPTION CONCEPTS TO CONSIDER:

*ALL EVIDENCE IS SELF-SERVING TO THE BE-LIEFS OF THE PERSON INTERPRETING IT.

*WE WANT AND THEN WE FIND REASONS.

*REASONS DO NOT SUPPORT WANTS, THEY ONLY CLARIFY DOUBTS.

*CHOOSING IS EITHER CHOOSING TO CONSENT TO MY WANTS OR GOING AGAINST THEM.

*KNOWING IS MOVING IN HARMONY WITH MY-SELF AND MY WANTS.

*WANTING TO BE HAPPIER AND MORE LOVING COMES FROM OUR KNOWING . . . FROM WHO WE ARE.

*WE DO NOT NEED A REASON TO BE HAPPY.

BELIEFS TO CONSIDER DISCARDING:

Wanting is bad if we have no reasons for it.

There must be something wrong with me.

I don't know.

Being myself is bad.

If I allowed myself to do anything I wanted, I'd screw myself.

SEVENTH DIALOGUE

Q. WHAT ARE YOU UNHAPPY ABOUT?
A. I'm an account executive at an advertising agency. I've been at this particular job for almost three years with the promise of becoming an account supervisor within a year. It has also been subtly hinted that I might get

V.P. stripes. Suddenly, from left field, I was offered another position by a competing agency, which would mean a bigger job and more money right away. There are pros and cons to staying and there are pros and cons to moving. (smiling) I can't seem to make up my mind. In fact, before this happened just a couple of weeks ago, I would describe my life as steady, settled and fairly comfortable. Now, as ridiculous as it might sound, I feel uncomfortable and possessed by this situation. I have to decide . . . and soon.

*Q. WHY ARE YOU UNCOMFORTABLE AND POS-
SESSED BY THE SITUATION?*

A. Because I can't make up my mind. It's ironic. When it comes to media commitments and decisions in business, there's never a problem. But when I'm dealing with my life, with ME, it's a bomb. I always end up feeling ambivalent. If I stay where I am, I might get screwed because I can wait from now to doomsday until I get my promotion. Maybe the divisional vice president is really just dangling a carrot in front of me. On the other hand, if I leave, there are no guarantees it will work out. New people, new faces and new problems. I'll have to prove myself all over again. Damn (pounds the arm of the chair with his fist).

Q. What's so upsetting to you?

A. This is not the first time this has happened to me. Every time I consider something important, I don't know why, but somehow it gets so inflated, I can't even grab it. I can recommend committing hundreds of thousands of dollars with the snap of a finger and feel really sure of myself. Yet here, I'm driving myself nuts.

Q. What do you mean "driving yourself nuts"?

A. When I'm dealing with something at a distance, like products and advertising, it becomes a game for me. When it's me hanging in the balance, I immediately get uptight. (pause) I really want to get somewhere with this. Let me tackle it from another point of view. If I move in a certain direction on a promotional campaign, we usually have opportunities to redirect if we're wrong. And even if we don't, it's just one of many decisions made. There's usually no "all-or-nothing" playoff. With staying or changing my job, with me deciding . . .

it's kind of all-or-nothing. When I know that, I literally drive myself nuts. I think about it day and night; ideas keep floating into my head until it becomes a blur, a confused mess. Then, instead of considering my alternatives, I just walk around hyper.

Q. Hyper?

A. Jumping back and forth like a rabbit. I can't even concentrate on the pros and cons (shaking his head from side to side).

Q. Why not?

A. Why not? Why not? If I knew, it would be solved. (exhaling an extended sigh) I can't stand it. I wish I would just make up my mind.

Q. What is so discomforting to you about not being able to choose?

A. If I don't get on the stick, it's going to be all over. I have to decide.

Q. Sure, I know you believe it would be better for you to make up your mind, but why are you uncomfortable if you don't?

A. Because I want to do what's good for me.

Q. Are you saying that if you don't make up your mind, you are doing something bad for yourself?

A. Yes, of course. While I'm pacing in my own cage, the world is moving by. By the time I make up my mind about the jobs, the new one will probably be gone. And then, Christ, I really blew it.

Q. What do you mean?

A. Like a relationship I once had. It took me so long to make up my mind as to whether I wanted to try to make it work or not that when I was ready to give it my all, she had already left. I don't blame her for not hanging around. Certainly when I was contemplating our problems, I wasn't dealing with them. This is sort of the same kind of situation. If I don't move, it will be gone. The door closed. Finished. And why? Because I couldn't make a decision. I don't want to spend my life tripping over myself.

Q. DO YOU BELIEVE YOU WILL?

A. Sure . . . it's part of my life-style. (pause) Well, no . . . not really. Come to think of it, I've done well in advertising because I could make judgments and could

160

decide. I guess I'm just talking about my personal life. (begins to tap his fingers on a table, stops and exhales a long, deep sigh) Listen, I don't want to be this way. Really . . . it's not a picnic. Sometimes I think I'm going to drown in my anger or get a heart attack. When I realize I'm being indecisive, I can feel my whole body tighten like a vise. A wave of anger just washes over me.

Q. *What is there specifically, when you become aware of being indecisive, that gets you so angry? (A version of, what is it about that that makes you angry?)*

A. If I was only more composed, more direct, then I would know what to do. It's like playing devil's advocate for both sides. I do a whole thing with myself. It's like jumping into an endless debate. I'm so busy going back and forth, I lose myself. If I stay at my present job, I have all the security and a probable future. But it may also be just stagnating . . . marking time. If I switch to the other agency, I immediately open new doors, face new people and create new opportunities. Yet, I can't be sure it will work out for weeks, maybe even months.

Q. *WHAT DO YOU WANT?*

A. I'm not really sure. Getting another offer is a beautiful ego boost, but so what. All I have now is my unhappiness about not being able to choose.

Q. *WHAT ARE YOU AFRAID WOULD HAPPEN IF YOU WEREN'T UNHAPPY ABOUT NOT CHOOSING?*

A. I . . . I might jump irrationally.

Q. *What do you mean?*

A. I might not be careful making up my mind.

Q. *So, are you saying that by being unhappy, you take better care or more care in deciding?*

A. Yes, that's what I'm doing. Seems strange, doesn't it?

Q. *In what way? (A version of, what do you mean?)*

A. To go through all this discomfort just to take care of myself. It's crazy because it just doesn't work. And yet, I guess I've already done this when I see the decision as really important to me . . . to my life. Whew. I never realized I was doing that before. That's quite a discovery for me. (smiling, a pause) When I see

161

what I was believing, it changes things . . . takes a lot of the fuel out of my unhappiness. Still, it only explains part of it. It feels like there's more . . . something else.

Q. Are you saying there is another problem that is also contributing to your indecisiveness?

A. Yes. Yes, I am.

Q. And what's that?

A. Well, I know it sounds like a little boy, but . . . I'm afraid.

Q. Of what?

A. That I won't do the right thing . . . that somehow I'll screw myself and end up really miserable.

Q. DO YOU BELIEVE THAT?

A. Yes. Because I've done it before. I've made other choices which didn't work out. Problems arose that I did not foresee.

Q. Sure. But why do you believe you weren't good for yourself if things happened that you did not foresee?

A. I guess if I were smarter, more perceptive . . . I could control it.

Q. Control what?

A. Things. People. Events.

Q. DO YOU BELIEVE THAT?

A. (laughing) Yes and no. In some cosmic way, sure. In a human statement, of course not. Wait. I want to stop for a minute. (long pause) Maybe the real question for me is why do I get so upset worrying about things not working out?

Q. Why do you?

A. Well, I'm not sure. If I stay at the agency and I don't get promoted, I'll feel I've lost a great opportunity because I was scared.

Q. Are you saying that your reasons for staying with your present job come from fear?

A. (more smiling) Yes, I guess so.

Q. Why are you smiling?

A. Admitting you come from fear is really a nice experience. I always thought letting it out and looking at it would be very painful. Wow, it's almost the opposite. There are very few places in the world I would feel comfortable saying this. In our discussions, it's

162

weird . . . it's just another piece of information. (chuckling) And that's marvelous. (sighs and distinct drop in voice) I'd really like to change. And that includes my job. I feel kind of bored and mindless. I can do most of it half-asleep. It's time to move on, but . . .

Q. *Is there something stopping you?*

A. If I move and it doesn't work, then I might end up even more miserable than ever.

Q. *WHY?*

A. No one would be thrilled about falling on their ass.

Q. *Perhaps. But maybe the question is if the worst came to pass, if you didn't make it at your new job, why would you be unhappy?*

A. I want to say I don't know, but that doesn't feel true. If I don't get into a whole frenzy about failing, I can always find something else. Somehow, I'd be unhappy about having poor judgment.

Q. *Why?*

A. Because it says something about me?

Q. *What do you mean?*

A. I'm not sure, Christ, there I go again with a namby-pamby answer.

Q. *Let's focus on it then . . . why does "not sure" upset you?*

A. It feels like part of the circle. Not sure is indecisive, doubting, confused.

Q. *WHY ARE YOU UNHAPPY ABOUT BEING IN DOUBT OR CONFUSION?*

A. It means I don't know.

Q. *AND WHAT ABOUT NOT KNOWING MAKES YOU UNHAPPY?*

A. I guess I want to know.

Q. *Sure, but what about the not-knowing upsets you?*

A. I guess I begin to think I'll never know. It'll go on forever.

Q. *DO YOU BELIEVE THAT?*

A. No . . . not really. I'm just so impatient.

Q. *If you knew you would come up with an answer . . . that someday, somehow, you would know what to choose, would you still be upset?*

A. No . . . then it would be okay.

Q. Are you saying that your indecisiveness upsets you because it will continue endlessly?

A. (laughing—no answer)

Q. Why are you laughing?

A. My initial answer to your question was yes . . . yes, I did most definitely envision the indecisiveness continuing forever. Yet as I thought about it, it suddenly sounded outrageous. But I guess that's what I believe.

Q. WHY DO YOU BELIEVE THAT?

A. (shaking his head) I don't know, I really don't.

Q. If you were to guess at an answer, what would you think?

A. (long pause) Still nothing comes. A blank. I really don't know why I believe it. I don't think I have any reasons.

Q. Okay, if you don't have any reasons to believe it, do you want to continue to believe it?

A. Do I want to continue believing it? No, why would I if it's not so. All it causes me is grief.

Q. What do you mean?

A. It's my being upset, not my questions that fog the issue. My doubts always clear . . . sooner or later. When I think about it, I always manage to find an answer and choose. I guess I've always had this internal alarm clock for perfection. If I didn't answer in a certain period of time, bang . . . it's bad, etc. etc. If I was more tolerant of not solving it, I'd probably solve it a lot easier. Could you imagine that I was really believing I would never decide?

Q. And now?

A. No way . . . I don't believe it any more. If I just let myself, I'll always manage to solve it. Oh, that's great stuff, I really feel I'm moving now. (His eyes close). I want to savor this. It's really nice to feel excited. (a deep breath) Just one thing, I'd really like to focus on my deciding on jobs.

Q. Okay. WHAT DO YOU WANT?

A. I want the new job. I really do (long pause, smiling). Can you believe I just said that so easily? A decision. Whew, it feels like a weight was just lifted off me. One thing bothers me though, why did I get so easily unnerved and worried about things not working out?

164

Q. Why do you think?

A. I guess, deep down, I believed it showed me I didn't take care of myself . . . maybe, it meant I couldn't trust myself.

Q. DO YOU BELIEVE IT NOW?

A. No, not any more. It was the game I had always played. Right here, right now, with my fears aside (smiling) or gone, it's very clear. I have and will continue to take care of myself. I always did, in the end. So even if things don't work out, it doesn't mean I didn't try to do the best for myself. (Suddenly, his face cringes.)

Q. What are you feeling?

A. Somewhere, somehow, maybe I still don't trust myself. I don't know if I'm ready to let go completely.

Q. Why not?

A. I'm not sure (reflecting on his comment, he begins to laugh). My classic line. Somehow, I was always taught I just can't jump into things. That's the way to break my legs. I have to deliberate, mull things over and then, maybe . . . just maybe . . . I could know what's good for me. It sounds so strange now, it doesn't even feel like my belief.

Q. No matter when you learned a belief and from whom, if you believe it now, it's active and a part of you in the present . . . in the now. In uncovering it, you can ask yourself the question: DO YOU BELIEVE IT NOW OR WANT TO CONTINUE BELIEVING IT?

A. What amazing questions for me . . . they really are! Do I believe it now? Do I want to believe it? I don't think so.

Q. Does "don't think so" mean that you're not sure?

A. Yes, but that's only my way of hedging right now. I am sure. I'm beginning to feel I can trust myself. Obviously, when I'm nervous and anxious, I'm too mixed up to see anything. The battle of reasons against reasons was never anything but a painful and confusing process. In the end, there were no absolutes. I feel really bizarre now.

Q. How do you mean?

A. As I'm talking, I don't think I can ever remember really ever trusting myself. The questions were always bathed in my anxiety; I never really felt I'd come to the right decisions. I really never believed I would know what's good for me.

Q. And now, do you still think you don't know what's good for you?

A. Not any more. And that's what's so strange. The questions of changing jobs . . . I know what's right for me now. In many ways, I knew it when I first got the offer . . . even then, but I was afraid to act on my first impulse. I just couldn't buy it without putting myself through my ritual of grief.

Q. How are you feeling?

A. New. A little strange with myself, but it's a good feeling. When I'm not afraid, I do know. It's funny how you're taught things, brought up in a certain way and just act it all out. Like a puppet. I never considered all the alternatives. It was as if I had nothing to do with it when, in fact, it has always been my ball game.

Q. WHAT DO YOU WANT?

A. To feel like this, to choose with or without reasons, but to trust that I will know and do the best I can for myself. As I say that, even mulling through the pros and cons seems like it would be a productive experience. (smiling) I really feel great! I realize now I could make decisions without all the fuss, without all the debating and reasoning . . . and it will still be the right decision for me. (laughing) I'm sure of it.

8

feeling good: health and questions of psychosomatic illness

The clear and colored oval platelets speed through the system in perfect harmony with the flow of energized liquid. Carrying their cargoes of food and other products, they whirl through the arteries, negotiating each turn and hairpin curve with professional expertise. This is the city of the future as it exists in each of us today.

Our body is a vast, complex and complicated world, yet it's beautifully orchestrated for its own function and efficiency. Our heart, the main cylinder, runs on its own momentum and pumps blood each and every day at a steady, melodic rate. Either by main avenues, or by small backstreets, connections are made with each individual cell for its supply of energy and nourishment.

Occasionally, a structure collapses as another grows to take its place. This modernization goes on continually as part of the harmonious process of the humanoid city. It is a designed utopia which is self-regulated and self-constructing. Millions of different operations take place each day without disturbing the balance of the organism as a whole.

Each part of our system has different characteristics, although they all remain connected by a network of tunnels and underground cables. Uptown contains the soft, spongy clump which is our computer. It fields millions of electric and chemical impulses along wires hooked into every location in our system. In another section in this part of town, there are some major bridges and tunnels to an outside environment. Sight, sound and environmental intake units are housed here.

The midtown area is not only the home of our master cylinder, but also a very populated section with different neighborhoods. The most complex area houses the digestive plant with its numerous satellite buildings that process sugar, starches, carbohydrates and other products. A long tunnel, which looks like a shriveled vacuum hose, leads out toward the rear of the city where the sewage plant is located. The respirator utility regulates air and oxygen intake. An elaborate fossil-type bone structure holds the city together and extend into the arms and legs.

Downtown is quite different from the other sections of the city. It begins with a whole network of caverns and structures in which several reproductive organizations have their headquarters. Also prominent are the major waste processing and recycling factories which eject products back into an outside environment.

Although the city of ourselves is intricate and partially incomprehensible, each section, each factory and each individual component participates with exquisite precision.

Then it happens . . . not for all of us and not at the same time. There's an explosion. All crisis systems are activated. Normally, these situations are handled as a matter of course . . . but, at times, sections, entire square blocks are destroyed. The city goes into a state of emergency.

Frequently, even after massive destruction, the city can survive although it has sustained irreparable damage. Any partial impairment, chronic disease, loss of limbs, certain bacterial and viral infections are called illness, sickness or more specifically, lack of health.

If the city has been completely destroyed, the passing is called death. Most of us share fears about losing our health because of the possibility of pain and loss ... and, ultimately, dying.

What am I telling myself when I focus on the fear of being sick? As a healthy person frightened of disease, I am fearing what "isn't." To concentrate on sickness would be the same as concentrating on the hole in the doughnut ... it's the part that isn't.

So when I say sickness, I am actually addressing myself to fears of what is not. Instead of focusing on my wants (good health), I attend to my not-wants. I attend to my unhappiness, which is fear of becoming ill or fear of an already existing condition becoming worse. The result is I drain my energy and divert my strength with tension and anxiety. In doing so, I render my body even more incapable of dealing with its distress. By concentrating on *nothing* (lack of health, future pain or death), I deprive myself of participating energetically in my wants for health. It is when I move *toward* something that I usually perform with much more effectiveness and clarity than while in retreat.

One of the most meaningful and illuminating words used in this arena is *"dis-ease"* "Dis-," from the Latin, means apart, away from or not. *"Ease,"* from the Old French, means comfort, a natural easy manner of flow. Thus, even the word that denotes the state of *un-health* in our language, makes a descriptive suggestion: *dis-ease ... moving away from the natural flow, not at ease or not comfortable with myself.*

Undoubtedly, it represents one of the most concise and accurate descriptions of *unhappiness*.

In Western medicine, the accent oftentimes has been on fighting illness, instead of seriously encouraging good health. Although important inroads have been made regarding preventive vaccines and serums, with some physical fitness programs highlighting the significance of exercise or diet, most of us consult a physician only *after* we have our diseases and malfunctions. Rather than concentrating on sustaining our physical harmony and health, we tend to fondle our fears and anxieties after a disturbance occurs in our system.

An opposite perspective might be gained by viewing the

founding concepts of the ancient art of Acupuncture, first recorded in about 400 B.C. The patient is treated as a whole . . . his mind (thoughts), his body, his diet and his life-style are all elements of concern. The Acupuncturist seeks not to fight disease, but to maintain health. If the patient does become ill, the concept is not to battle "illness," but to find its cause and rectify it by helping the body maintain its balance. Rather than "treat" the infection, the Acupuncturist concentrates on helping the involved organs correct the situation by energizing or sedating the flow.

The aim is to help the body come back to its own harmony, and through this, correct itself. The hallmark of a good Acupuncturist in ancient China was having not one sick patient. Using his points and meridians of energy, he could detect imbalances before they became disease . . . in that way, he could then help energize or sedate organs to function properly. If he was inattentive or not thorough enough, his patients might become sick and die. When this happened, he would have to hang a lantern outside his office door. This enabled a prospective patient to have a guide in choosing his doctor.

Interesting, you're thinking . . . but that was ancient China. Sure. But what's relevant here is a perspective, a focus and, perhaps, some beliefs. The concept is treating the human being as a whole, not as an isolated kidney disease, or a heart attack or another case of diabetes. Also the vision is on what IS, health, rather than on what isn't, lack of health. The Acupuncturist tries to help the person maintain his health. Naturally, a healthy body is free-flowing and efficient in dispensing with germs and bacteria.

Western medicine, in contrast, wages "war" against disease. It moves against and away, rather than toward. Most of the energy expended is to "beat the disease." Hit it with everything you've got . . . harsh drugs, amputation techniques, radiation treatment. Battle it until the disease surrenders.

If the methods of warfare are extremely severe, the body may not recover from having served as a battleground. The drugs used in cancer treatment often destroy as much healthy tissue as they do diseased tissue. Ritalin hydrochloride, which is utilized to help "calm" hyperactive children, is actually a stimulant, similar to an amphetamine, or "speed" . . . it can create a disabling neuromuscular syndrome and destroy brain cells when introduced into the body's system. Insulin, used in controlling diabetes, after prolonged usage can cause blindness, kidney failure and lowered resistance to infection. So often the methods are extreme, but they seem unavoidable. To help a child. To save a life.

And yet the question arises . . . are these methods necessary? Many cases of diabetes would never have developed if our diets and our life-styles were consistent with our nature.

Everything is treated separately, in a disconnected fashion. When was the last time my doctor inquired about my diet as well as my physical activity, my emotional state and my work schedules as an adjunct to my visit? Unless I requested the "classic" physical checkup, my physician only dealt with that specific cold or infection or virus. But my state of health is not separate from who I am and what I do and how I feel.

These concepts are more than just metaphors. They might stimulate questions we would want to ask ourselves now. Words have as much power and reality as we give them. No one will suggest that we should not fight disease if we get sick or consult a doctor for our medical ills. No one will try to convince us of anything here . . . but only present an alternative vision that we can apply or not apply as we see fit.

The accent of medicine could be preventive and curative rather than just reactive. Do I have to battle disease? Isn't my biochemical system affected by my thoughts and feelings . . . thoughts and feelings most physicians ignore? And ultimately, who will be more conscientious about my well-being than *me?* Consider the statistics released by a House subcommittee of the United States Congress. The conclusion of their research and investigations illustrated that in this country during 1974 there were at least 2.4 million unnecessary operations performed at an expense of 3.9 million dollars causing 11,900 fatalities.

An argument frequently marshaled in defense of the strategies of contemporary medicine can perhaps, here and now, be laid to rest. There are those who would show us statistics suggesting life expectancy over the last seventy-five years has increased dramatically as a result of doctors, drugs and surgery. But those statistics are very misleading. I might

171

assume that if I had been born in 1900, I could have expected to live to about 47 years old. If I were born in 1977, I could expect to live to about age 72. Now that is progress, but what does it really mean to me?

The major factors in the lengthened life expectancy are the highly improved techniques of child delivery and child care, as well as an improved standard of living. At the turn of the century, fatalities during childbirth were extremely high. And many other children did not survive their first year. The result on a graph lowered the life expectancy for everyone. But if we read these figures with one change, the message is very different. When we put aside the data on all those who died under five years of age and concentrate on you and me, who did survive our first five years of life, we find that even after all the research and "medical progress" our life expectancy remains just about the same as it was seventy-five years ago.

Over the last thirty years medicine has become more yielding and willing to accept certain relationships between states of mind and physical conditions. Psychosomatic illness is the general label given all those diseases in this category. It refers to those problems in the body that are believed to be mentally or emotionally generated or triggered (psychogenic problems).

Within the skull there is a mass that receives, processes, stores data and sends impulses to all areas of the body. This computer processing unit is called the brain . . . but is it all of what is considered the mind? The brain is a mass with many functions, some of which consist of automatic and reflexive triggering mechanisms. The mind, which is the cognitive center, does have its physical seat in the brain. But who's to say that although the processing takes place in the brain, our best formulating, knowing and meditative Nirvanas are not done in our thumb or kneecap?

Off the deep end? Well, perhaps, but then again, maybe there is some bit of information here that can be explored and utilized.

Even if the "kneecap" concept of thinking is discarded, medicine will not dispute the millions of neurons that connect the so-called thinking center with all parts of the body. Nor would they dispute that feedback in both directions is

172

married electrically as well as chemically. Thus, the mind-body marriage is linked at every level.

The suggestion here is that although different parts of our system contain dissimilar elements, when placed in a single harmonious unit (the body), each part functions as an integrated and responsible part of the whole. When there is a malfunction in one organ, it ultimately affects all organs. Our anger and fears alter body chemistry and electrical impulses in every part of our body. Decision by one element of us (mind) to ingest drugs or alcohol certainly affects our other elements.

What then is the supposed difference between psychogenic and organic illness? Types of heart disease, high blood pressure, ulcers, colitis, diarrhea (some forms) and headaches (other than brain tumors or inflammation) are considered psychogenic. The person is somehow a causal agent in the genesis of the problem. Cancer, diabetes, kidney disease and other internal malfunctions are defined as organic . . . outside a person's control. Typhoid, Asian flu, malaria and plague are labeled as communicable diseases that originate external to the body . . . and, in part, are also outside the person's control.

The categories appear clear and specific. Psychosomatic problems are illnesses I participate in generating; in contrast to organic diseases over which I supposedly have no control. In that context, the separation does not seem arbitrary, but is it?

How do I know which diseases are which? Consult my doctor! It is supposedly very simple . . . bacterial and viral triggers versus emotional and mental. Yet, certain types of disease that were called organic twenty-five years ago are today viewed as psychogenic. Twitches, rashes, a variety of digestive disorders, certain heart and blood pressure malfunctions are just a small sampling of illness reclassified. The list has been dramatically expanded in the last decade alone.

There are medical people who will even dispute now among themselves as to the origins of disease. One doctor will tell you that the idea of cancer being psychosomatic is absolutely absurd while his illustrious colleagues work dedicatedly in some large university to prove the opposite. Many will argue that schizophrenia is organic and should be treated with drugs and megavitamin therapy; others will say it's emotional or psychological and must be dealt with on a cognitive and verbal level. What does it all mean?

It illustrates that even among the so-called experts and professionals, there is heated discussion and dispute about the genesis and treatment of disease. All doctors, to different degrees, will admit to the reality of psychosomatic sickness. Some are investigating whether all diseases, in fact, fall into this category. But in terms of experiments and substantiated scientific proofs, their investigations are still embryonic.

Okay . . . so what can I, as a medical nonprofessional, know now? First, that what I think and how I feel *does* affect my body system as a whole. Second, perhaps the missing vision is not that I cause my own sickness or lack of health, but that *I precipitate receptivity to sickness insofar as I might divert the body from working properly in harmony with its own flow.*

One person gets a dreaded communicable disease, while others do not. One person suffering a serious heart attack never recovers while another does. Two people with the same brain damage (where cellular structure is irrevocably detroyed) from a stroke exhibit dramatically different capabilities during the rest of their lives. One never learns to talk or walk again; the other does. Even most doctors will admit that the difference, in part, has to do with the "will to live" or the person's "attitude."

The inference here is that the operative factor in "getting well" or surviving is motivation . . . *wanting.* One person might clearly be in touch with wanting to talk or walk again while another person is depressed and founders in his own hopelessness. Perhaps, in his depression and unhappiness, he is distracted from attending to his wants while he grapples with his fears and anxieties.

When I am distracted, I divert my energy and will power and appear to have less motivation or less will to live. The result is increased susceptibility to disease and a decrease in capability of repairing breakdowns in the system I call myself.

The contrasting implication might be that in wanting to be happier and in being happier, I'd be in harmony with my natural flow. I would attend to my health and maintenance

174

by simply allowing my body to function properly and not inhibiting it with the chemical, electrical and attitudinal short circuits of fear and depression that dramatically interfere with my physical functions.

One step further . . . if worry and tension could result in a heart attack or an ulcer, could they result in a tumor? That's just a question! Unhappiness certainly can prolong a cold or respiratory infection. *When we are unhappy, we sap self-sustaining energy of the body and that drain can result in short circuits and breakdowns.*

Is a cancer cell a passing experience for the tuned body, but a blockage in the system that is out of balance? Numerous medical people would attest to the fact we all have cancer cells in us; but in many, they do not grow or create a problem. Why do they in some?

Also how strange to find that many people seem to share fears and even guilts about illness. Their colds, their headaches, their stomach aches and their high blood pressure all seem to be illnesses they feel they had some part in creating . . . and for which they even might feel guilty, as if they had done it for a particular reason they now regret. In a counseling session, a student said quite casually, "When I gave myself a heart attack . . ." It was as if our specific illnesses do have meaning and say something about us.

With several associates, I created a score of profiles of people we knew intimately who had recently died. Very quickly, we were confronted with an amazing realization. Each person had died of a disease appropriate to him or her. In most cases, it seemed to fit so exactly, almost as if each person had *chosen* their way to die.

One person's father went to the hospital to undergo a routine hernia operation. When he came out of the recovery room, he was very upset by the pain. The doctors had promised this was to be a quick and comfortable procedure. Characteristically, he became angry and furious with the attending staff. By late afternoon, he had brought on an asthma attack. Since he had always been intolerant of his respiratory disorder, he became angry with himself and rigidly fought his body. By late evening, his right lung had collapsed. An hour later, his left lung began to fill with fluid and he was put on a respirator. By morning, to everyone's

175

amazement, he had died of heart failure.

A friend of mine had an overwhelming fear of cancer. Ever since his college days, he would run to the doctor with every pain, every swelling, every infection to see if he had contracted it. Finally, at the ripe old age of twenty-seven, a lump was diagnosed as a tumor and surgically removed. It was malignant. Ironically, I remembered our meeting only weeks after the operation. He was more relaxed than I had seen him in years. His search and fear of getting cancer was over and somehow, I believe, having the illness actually relieved him of the fear of getting it.

There is an old adage that says we often get what we fear most . . . but perhaps this is not as some mystical retribution, but because fearing something is often more painful than getting it since in getting it there is a release from the fear (the man who loses his job is a lot more accepting and more relaxed than the one who sees and fears the hatchet falling).

Another person recalled her mother affectionately. She died in her late forties of myeloma, which is a progressively destructive form of cancer that attacks the bone marrow. This woman had always seen herself as frail and weak. Since early adulthood, she had been plagued by severe anemia. In her last years, when cancer wrought havoc throughout her system, it is curious that the disease she contracted rendered her bones brittle and easy to fracture—frail and weak and not unlike her self-image.

Someone else recalled that his father-in-law was a very uptight and prudish man. His manner was stiff, even his stance was rigid. Behind his back, they nicknamed him tight-ass. He died of cancer of the colon and rectum after having a colostomy. Anther person talked about her aunt who had always been quick to anger. Her fury was almost constant, although often repressed beneath the surface. She died of complications from a severe case of high-blood pressure. Another talked about how her grandmother had always been extremely dependent on her husband for support and comfort. She always said that if he ever became sick or died, she simply could not live without him. Two weeks after he had surgery for a brain tumor with a terminal prognosis, the woman dropped dead as she sat on her balcony. Everyone who knew her and loved her easily accepted that she had fulfilled her promise to herself and had somehow managed to turn her motor off by an implicit act of will.

These examples of disease and dying are not evidence that people intentionally hurt themselves. But they might suggest that our unhappiness and fear are related rather specifically to whatever short circuit might ultimately develop in the body. Certainly the woman who saw herself as fragile did not willfully want to contract cancer and experience her bones cracking. But her fears of being vulnerable had to sap the energy from her system and perhaps resulted in a sympathetic body malfunction.

People who are depressed (from fear, anxiety, frustration) are statistically more "susceptible" to disease than others who are generally optimistic and vivacious. Unhealthiness may not be so much the result of an attacking virus or bacteria, but the result of the vulnerability of the body that's out of balance.

If I am willing to consider a real marriage among all the parts of who I am (body and mind), perhaps I can trace the function and effects of unhappiness on health. When I am unhappy, I usually express it verbally as *feeling bad*. If pursued, I can often detect parts of portions of my body that reflect the discomfort. My head hurts, my stomach is upset, and my body is exhausted.

Ask anyone how he knows when he is happy, he will probably tell you he *feels* good . . . and what he means is that he and his body (which are one) are free flowing comfortably without any blockages.

When I am unhappy (fearful, anxious, guilty), my body processes its food differently, alters its chemical output and functions in a *state of stress*. In order to cope with this disturbance, internal physical operations change. Often these emergency alterations, if sustained, result in certain breakdowns. Acid in the stomach for one afternoon is easily coped with by the body; but after weeks and months, the imbalance starts to destroy tissue. High blood pressure for a short period of time is common to all organisms, but here again, sustained imbalance weakens the entire cardiovascular system. Some of these difficulties can be repaired by surgery, diet, programs of relaxation and drugs. Others are either so chronic or catastrophic that they destroy our systems. As I come to understand this cycle, I can begin to see that my unhappiness has very dramatic and self-defeating by-products ... such as loss of health. When my mother scolded me for not feeling bad when *she* felt bad (she didn't want me to be heartless and inhuman), neither she nor I realized that feeling bad always has profound side effects (aborted goals, illness, etc.).

If my system is so interrelated, what can I know or do when I have a pain or illness I believe is psychogenic? (Perhaps all illness is psychogenic!) *I can use psychosomatic illnesses as signs. Signs of my unhappiness ... not indictments that I am stupid or bad for myself.* Since my thoughts and feelings register chemically in my body (getting nauseated when I am frightened), I could use them as a guide. *My body is one way of letting me know that I am happy or unhappy.*

I can use it as a conveyor belt to my beliefs in an Option dialogue. If something hurts, I can ask myself: Am I unhappy about anything (even the pain)? If so, what am I unhappy about? It could provide me with an internal radar system I could effectively utilize.

Yet, ironically, I could choose to see my illness as an indictment that something is wrong with me ... that I am bad for myself. With such a belief, I might decide to "fight" the illness ... hate my ulcer, be angry with my headache and furious over my high blood pressure. But in doing battle, I am actually feeding my pains and malfunctions by further disabling my body (my anger and fear increases my blood pressure, contracts my muscles, overacidifies my digestive tract). So in fighting the devil, I give it power.

Since I might interpret this as proof of hurting myself further, I could see it as a reconfirmation of how bad I am for myself. But how could that ever possibly be if I am always doing the best I can based on my current beliefs. When I fight my illness by feeling angry or frightened, I do so because I believe at the time it is the best way to handle the situation ... a way, perhaps, to stop the illness from getting worse. If I contracted a serious disease, I might easily and immediately focus on not wanting to die ... which is very different from staying in touch with *wanting* to live. When I am fearful, it is almost as if I can hear a little voice in my body whisper, "You're not going to make it." But it is not true, unless I help it become true by believing in it. There is no situation that is hopeless or irreversible. Although I am always trying to take care of myself . . . maybe, there is a better way.

The only thing my pain or psychosomatic symptoms could possibly be saying is that I am not flowing with my wants, with my nature . . . that I am upset or uncomfortable about something.

Symptoms are neither indictments nor accusations, unless I choose to see them that way.

In order for me to buy the concept that psychosomatic illness is an indictment, there would have to be another supporting belief . . . that my body is my enemy; that it is doing something against me. How can that be so? Yet the belief can be its own self-fulfilling prophesy . . . for out of the worry and doubt comes the tension and the discomfort, which in turn causes an imbalance and facilitates increased susceptibility to all diseases and sicknesses.

And in terms of this perspective, what could anyone mean by self-healing? It would simply be disconnecting the short circuits of unhappiness, allowing myself to flow from my wants and good feeling, permitting my body its own natural harmony . . . and in the balance, my body would be freer to take care of itself. Perhaps this attitude would then generate other alternatives we could put into effect to help ourselves (changing diets, altering life-styles, eating herbs, etc.) This is not to say that a doctor or surgeon can't be of crucial assistance to each of us.

The suggestion here is that my psychic comfort is a significant element in the continuance of my good health. In choosing my beliefs and their consequences, I choose my physical destiny.

Feeling good is my body's way of experiencing my happiness. Pains, dysfunctions and psychosomatic illness can be used to help me dispel my discomforts. If I dismantle the beliefs which generate my unhappiness, I dismantle the energy of my symptom and, perhaps, its lifetime.

Years, ago, I used to concentrate on knowing that being overweight was unhealthy, that overeating creates excess fat and therefore concluded I must diet. My diet was a not-want.

179

I would badger myself, "Don't eat!" I attended to my fears and pushed against myself . . . as if I wanted to eat and be fat. Ironically, in fearing that I would stuff my mouth, all I could think about was food. The whole procedure backfired. But I did not do it because it was going to backfire, I did what I believed would stop me from eating and help me to be healthy. That was the best I knew to do at that time.

What I had not realized was that I had lost touch with wanting to be healthy and trim. If I had taken the Option alternative and had chosen to uncover and perhaps alter my beliefs creating my fears about weight, illness and my physical appearance, I might have freed myself to focus on my wants . . . to be healthy and trim. My appetite and food intake would then have been adjusted to my wanting, to going with myself . . . instead of being fed by my anxiety.

Isn't the person who mournfully proclaims he is addicted to cigarette smoking doing the same thing? "I don't want to smoke . . . it's awful, but I can't help myself." "It's going to make me sick." "I wish I could stop." All those pronouncements are negative. They speak of fears and unhappiness about sickness and addiction . . . none of which has to do with wanting to be healthy.

There is no reason to judge this behavior and commentary as good or bad, right or wrong. There is only a question. If I originally believed there was a path to travel in taking care of myself and subsequently found it did not work, would I want to continue? And if not, then I would have changed a belief, which would change my behavior.

One of my students, who had constant stomach cramps, would become furious with herself and literally scream to herself, "Stop being tense, damn it!" In fighting her stomach pains, she made them worse as she increased her tension. In being so busy with her symptoms as an indictment and proof of how bad she was for herself, she deprived herself of getting in touch with what she wanted. Later, after changing some of her prime beliefs, she noticed she was completely free of abdominal pain. "Wow," she exclaimed one afternoon, "I've finally made friends with my body." What she meant is she had finally made friends with herself and no longer sat in judgment on herself. The Option attitude of *to love is to be happy with* was ultimately the vision with which she chose to embrace herself. Without expectations. Without conditions.

Awareness of what each of us does is a major step toward change. But actual change is a *decision*.

As I live more in the Option mode, I find I allow my pains and go with them. In doing so and asking myself what I am uncomfortable about, I can usually uncover underlying beliefs. When I see that the unhappiness is a product of judgments which are either unfounded or self-defeating, it is easy to dispense with them. And as I discard those beliefs, my pains and physical problems resulting from them usually dissipate and disappear. I do not fight or even work on my bodily discomforts . . . I try to free myself from the beliefs which feed them and clear a path so I can stay in touch with my wanting to be healthy. If there is no time to explore my beliefs, I can quickly ask myself: What do I want? The answer, which usually comes easily, becomes an immediate affirmation of my nature. I use it to turn my head in the direction I want to travel.

Each physical malfunction becomes an opportunity to explore and restore . . . which is not a question when I am healthy, but certainly becomes one when I am not.

But I don't have to wait for a body malfunction. *I can affirm my wanting to be healthy now, which is just another way of accepting and allowing my nature. It is a way of loving myself.* In choosing that direction, the many things I can do to maintain my health or reestablish it become apparent (alter my diet, create an exercise program, etc.). When we are clear and comfortable, we each know for ourselves what we can do to enhance and support our health.

The gift I can give myself, right now, is to *stop* stopping my body from doing its thing by discarding the beliefs which short-circuit it. And then, after I've read all the books and consulted all the doctors, I can listen to the voice within me and trust my decisions. *Although professionals and experts can be extremely knowledgeable and authoritative in specific areas, the relevance of their information as it affects my life is for ME to decide.* Whether I choose to buy their concepts and predictions, take just a portion of their advice or decide to walk alone on untrodden ground, I will know the best route for me. I am the only expert on me as you are the only expert on you.

THE "THINK" PAGE (FEELING GOOD: HEALTH AND QUESTIONS OF PSYCHOSOMATIC ILLNESS)

QUESTIONS TO ASK YOURSELF:

Are you aware of fearing sickness or wanting to be healthy?

Does your doctor treat you like a total person or just an isolated problem?

When you feel physically unhealthy, do you think of fighting the problems or restoring harmony?

If you have a psychosomatic pain, do you become upset with it and fight it, or do you try to understand its meaning?

Do you see yourself as healthy or sickly?

Do you fear disease and death? If so, what do you believe about them?

OPTION CONCEPTS TO CONSIDER:

* FEARING ILLNESS IS CONCENTRATING ON WHAT "ISN'T."

*"DIS-EASE" MEANS NOT AT EASE OR MOVING AWAY FROM OUR NATURAL FLOW.

* ILLNESS IS ONE POSSIBLE CONSEQUENCE OF UNHAPPINESS.

* UNHAPPINESS SAPS THE ENERGY FROM OUR BODIES, CREATING AN IMBALANCE AND AN INCREASED RECEPTIVITY TO SICKNESS.

* PSYCHOSOMATIC SYMPTOMS ARE SIGNS FOR US . . . QUESTIONS, NOT STATEMENTS OR ACCUSATIONS.

* WE ARE ALWAYS DOING THE BEST WE CAN.

BELIEFS TO CONSIDER DISCARDING:

My body is against me.

The best way to treat disease is to FIGHT disease.

Psychosomatic illness proves I am stupid and self-destructive.

EIGHTH DIALOGUE

Q. WHY ARE YOU UNHAPPY?
A. (sigh) Because less than one week ago, I found out I have diabetes.
Q. What is it about having diabetes that makes you unhappy?
A. Where do I begin?
Q. Where would you like to begin?
A. With me. I'm a thirty-six-year-old man who would like to live for at least another thirty-six years. But now, the odds are against it. Every morning for the rest of my life, I have to get up and shoot myself full of insulin

183

with a hypodermic needle. I'll be like some sort of a junkie. Hooked . . . but it's a habit that I can never kick. It's disgusting.

Q. *Why is it disgusting?*

A. It's not normal. I've always been pretty healthy. Now, suddenly, I'm a cripple.

Q. *What do you mean?*

A. For the rest of my life, I'm dependent on a needle . . . otherwise, with my sugar count, the headaches, dizziness and blurred vision will ultimately lead to insulin shock and then . . . well, it can get pretty hairy. I can't believe it. Each morning, I take a disposable syringe out of its cellophane wrapping, insert the needle into the insulin vial and then, my God, I push it into my arm and press down on the plunger. The second morning I did it, I looked up at myself in the medicine cabinet mirror and a wave of nausea came over me. Me. I looked like some sort of a freak. It's only been four days, but it already feels like a lifetime. I don't want diabetes. God, it's awful.

Q. *I know that you don't want diabetes, but why are you unhappy that you have it?*

A. Because I don't have a choice anymore. I'm stuck.

Q. *WHY DOES THAT MAKE YOU UNHAPPY?*

A. I want to get unstuck. How's that for a sick pun!

Q. *And if you can't get "unstuck," WHY WOULD YOU BE UNHAPPY?*

A. Because in twenty years, when I'm in my mid-fifties, all kinds of exciting things will begin to happen to me. My eyesight will start failing. My veins and arteries will continually fill up with sludge from the injections and the circulation in my legs and arms will start to diminish. And if I'm fortunate enough to get a bad cut or a small clot, gangrene could easily set in . . . and you know what that means. Do you? (pause) Amputation. A leg here, an arm there. Piece by piece. Before my time, I will start to disintegrate. And since I might be blind, I could experience all this in darkness. That's a bird's-eye view of my future. Three weeks ago everything was okay . . . now, it's turned to mud. (voice breaking) I can't believe how miserable this is!

Q. *I understand what you believe are the future ramifica-*

184

tions, but why are you miserable about it now?

A. Because I don't want all those monstrous things to happen to me.

Q. *WHY DO YOU BELIEVE THEY WOULD?*

A. I don't know for sure. But I'm telling you what's in the books . . . what's on my doctor's lips.

Q. *WHAT ARE YOU AFRAID WOULD HAPPEN IF YOU WEREN'T UNHAPPY ABOUT THOSE FUTURE CONSEQUENCES?*

A. Ah . . . I guess I believe they're more likely to happen.

Q. *Are you saying that your unhappiness somehow might hold off those possibilities?*

A. Maybe! If I wasn't unhappy about it, I might then just welcome it by doing nothing about it.

Q. *DO YOU BELIEVE THAT?*

A. As I was saying it, no.

Q. *Do you think it's possible to not be unhappy about it and still try to prevent it?*

A. Yes. Yes, I do. (long pause)

Q. *What are you feeling?*

A. I was beginning to feel okay, but then I felt this anger . . . from deep down, way inside.

Q. *WHAT ARE YOU ANGRY ABOUT?*

A. (His face becomes flushed.) You really want to know . . . that damn doctor. We're talking about the crisis of my life and he just keeps me waiting in a small cubicle for over an hour. It's like being stuck in a glorified closet. Then, he enters. Poker-faced. And very casually, he tells me my sugar count is unbelievably high, which would explain my symptoms and then he hands me a box. As I'm reading instructions on how to take insulin, he gives me this quick, cool rap on diabetes and insulin like I'm an idiot. I told him I know what it means and what I know differs from his pretty pictures. He laughs condescendingly and assures me by the time I'm in my fifties, they'll have discovered new methods of treating my problem. And that's it, fella . . . too bad. The doctor had about as much grace as a firing squad. I even asked him if there were books he could recommend. Immediately, he became indignant, suggesting that he would worry about the problem . . . that was his job. Bullshit! The moment

185

I left the office, he went on to the next body.

Q. WHY DOES THAT GET YOU SO ANGRY?

A. We're talking about my life. That's my arm I'm injecting, my veins which are going to clog, my eyes which will grow dim. I don't mean to be melodramatic, but I don't want to be crippled . . .

Q. THEN WHY DO YOU BELIEVE YOU WOULD?

A. What? (stares intently at the floor) Why do I believe that? Because it's going to happen . . . all I have to do is keep shooting up for twenty years and I'll be wasted.

Q. I understand the possible effects of insulin injections, but what is it about those eventualities that disturbs you?

A. I'm helpless. I can't do a damn thing about any of this. I feel like a defenseless victim. And you know that kills me; I can't exactly call this totally unexpected. I come from a family with a long history of diabetes. Yet, I was brought up on Rice Krispies, sugar-coated flakes, candy, ice cream and cake. Whoever talked about diet and balance? Everyone was supposed to eat their way to good health. And it didn't matter much what you stuffed into your mouth. Unbelievable. It just drives me crazy to think about it.

Q. About what?

A. That as a kid I was stuffed with garbage and then, as an adult, I continued the insult to my system. Look at me, thirty-five pounds overweight, three teaspoons of sugar in my coffee at least three times a day and a history of diabetes in my ancestry. No small wonder I'm sick. I guess I put the final touches on . . . I did it, I'm responsible.

Q. What do you mean?

A. I didn't take care of myself. I did everything wrong. The result is my pancreas died before its time and I'm condemned to the needle. (He pounds his fist on the table.)

Q. WHAT ARE YOU ANGRY ABOUT?

A. Why didn't I do something when I could? Why didn't I take care of myself?

Q. What you did is done . . . part of the past. Why are you unhappy about it now?

A. Because I was an idiot. Dumb, just plain dumb. How

could I ever feel happy about that?

Q. *WHAT ARE YOU AFRAID WOULD HAPPEN IF YOU WEREN'T UNHAPPY ABOUT NOT HAVING TAKEN CARE OF YOURSELF?*

A. I guess that I might be doomed to repeat it . . . ignore my health even more.

Q. *Are you saying that if you weren't unhappy about what you did, you wouldn't take care of your health?*

A. Yes.

Q. *WHY DO YOU BELIEVE THAT?*

A. I don't know. (pause) Wait a minute. That's ridiculous. I don't believe that. I don't have to be unhappy to take care of my body. I never quite looked at it that way before. That's nice to see. Okay, okay . . . but it doesn't solve it.

Q. *What do you mean?*

A. I don't want to be hooked on insulin the rest of my life. I couldn't stand it!

Q. *WHY DOES THAT MAKE YOU SO UNHAPPY?*

A. Because I don't want to be an insulin junkie.

Q. *Sure, I see that, but there is a difference between not wanting to use insulin and being unhappy about using it.*

A. I'm unhappy about using it because of what it ultimately does to your body.

Q. *Why?*

A. You sure as hell would be unhappy if you knew you would be blind and maybe crippled in twenty years.

Q. *If I did, I'd be unhappy for my reasons. What are yours?*

A. I want to find another way; that's why I'm so unhappy.

Q. *WHAT ARE YOU AFRAID WOULD HAPPEN IF YOU WEREN'T UNHAPPY ABOUT TAKING IN- SULIN?*

A. I might just take it . . . without questioning, without searching.

Q. *WHY DO YOU BELIEVE THAT?*

A. I don't know. If I was loose and cool about it, maybe I wouldn't do anything.

Q. *DO YOU BELIEVE THAT?*

A. No. Not exactly.

Q. *Let's take the "not exactly." Are you saying that by being unhappy, you would be more motivated to search for alternate ways?*

A. (smiling) I guess so. It sure seems like that . . . but there it is again. I do that a lot. I never realized how much being unhappy is part of my system. I can see not being miserable and still trying to find other solutions.

Q. *WHAT DO YOU WANT?*

A. Well, it's going to sound crazy, but my brother is into acupuncture, cell salts and herbal healing. He researched the situation with all his cronies and was told by one Eastern doctor that certain herbs and leaves boiled in water and served as tea four times a day will retard the manufacture of almost all of the glucose made by the body. They say this would completely alleviate the need for insulin. We've talked every night and he's pushing. But it's my body and I'm afraid.

Q. *Of what?*

A. Of going into shock . . . insulin shock . . . and ending up face down on the sidewalk.

Q. *DO YOU BELIEVE THAT WILL HAPPEN?*

A. Sure, if I'm not careful.

Q. *Are you saying you won't be careful?*

A. No, of course not. But suppose I don't know and something happens. I'm afraid to hurt myself and yet I know using the insulin is hurting myself. You see how confusing it all is. I don't know what to do. I get so mixed up with all the anger and fear.

Q. *What do you mean?*

A. My brother's suggestions are really interesting . . . they're beautiful because, if they worked, you'd be healing the body in a natural way. But sometimes I think I listen to him only because I'm so afraid of the insulin. And yet, that's not altogether true. I'd like to go a more natural way . . . a special diet and exercise feels right to do, but not the injections. When I told the doctor about the herbs, he laughed in my face. He said it was ridiculous and that I must not ever dare to go off the insulin. His tone of voice scared me. But it's more than that; I can't stand him.

Q. *Why?*

A. Because he doesn't give a shit. Whether I lived or died, it doesn't matter to him. He just goes by his book.

Q. *Even if that's so, why does that disturb you so?*

A. Because he's playing God with my life.

188

Q. How's that?

A. He prescribes insulin and I have to take it.

Q. Do you see yourself as forced to take it?

A. No, no . . . but what else can I do? He's supposed to know, so I follow what is said to me.

Q. Then WHY ARE YOU ANGRY WITH HIM?

A. Because sometimes I think he doesn't know or care to know. I tell him what an herbalist suggests and he laughs in my face. But just maybe it could work. I'm not saying it's the solution, but how about considering everything. After all, this is supposed to be the man's medical specialty.

Q. And if he chooses to see it only one way, WHAT IS SO UPSETTING ABOUT IT?

A. Like I said, I don't think he goes beyond his nose.

Q. And if he doesn't, that's for him to do, but WHY DOES THAT MAKE YOU UNHAPPY?

A. Because I have to listen.

Q. Why is that?

A. (pause) If I don't, I'll get sick.

Q. Why do you believe that?

A. Because he's supposed to be the expert.

Q. Then, are you saying that you are listening because you believe it's in your own best interest to do so?

A. Yes.

Q. Do you have to do that or do you want to?

A. (smiling) I want to. I see. I see. By following him, I'm deciding to do that. Okay . . . that's good to understand because now, more than ever, if I'm choosing, I want to give it my best shot.

Q. And what's that?

A. To move in another direction, but, you know, I'm still afraid.

Q. Afraid of what?

A. Of making more mistakes. After all, if I had been more aware and more concerned, I could have lost weight, changed my diet and perhaps avoided this entire mess. So I'm part of my diabetes. How can I be sure that I would know what to do?

Q. WHAT DO YOU WANT TO DO?

A. Try the herbs. You know, my brother has always been the odd turkey of the family with his weird friends and unorthodox way of life. Yet, he really made sense. In a way, he made more sense and explained more to me than the doctor. Man, I'm almost there. I keep trying to decide whether I want to try the leaves and roots because I believe they could work or just because I'm frightened of the insulin. I don't want to act out of fear.

Q. *Then why would you?*

A. That's a good question. Before I came in here, I was ready to jump at anything. I was so afraid and so angry at myself and the physician. But now, I feel much, much better . . . calmer, not afraid. Now I know I'd like to try the herbs. (chuckling) I'm really trying, but I still feel a lump in my throat.

Q. *What do you think it means?*

A. I'm still uncomfortable . . . not like before, but something is still there.

Q. *WHAT ARE YOU UNCOMFORTABLE ABOUT?*

A. Suppose I'm wrong?

Q. *WHY SHOULD YOU BE UNHAPPY IF YOU WERE WRONG?*

A. I might hurt myself.

Q. *WHY DO YOU BELIEVE THAT?*

A. You know, when you asked me that before, it seemed like an insane question. I'm not sure I believe I would hurt myself . . . I think I just assumed it. After all, I can set it up so that if the symptoms appear again, I can take the insulin. Maybe, I can slowly replace the dosage of insulin with the herbs . . . while having my blood checked every day. (laughing) That's the way right there. Why couldn't I do it?

Q. *WHAT DO YOU WANT TO DO?*

A. I want to try the herbs. I do. I'll still drop weight and do the exercise too.

Q. *How do you feel?*

A. Good. Excited. I'm not totally clear about why I didn't take care of myself all these years, but now I want to try. I feel more connected with my body than ever before. It's like I just opened up a whole new world.

NOTE. Over a period of four weeks, this student, whose sugar count had been extraordinarily high, withdrew from using insulin by replacing it with a specially prepared herbal tea. His count was restored to normal for a person his age. When he informed his doctor about his successful experiment, the physician did not believe him and immediately dismissed him as a patient. Not once did this man of medicine seriously question his patient about the nature of the alternate therapy.

Although there is no attempt here to suggest or to draw attention to herbs as a new, applicable or even useful treatment for diabetes, this dialogue does stand as a testament to one man who actualized his wants and found another way. Like many of us, he had initially given up his desire to explore and decide his future because of fear and the belief that someone else knew better than he did about what to do for himself. When coming from comfort and clarity, he, indeed, had become his own expert.

9

sex and your own natural expertise

He slid his athletic body subtly across the soft suede couch as he watched her out of the corners of his eyes. Staring into the magic one-eyed cyclops during a noisy soap commercial, she steadily consumed cocktail pretzels. He had been waiting for several hours for this precise moment. Calculating. Everything was perfect, even his timing. The movie they had come together to see on her cable T.V. had ended several minutes ago. And he noted with excitement that she had already made herself comfortable in her apartment by exchanging her denim pants for a robe. Without hesitation, he gently placed his hand on her shoulder, paused five seconds to wait for a cue. Then assuming her lack of response was her signal for him to continue, he kissed her lightly on the neck, letting his hands explore her breasts. With great bravado, he expertly worked his way down to her waist. Faded old movie images of Errol Flynn making it in the Casbah.

Then it occurred to him—the realization that he had

just started a sexual passage for the amusement of only one person. It was as if he was massaging a cadaver. Nothing moved, not one part of her body was active except her mouth. The chopping action of her teeth munching pretzels and the weight of his own breathing were the only sounds competing with the commercial. The sweat in his palms began to dry and grow stale. The passion drained from his hands. "Maybe, later," he assured himself. "Maybe now is not the time." As casually as he could he removed one hand from the inside of her bathrobe and the other from the top of her thigh. And he waited.

An hour passed, then another. He decided now was the time to try again. Decisively and aggressively, he made his move. This time she responded, but without the life and passion he was expecting. Even as they settled into the deep pile of her area rug, he could feel that his emotional pitch was much higher and more intense than hers. He was continually distracted by her suggesting he move just a little to the right, then a little to the left. It didn't seem possible there could be so many uncomfortable positions for her.

Her hands tracked a repetitious circular motion on his back as if they were battery operated. He could feel the perspiration pouring from his body onto her cool, dry flesh. Anger began to swell inside him. The more he tried to involve her, the more aware he became of her lack of enthusiasm or participation. He almost wanted to scream at her to put some life into it. But he couldn't. He couldn't even ask why. The fury just continued to build in his chest as he lost his capacity to continue. Once he realized what was happening, he panicked.

Jumping to his feet, he announced that he had a sudden pain in his chest. Very apologetically, he began to dress furiously, clutching his hand to the left side of his chest. She wanted to call a doctor but he flatly refused. He insisted he would be okay . . . he just needed to get home and take some pills. As he hurried to the door fully dressed, he looked at her standing there nude in the clarity of the hall light. She no longer seemed attractive. "Maybe, that was it," he frantically told himself as he began to dismiss her from his mind. They said their good-byes, and he raced down the corridor.

Out on the street, he paused for a moment, trying to catch

his breath. Now that he had left the source of his discomfort behind, he could think. He began to laugh as he considered the cleverness of his exit line. Thinking on his feet. He liked that.

Now he confronted himself. That was not just an isolated evening. It had happened many times, which had resulted in his feeling asexual.

It was as if he had convinced himself that he really didn't care and had little or no desire for sex. Most of the time he pursued it because he believed he should. And besides, this girl really was unattracttive, he reassured himself. Certainly, this would affect his virility. But did that explain it sufficiently? Even he couldn't deny the obvious. His loss of potency was an all-too-frequent occurrence. The thought triggered a rush of pain in his stomach. When it passed, he decided it would be more productive for him to think about something else.

Sex can be beautiful or extremely problematic. It can be the extension of love or hate . . . a gentle or a violent act. When I flow with my sexuality, it enriches me. When I don't, it preoccupies my thoughts and precipitates all sorts of discomfort.

What is sex? What is its nature? On a physiological plane, sex is frequently interpreted to be the act of and all secondary acts leading to copulation. The more liberal definition would include any erotic stimulation whether self-induced or initiated by another. Sexual activity has many varieties . . . it can be performed alone, in pairs, in groups with members of the same or the opposite sex.

It is as romantic and mysterious as I choose to make it. It has no consistent and absolute properties beyond its physical aspects.

How we view sex is how we view the world and how we view the world is how we view sex.

The aggressive usually goes marching in determinedly. The timid moves quietly, with much hesitation. The guilty, perhaps, never turns on the light. The fragile does it very elegantly, like sipping fine wine from delicate crystal. The free-thinking jump in enthusiastically, ever anxious to experiment. The uncomfortable carry their discomfort in their underwear. The drifter coasts right over the experience as if it never occurred. The angry move in with a heavy assault, crashing their units right into the beach. The nervous and the giddy laugh at the beginning, in the middle and at the end. The alcoholic does it drunk, the pot-head does it high and the speed-freak races through it at a thousand miles an hour. The connoisseur sets it up perfectly, the sheets in place. The celibate monk never does it.

My sexuality is no different from any other manifestation of who I am. *I bring to my sexual contact the same vision and consciousness I bring to any other activity.* Just as I might use happiness in motivation and creating expectations, in turning wants into needs in other activities, so I utilize it in my sexual relationship. And conversely, when I allow myself to flow from my own nature, happily and freely, so I also bring that acceptance and permissiveness to my sexual contacts.

Unfortunately for us participants, sex has been distorted and dramatized by a culture uptight and uncomfortable about its sexuality. The subject has been inflated, twisted, warped and made special in such a questionable fashion that it has become one of the major epidemic areas for unhappiness.

Our concepts of sex are filled with shoulds and should nots. They are subjected to explicit and implicit taboos. Sex is the Mt. Everest of our expectations. And yet, amid all this difficulty, there is no such thing as a sexual problem. *It is a question of beliefs, not sex.*

Perhaps uncovering and exploring the lessons of others will best portray our sexuality. Their experiences can be mirrors . . . mirrors through which we can observe, not just as voyeurs, but to gain perspective and insight into unraveling, clarifying and changing our own beliefs. Many of the judgments and expectations operative in our love relationships are the same ones we trip over before, during and after our sexual encounters.

A child experiences his sexuality even as an infant. Many well-meaning parents tell their sons and daughters not to touch and play with their genitals . . . communicating a primal restriction. Many children hardly ever see or experience themselves or their private parts before the age of three or four because of all the years closed and sealed and pinned into diapers. What are they to think about their sexuality? Already,

196

they have absorbed attitudes from their parents. Certainly, the prohibition against exploring themselves is the first explicit taboo.

Later, these same children (was it you and me?) grow up and play "doctor" behind closed bathroom doors and in paneled basements. Their beliefs about their experiments are reflected in their secretiveness and embarrassment about being caught by disapproving parents. Initially, they confine their exploration to members of the same sex. As time passes, they become bolder and decide to move into the expanded arena of heterosexuality. They talk their parents into inviting playmates of the opposite sex. Off and running.

At this juncture, several dramatic events may occur. Often, children are discovered playing "hospital" and are reprimanded in tones of anger and disappointment. Although this, of course, is not the only response, it is often the reaction of a well-meaning parent confused about how to proceed in such a situation. Later, the children might be lectured about "good" girls and "bad" girls, "good" boys and "bad" boys. Although they have felt the spirit and delights of their own sexuality, they are suddenly confronted with many emphatically stated taboos. Parents, religious institutions and schools tend to support the concepts of "don't touch" until later (whenever that is).

In adults' attempts to caution their children, a diverse cluster of beliefs and superstitions are dramatically invoked. Fears of pain, of frustration, of loss of respect, of rejection, of disease, even of insanity (in cases of masturbation taboos) and of guilt proliferate. The growing adolescent is caught in a cross fire of confusing thoughts and feelings. Even some of the more free-thinking adults, in their efforts to counterbalance the taboos, tend to color sexuality and the sex act with the vivid hues of Hollywood romance. Ultimately, this creates a world of improbable expectations for young people to try to match.

Before I embarked on my own first adolescent sexual experience, my head was permeated with rules, images and fantasies. My desires were intertwined with a collection of diverse beliefs, most of which had been taught to me supposedly for my own protection. So my early sexual problems were the result of self-defeating beliefs.

197

Unless we move with absolute freedom from judgments and come from our own nature, beliefs will always lurk beneath our sexuality. But the beauty is, a belief can be changed, altered or discarded . . . which in turn, can result in increased, or even absolute, comfort and ease with our sexual acts.

An eighteen-year-old girl, who later became an Option Process student, permitted herself to discuss a milestone in her life. She had been spending a warm summer evening on the beach with her boyfriend. They had both repeatedly discussed having sexual intercourse. She insisted emphatically, that if he loved her, he wouldn't continually push her. She told him she would do "IT" in her own time. Nevertheless, he argued that he had the perfect right to express himself, explaining that in loving her, he wanted everything . . . everything. He promised she would love it and there would be no pain. He promised he would be very gentle. As the night wore on, their games of tossing and turning on the blanket became more serious. Her desire to be caressed and touched increased. Their gentle kissing grew more intense as their passions swelled. The hot breathing triggered a crisscross response. Each of them became more aggressive and daring in their exploration and involvement, thirsting to love more . . . to be loved more.

Realizing they were about to make contact, she, almost automatically, said "no," but really meant "yes." Her boyfriend intuitively recognized her assent and continued. She opened herself and within less than a minute, they had bridged the gap and were moving together. Within twenty seconds he ejaculated. She felt nothing but pain and discomfort. He abruptly withdrew, rolled over and looked away in his embarrassment at having finished so soon. He left her panting to the discords of her own music.

Alone. She lay there bewildered and tearful as the thin layer of heated perspiration covering her body began to cool in the night air. She had saved herself, kept her virginity intact because it had meant so much. Yet, this definitely was not what she had anticipated. Where was the joy and ease? Where was the music and the euphoria? What about the promised tenderness?

Sexual intercourse was "supposed to" be an intimate sharing that brought people closer together, but she felt distant

198

and incomplete. Her expectations had definitely not been met. In fact, she recalled her first sexual interlude as abrasive and frustrating. Anger possessed her. Judging her boyfriend harshly because he was inexperienced and did not fulfill his promise (he told her she would enjoy it), she concluded he did not really love her. After all, she reasoned, the least he could have done is not turn away. She was unaware his movement said nothing about his love and caring . . . he was now acting out of his own discomfort and self-consciousness. She drifted further into herself.

As she explored her awareness and beliefs, she realized that during the entire period of foreplay, she had been hyper-sensitive to the possibility of getting caught. Fearing exposure and rejection if anyone knew, she had had difficulty concentrating and allowing herself to enjoy. Originally, the taboo against premarital sex had been used to help her keep her distance from it. Though she had now changed her mind and desired sexual contact, the same belief still blocked her. Anticipating the negative judgments of others restrained her from participating freely. She also began to understand how she used her expectations as an enticement . . . yet those visions and prejudgments brought their own pressures and unhappy conclusions. Because sex was "supposed to" be a beautiful dream-like experience, she used the fantasy as a yardstick for judgment, against which her reality on the beach could never compare.

Beliefs, expectations and judgments dramatically influenced her first sexual encounter.

Her reasons for unhappiness existed before, during and after the sex act. All the taboos she had heard since childhood still haunted her because she continued to believe them. All the frustration over broken promises was operative because she had expectations. In taking her beliefs to the beach, she brought with her an underlying network of cables controlling the tone, feelings and intensity of her sexual behavior. Her beliefs did not disappear in the heat of passion. They surfaced only to sabotage her flow. But now, as she explored and uncovered them, she created an opportunity to discard or change them.

Another student viewed his own sexual philosophy with anxiety and discomfort. He had created a rule that he "had to" make it with a woman at least three times a week. This figure was determined from various surveys he had taken at his Thursday night backgammon game. If he missed, he believed that meant he was failing as a man. He presumed his masculinity was provable through sex—that having an affair with a woman reaffirmed his sexuality, his manliness. In many ways, the sex act for him had nothing to do with sex.

When he began his artful buildup, when he carefully manipulated the other person toward his goal, when he climaxed, it had little or nothing to do with anything other than his own unhappiness and beliefs about himself. It was his style of confirming the opposite of what he feared. His statement was, "This proves I'm not inadequate."

But as he talked about how hollow and exposed he felt after intercourse, he realized his goal was, in fact, unfulfilled. It only served to heighten his awareness of his discomfort . . . pushing him compulsively toward the next sexual encounter in search of solace. He knew he had proved nothing.

The more he explored his erroneous beliefs about proofs, the more he realized the self-defeating nature of his behavior. As he discarded that single belief, he found he no longer needed to "score" even once a week . . . he no longer needed to "score" at all. He was free to have sex when he wanted or to pass. Uncovering other beliefs about himself and his concepts of self-worth became an exciting prospect. He was enthusiastic about having the opportunity to *choose* to change his beliefs. Even at this point, as he discarded his belief about sex being a proof of manhood, he knew his feelings and behavior toward women had dramatically changed. The pressure was removed, in part, from those relationships. It was a beautiful beginning.

A housewife, whose marriage had disintegrated, defined her dilemma as a sexual problem. After sixteen years of marriage, bedding down with her husband had become an infrequent and dull experience. Although she valued their relationship and admittedly loved her husband, she felt incomplete and unattractive. Yet, she believed her body, her technique and her enthusiasm were still intact. Perhaps, she reasoned, he was having difficulties. In any case, she envisioned a discussion on the subject with her partner as directly threatening to the sanctity and continuity of her marriage. On one occasion, after working up courage for almost a year, she opened the door to a conversation on the subject, but her husband declared there was no problem and refused to discuss it further. Intimidated and angry, she elected to go outside her marriage to satisfy this one unfulfilled desire. Initially, it began with a single brief affair. Then she explored her sexuality with many different men until finally settling for one steady relationship. She constantly boasted about the quality of her marriage. Privately, she assured herself that her marriage was fine, except for this "slight" sexual difficulty. In order to reinforce her proposed belief, she told each man she ever bedded with that she could not get emotionally involved because she still loved her husband. As years followed years, her life-style became a set pattern as did the guilt and discomfort accompanying it.

Initially, she insisted emphatically that her marriage was excellent. Yet, as she investigated her boredom and sexual incompatibility, she began to uncover the many beliefs and judgments she held in regard to her husband's performances and caring. She even came to understand that his aversion to approaching this subject could easily have come from his own fears about questioning his masculinity and pride.

Doing the best she could, at the time, and rather than face the unspeakable (problems in marriage that lead to fighting and divorce), she settled to live with what she envisioned as the lesser threat (infidelity). Unfortunately, her alternative approach also had its liabilities. The meetings and interludes required creating an extensive network of lies. She was constantly pressured by her fear of exposure. Eventually, she realized how her escapades had drawn her attention and focus from her marriage and how the guilt and discomforts had actually resulted in an even wider gap between her and her husband. Now, she watched her marriage crumble.

Sitting on the hard bench of a divorce court, she avoided her husband's eyes . . . embarrassed, yet simultaneously furious at his lack of awareness and concern. If he had loved her, she assumed, he would not have let this happen. The years of separation and silence created a communication barrier neither partner, each for their own reason, could surmount . . . for their fears as well as their anger prohibited them from even trying.

A multitude of beliefs were uncovered. But essentially, the fear of aging and the fear of divorce precipitated this woman's predicament. And those fears were chained to other unhappy beliefs. In the process of attending to her discomforts, she had not only contributed to undermining her sexual relationship, but also her entire marriage. As she exposed and discarded many beliefs, her ability to accept herself improved dramatically. This, ultimately, had ramifications in all sectors of her life. *Sex problems were just a sign of her unhappiness.* It was her beliefs that had short-circuited her flow.

It was not any different for the divorced multi-millionaire just approaching the watershed of fifty, astounded that he was middle-aged. Believing himself to be "over the hill" and imagining the quick descent into a wooden box, he contemplated his old age with fear and disdain. He saw impotence as an inevitability. Using the energy of this unhappiness, he decided on a procedure to test and verify his virility . . . to recapture the fervor of his youth.

He began to date younger women, not just five or ten years younger, but twenty years younger. He would slip beneath the sheets with almost anyone under twenty-five who gave him the chance. He gloated over having broken his "youth" record when he spent the evening with a girl younger than his own daughter. But this support of his self-image had to be continually fed, an appetite incapable of being satiated.

The pressure built in his life and his sexual relations. Scoring became all important. What mattered was making it, staying young. His fears were his fuel. Yet, he hated himself in the early morning light and was angry each evening even though he was not alone. He was uncomfortable with his sexuality despite his efforts and indulgence. As he realized he was buying his youth, not living it, he resented himself further for having to do this charade in order to sustain his good feelings. Stripped of a sense of dignity, his act to mask the pain and the anger brought more pain and anger.

Each tumble onto the mattress of intimacy brings with it different experiences—experiences determined by the beliefs of the parties involved. Although the examples cited seem to derive from unhappy places, this is not because sex is unhappy. I only begin here as I had once begun with myself. It was only after I explored and uncovered my beliefs which short-circuited my own sexuality that I created myself the opportunity to change . . . to change dramatically and irrevocably. As I chose to discard certain self-defeating beliefs, I began to stop stopping myself. The process was one of undoing. And then it became just a matter of allowing, giving myself permission to follow my wants and good feelings.

People enjoy sex to the extent they are happy.

Far from being unhappy or difficult, sex in an allowing and nonjudgmental context is a beautiful and intimate experience. Even sex manifested in the name of just expressing a physical inclination can still contain qualities of beauty . . . beauty in sharing, beauty in passion, beauty in touching, beauty in doing what I want. When it moves smoothly with great ease and tenderness, it feels good before, during and after. When it's physically delightful and fulfilling, then the attitudes of the participants are much like the Option attitude: To love is to be happy with. And to be happy is to love.

In loving my partner without judgments or expectations, I am also loving and accepting myself. No matter what turn of events takes place, if we are happy with each other and aware that each of us is doing the best we can, then certainly our experience of being together and sharing will be soft and easy . . . flowing and consistent to our nature.

When it's good, I notice I'm happy and when I'm happy, I notice it's good. How I am and see life is how I am and see myself sexually. Only my unhappiness short-circuits my sexuality and sex acts. The unhappiness operating in illness, in love relationships, in guilt, in fear of the unknown, operates in this arena too. Cardinal beliefs: *If you loved me, you would . . . and I am responsible for another's unhappiness* continue to be sustained. Every sexual problem discussed is an excellent illustration of how *expectations* affect our lives. Fear of failure and rejection and the belief that something is wrong with me infiltrates many sexual experiences.

My body, how it moves, its sexuality and spirit is not separate and unrelated to who I am. My sexuality is a function of my totality . . . my beliefs and the subsequent feelings.

The following overview of the searching of one Option

203

student details how when we unravel the beliefs, we create real opportunities for change.

Her major difficulty, as she assessed it, was her unhappiness about her sexuality and her sexual experiences. Why was she unhappy? Because her mate did not seem to be interested and when he was, he responded mechanically. What about that made her unhappy? She felt that her partner's lack of enthusiasm was her fault . . . there must be something wrong with her. Otherwise, she believed he would always be wanting to jump in bed with her. She also decided his lack of pursuit of her was a sign she did not do it well. What did she mean? Somehow, no matter how she tried, no matter how good she was in her fantasies or dreams, when lying on the bed with a real partner, she suddenly had two left hands and her mind went blank. She felt awkward and super-uncomfortable. Why did this happen? Because she was afraid. Afraid of what? She was concerned that if she was free, the aggressor and initiator, it would mean something "bad" about her. She was afraid her advances and uninhibited involvement would be misconstrued and actually chase her partner away. Her fear of being rejected had been intense.

Why should she be unhappy if she was rejected? That would be proof she was no good, that her failure here signified failure everywhere in sex. Did she really believe that? No, she did not as she said it. The more she reviewed that belief, the more she decided that it was unfounded. What was she afraid would happen if she did not worry about failing? That she might then do what she did in her fantasies and then be rejected. So in her way, she was really protecting herself . . . at the time, it was the best way she knew how to be in order not to be rejected.

Ironically, in exploring her unhappiness, she realized that her being afraid brought about the exact opposite of what she had wanted. Protecting herself from her fear had also rendered her incapable of acting freely and moving affectionately in accordance with her inclinations (which she only expressed in her fantasies). In fact, her vision of her mate as mechanical, although possibly accurate, was also a description of herself. *By attending to her fears and not-wants, she lost touch with her wanting.*

Her belief that SHE WAS RESPONSIBLE for her partner's enjoyment set up another series of concepts . . . with corresponding pressures. She felt she "had to" perform with a certain expertise and lived with the anxiety of being judged and rejected after each sexual encounter. Since, in her recent relationship, the responses of her lover were unenthusiastic, she used it to support other beliefs that she was sexually inept (again, something was wrong with her . . . her face, her body, her talent).

She came to understand that, as she reacts in bed from her own fears as well as comforts, so does her partner. Therefore, he, like she, reacted from his own set of beliefs. His enjoyment or view about their sex act was his . . . derived from his own frame of reference. If he chose to like it or dislike it, that was his choice coming from his reasons . . . he was the one who set his own stage, saw and interpreted the experience as he wanted. As she began to realize that she wasn't responsible . . . that another person's unhappiness or lack of enthusiasm was theirs, she discarded that belief. And like a wall of falling dominos, many other beliefs fell to the side. She tasted a new sense of freedom.

Yet, she still did not permit herself to feel absolutely comfortable. What concerned her was failure. But if she was not responsible, if she did not "have to" do this or that, then she could not have failed . . . because how her partner decided to view his side of the affair had nothing to do with who she was. In fact, she could have been the "great" lover of all time, but be viewed as aggressive and crude by a frightened and uncomfortable person. As she became aware of these realities, as she started to understand and digest her involvement with a new clarity, she realized that she would no longer have to protect herself or worry about failing. Removing her self-defeating beliefs in a series of Option dialogues freed her to be and do more of what she wanted. It was not even a question of "daring"; it was simply the act of doing.

What about her "ineptitude"? She still wasn't sure she had dispensed with that hobbling belief. As she reviewed herself in her fantasies, she noticed that she really seemed to know what to do . . . that she wasn't really "incapable." She had just stopped her natural flow with fears and had actually gone against herself. Since she no longer believed there was anything to be afraid of, she began to trust herself. If her partner became uncomfortable during relations, she could try to help him, to comfort him, to even play to his wishes. Yet, how he viewed what occurred was his personal, private vision.

A new excitement dawned on her. If she couldn't fail, if nothing was wrong with her, if she knew "how" to do it, if her partner's lack of enjoyment was his own thing from his beliefs, if she was only responsible for her . . . well, then she felt relieved and much freer to move with her inclinations instead of against them. Moreover, she now decided, she could even ask him to do what pleased her if he forgot or missed. If he did not comply, she would understand he was coming from his beliefs and it would mean nothing about her or their relationship. Once those fears were dispelled, it was easy for her to stay much more in touch with her wants.

As the unhappiness infiltrating her sexuality disappeared, she found herself happier and excited about her sexual encounters.

Her sexual experiences were more satisfying as she became more permissive of her own desires and more accepting of her partner. She reported that since she was more active and more allowing of his inactivity and mechanical performance, he seemed more willing to participate actively and more spontaneously. Her accepting attitude and nonjudgmental approach had provided an environment where *he* felt more comfortable with himself in accordance with his beliefs and fears. In this arena of no conditions and expectations, her partner became more desirous of exploring his wants and his not-wants. It all began with her changing one belief . . . and that is the beginning of changing everything.

Another Option student also described himself as having a severe sexual "hang-up." All he wanted and thought about was sex. In fact, having a sexual encounter was all he did when he had the opportunity. Yet with all the pillow play, he felt empty and unloved. Each time he jumped between the sheets, he scored in accord with what he believed he wanted. He would consummate a union and climax. But at the end of each evening, alone with himself, he became aware of that hollow feeling. He called his problem a sexual one . . . it was the cause of his current melancholy. Why? What was he unhappy about? He believed sex did not satisfy him. What did he mean? That although the women he slept with were desirable and enthusiastic, he felt there "should" be more than just a physical thrust. He then unhappily deduced that when he went to bed with someone, it was just the mechanics that counted. He remembered sleeping with one specific woman who performed all sorts of new and innovative acts. He assumed this meant he really turned her on. Later, he found out she did those very same things with just about everyone. Suddenly, he became upset and judged her a cold mechanic.

Why did that make him uncomfortable? Because then sex was still just a mechanical activity. Although he insisted that making it sexually was important to his virility, he found it uncomfortable for other reasons.

What was he saying? He did not feel loved. What does he mean? That sex was cold and callous; he wanted to be loved. If he was not loved, it meant he was no good (had little worth in his own eyes). Ironically, this was the reason he had had all these encounters in the first place . . . he wanted to feel good about himself. But the very activity he engaged in made him feel more uncomfortable and unhappy. Why? Because he had used unhappiness to fight unhappiness. Because he had expectations of what the sexual act "should" be and mean. Fearing sex would not be what he anticipated, he continually looked for evidence that it was bad . . . and he always found it (for it was through his fears and judgments that he gathered and interpreted his data). This provided additional proof that *something was wrong with him.* In fact, it confirmed he was unlovable. Why? Because women did not really care about him and he always ended up alone. But as he explored it, one fact became clear to him. His proof was really not a proof, just a judgment based on his beliefs. And his implicit disapproval of his partners, his reacting from unhappiness during and after intercourse had to put even more distance between him and his lover . . . and it was his distance. A self-fulfilling prophecy. Wasn't he also saying . . . love me even though I don't love myself?

Like the girl who believed she could not do it right, he shared with her the belief that he was responsible. This belief resulted in his using expectations and *standards of proof* as criteria for judgments. His sexual problems were not

207

problems of sex as much as they were problems of loneliness and self-criticism. He also discovered he was using unhappiness as a tool to maximize his skill—he promised himself that if he did not get what he wanted in sex, he would be unhappy. Ultimately, he obliged and fulfilled his threat. But once he realized what he was doing and believing, he removed the promises and the threats, freeing himself from his own vicious judgments and incriminations. Once he gave up his expectations, he participated more easily.

Another student located her "real" problem as a sexual one she was having with her living companion. She did not seem interested in sex any longer . . . in fact, their sexual relations were so infrequent that she believed they were a classic case of sexual incompatability. They both used "infrequency" and their mutual "lack of enthusiasm" as proof. Even as they discussed it together and reaffirmed their love for each other, they openly admitted and agreed that they had ONLY this one specific problem: sex. Unwilling to dig for the beliefs which resulted in their "problam," they each separately, without telling the other, decided to go outside their relationship for sexual gratification. Everything progressed well, until she realized that they had become very distant and cool to each other. She was now even concerned she might loss the very thing she had wanted, her lover.

The crisis revolved about her belief that she did not know what to do now. What was she unhappy about? That her lover did not desire her. What did she mean? Well, he never responded as if he was involved and he never touched her first. Why did that make her uncomfortable? Because if he loved me, he would be more aggressive and excited. What she was saying is that sex and, in particular, her specific image of "good sex" was a proof of love. Another version of the cardinal belief: *If you loved me, you would desire me sexually.*

As she investigated her belief and interaction, she remembered they had always had problems from the very beginning . . . shared fears about attachment, an unwanted pregnancy, the abortion and the guilt. She realized that sex always suggested another pregnancy, which they both feared and desperately wanted to avoid. She began to uncover other

208

beliefs feeding her judgments and finally understood that resistance to sexual contact and *poor sexual performance said nothing about their loving, but everything about their fears and difficulties.*

She discovered her proof was not a proof, but only a belief substantiating itself. Ironic how she was never willing to discuss the matter with her partner in depth because she feared she would discover she did not find him desirable any longer and maybe did not love him. Now, the relationship she sought to protect was on the verge of ending just because of her defense and her fear of losing.

As she began to discard many of those beliefs, she considered another question. What did she want to do? Salvage the love if possible, create a beautiful and happy relationship. But she was frightened. Why was she anxious if that's what she wanted? Because she was afraid to try . . . really try and then fail. To be rejected. Again, the pendulum swings back to her own belief . . . sex was merely the stadium in which some of her beliefs were played out, proved and disapproved. For her, this awareness became a sign and the first step in discarding self-consuming and self-defeating beliefs.

Viewing himself as incurably timid, one student was frustrated by his hesitancy and difficulties in making advances toward women. Often he felt repulsed by them. Subsequently, he concluded he had a major sexual hang-up. What was he unhappy about? That he didn't have enough sex . . . for long periods of time, months and months and months, he did not have sex at all. Why did that make him unhappy? Because he was lonely and believed he was undesirable. What did he mean? Well, if people did not want to sleep with him, then he must be unattractive, unlovable, repulsive. Why would he be unhappy if he were unlovable? Because he might end up alone, and if it's because something was irreparably wrong with him, he suspected the situation would last forever.

Did he believe that? Yes and no. No, nothing is forever . . . even when he did not have relations for months, he always managed to score again. What he feared was that the hiatus could last a long time if he allowed it. What did he mean? If he didn't hustle on solving this problem, he would end up alone.

An important note is that he did not mean alone . . . he meant lonely. *Lonely is unhappy about being alone.* Why would he be unhappy if he were alone? It would be okay for awhile, but not for an extended period. Why not? Because it might last forever. How would that happen? If he allowed it. Why would he allow it? He guessed he really wouldn't. As a shadow lifted from his face, he stopped himself. The question: What was he afraid would happen if he were NOT unhappy about being alone? That he would have remained alone. So he was believing if he was not unhappy, he might not take care of himself and pursue his wants. When he explored that belief, he realized he could do what was best for him without being unhappy.

Suddenly, he became excited. Yes, that's it . . . just as he has been using fear and unhappiness to protect himself from loneliness, he decided he could take care of himself without being miserable. In fact, he found his focus altered as he, for the first time, permitted himself to clearly concentrate on what he wanted.

Great, but he was still concerned about being rejected by all those women. What did he mean? When he made advances, the woman in question usually said she wasn't interested now, and sometimes suggested: "Later." But there was never a "Later." As he considered his discomfort, he realized he felt so intimidated by the first refusal or lack of enthusiastic response, he never tried again in the same evening (or week) for what he wanted. Why did the refusal make him so uncomfortable? It meant he would not get what he wanted . . . he would not have sex. Why did that make him unhappy? Because that meant that he was no good, that something was wrong with him. He believed he "should" be able to motivate his companions to want sexual relations with him.

Each time he said "should," his face tightened. He then became aware that because he believed he "should" be able to move her, he felt pressured by an almost unbearable burden.

The interplay here is with beliefs of responsibility and expectations. As a result of believing he needed to score in order to be happy, he found himself stopping his wanting. In fact, sometimes it seemed as if he did not care anymore. The meaning and ramifications of not getting, after he had tried, were so intensely disturbing that they actually extinguished his original desires and diverted his attention. They left him in a place which was exactly opposite of where he wanted to be.

Again, even the cardinal belief was operative here: If she loved me, she would want to have sex with me. The beliefs of being *responsible* for her lack of interest provided a base for feelings of rejection as well as the judgment that something is wrong with me. The using of unhappiness as a motivator and reinforcer was rampant.

As he freed himself from those beliefs and lifted the shackles of unhappiness, he immediately stayed with his *wanting*. Understanding that rejection of one person by another is only a comment about themselves and their beliefs, he felt freer to make advances and explore. As a result, without using unhappiness to solve his problem, he became more sensitive to a new relationship he had just formed and more cognizant of his own desires and pleasures as well as hers.

Since he saw himself as having nothing to lose, he made no judgments and created no expectations. He just found himself wanting more . . . and getting more. He was aware the happier he became, the more alive and sexual he was.

Sex is again the arena; unhappiness is the cause of the short circuit . . . and only we are the cause of our own unhappiness!

One woman who was extremely overweight was transformed dramatically by exploring her beliefs. Her fear centered on being thin. She was afraid to lose weight because she might then have sex all the time . . . yet, she desperately wanted to lose weight. By exploring the beliefs surrounding her fatness, she concluded her dilemma was sexual. She now realized that her fatness, as she stated, made her undesirable and therefore, kept her from becoming "bad." She reinforced this concept by rejecting all advances while she was heavy . . . dismissing suitors as lacking good taste.

What was she unhappy about? Being fat. Why? Because she did not like the image in the mirror, because she felt ugly. What did she mean? She believed that in being fat she was truly undesirable, which was what she might have wanted at first, but now she had definitely changed her

211

mind. She wanted to be thin; she "must" be thin . . . but she was scared. About what? That if she was thin, she would have too much sex. Why would that make her unhappy? Because she would be "bad." What about having "too much" sex would be bad? Well, she'd be easy, an easy mark . . . she would only be wanted for her body. Why would that make her unhappy? Because then she would not be having sex or be loved for the right reasons.

Those who love her now while she is fat really love her because they are with her despite her fatness. If she were thin, she also suspects that if she were rejected, it would then be because of HER, and not her fatness. Why would she be unhappy about that? That would prove that something is really wrong with her, that she is unlovable. Does she believe that? Yes, she guesses, in a way . . . that's why she has so much trouble with sex. But then, she doesn't believe it; she kind of knows she is okay. What is she afraid would happen if she wasn't unhappy about having too much sex? That she would have it. Her unhappiness, her fatness, were her way of protecting herself from what she believed she wanted which was no good to want. These were her way of dealing with her guilt, not for the way she acted, but for the way she thought she might act if she were thin.

As she became more and more focused on how she used her unhappiness to keep her where she was for protection against some mythical wrongdoing, she decided she could look out for herself without being unhappy. She could dispense with those beliefs and fears . . . nothing was wrong with her; even having all the sex she could imagine seemed okay.

Great, but this still left her fat. She then decided to deal with her fear of not losing weight now that she wanted. Once she accepted her current fatness, her fears and pressure disappeared. Slowly, she began to lose weight. She concentrated daily on her wants (thinness and health), rather than on her not-wants. Thus, her energy was not concentrated on not eating or a diet, but on thinness and comfort. The result was that she began to move with herself (with her wants) instead of against her fears, which is a much more difficult battle.

Once she became thinner, her sexual activity increased just as she had predicted (self-fulfilling prophecy). Although she was feeling much better about having sexual relations, there was still an unresolved uneasiness for her.

As she pursued herself further, she realized she still harbored another belief she had acquired in early adolescence; if he loved you, he wouldn't have sex with you and make you a bad girl. Instead of feeling loved, she began to feel more unloved. While she operated from that belief, she gave it power and substance. She had even forgotten the circumstances or the individual who first presented it to her. But those aspects were not important. What was significant was the now of her life and in the now, that belief was operative and it belonged to her. She laughed as she verbalized the belief, amused such a concept actually molded her behavior and generated all sorts of unhappy feelings.

What she had created was the double bind of unhappiness . . . whichever way she moved, she'd always decide the result was bad for her. "If he did have sex with me, then he really didn't care (he violated me)." "If he did not have sex with me, then he did not find me attractive and also didn't care!" Either way, she was caught in unhapppiness. Her belief supported a negative judgment no matter which way it went.

Later, when she discarded it, she began to find herself enjoying sex much more and feeling good about herself. Now that contact and copulation were not threatening, the danger was over. She felt freer with herself and her wants, no longer preoccupied by her judgments or her partner's judgments. All this enabled her to explore her sexuality as aspects of physical sensation, sharing, communicating, participating, loving and being happy with.

There are three seemingly dissimilar situations that derive some of their input from a common dynamic and belief. The woman who cannot reach a climax, the man who ejaculates prematurely and the man who often finds himself incapable of an erection. They are all believing their behavior is "bad" . . . that they "should" be able to perform "correctly" and therefore they are always fearing they won't.

The man who is impotent concentrates on his fear of impotence, diverting his attention from the sexuality of the moment and suddenly finds himself limp. The woman who always has difficulty reaching a climax concentrates on the fear that she won't. Rather than trying to reach orgasm and failing (since she believes she will not succeed), she often gives up. Or, she pushes herself, NEEDING to reach a climax, and in the tight anxiety of fearing she will not have it, her unhappiness gets directly in the way. The result: a short circuit. She brings about what she had dreaded.

The man who ejaculates very quickly takes a first occurrence and uses that as evidence that something is wrong with him. He concentrates on his fears of ejaculating early and actually brings about that reality *so that he can at least stop the anxiety.*

Fears often become their own self-fulfilling prophecies. The dynamic of getting what you fear most goes something like this . . . I become so unhappy or anxious fearing it, that if it actually happens, it couldn't be any worse. So rather than drown in this discomfort, I'll let it or make it happen; at least when I get it over there is no more need to worry about it happening. The intensity of the fear is more painful than the event.

If each of these individuals knew nothing was wrong with them, if they knew they were okay whether or not they performed to the expectations of another, it would help free them from their bind.

Of course, I am not suggesting that the solution to such problems is always so one-noted or the manifestation of a single belief. Often, other beliefs also underlie the behavior. *The significant aspect here is when I need it to happen and fear it won't, I fuel the not-want.* That dynamic of thinking is usually very common and influential in the situations discussed.

A view of multiple beliefs tied to a single problem can be seen through the example of the woman who had difficulty reaching orgasm because she feared not reaching it. She also might have been believing, at the very same moment, that if she does reach a climax, it means she is a "dirty" and "vulgar" person for enjoying sex and "letting herself go." Also, she might believe that her partner facilitates her orgasm . . . if she really enjoys it, she might come to need him for it, which she dreads. So, she withholds for many reasons. In the same situation, the sable brush of expectations, which paints images of orgasm tied to one special love relationship, can create a barrier. Beliefs, beliefs and more beliefs. They short-circuited and sabotaged her flow—*but the beauty is that she can change all of it if she wants.* There are no dead ends here, just opportunities.

One student, who had "come out" and moved to center stage with his homosexuality, viewed himself as reasonably "together" . . . yet wanted to shed what he called the last remnants of discomfort. But first, he decided to try to reconstruct, from an Option perspective, the development of some of those beliefs which affected his sexuality.

When he was a youngster, his father, a strong and self-reliant man, had always counseled him to "be a man . . . don't be weak." The implications and transmitted beliefs exerted a strong pressure on his development and behavior. "Crying is weak." "Softness is weak and unmanly." Each time he would either withdraw from a situation or respond meekly, his character would be questioned. "What's the matter with you? Don't act like a sissy." "No son of mine would have run away." Even his athletic talents were scrutinized. "Can't you catch a ball? Don't tell me you're afraid of it?"

Eventually, he began to see these questions as accusations and indictments. He permitted his father's continual commentary to erode his own beliefs about his strength and manliness. As he began to envision his feelings and responses as inept and inappropriate (acquiring the unstated, yet communicated, beliefs of his father), he reflected, "Maybe something *is* wrong with me. I'm afraid I'm really different . . . It's true, I am afraid I'll get hit by a baseball and often I do feel like crying. But only girls cry." The adopted beliefs, also supported by the comment of his peers, flooded him with fears and anxieties.

His mother, a very "possessive," "protective" and "competitive" parent, helped support his self-image of weakness. Although she played a distinctly feminine and subordinate role with her husband, her domineering relationship with her son reinforced his beliefs about his frailty and femininity. Although she would applaud his sensitivity, he suspected it was yet another sign of his growing "differentness." "I know what I usually want to do, but I'm afraid . . . which means I must be soft, which further suggests I am not a man."

Now the fear of being different gave birth to a self-consciousness and heightened sensitivity to being different. In effect, he began continually to search for signs that would confirm his fears and substantiate his beliefs. "What I am afraid of being is softhearted, like a woman . . . a sissy." Each judgment compounded the impact of the next. As he became older, he began to sense an equation between his role and the role of a woman. One day, when he found himself admiring a male body, he presumed his attraction was another indication that he was different, womanlike and, perhaps homosexual (his worst fear).

The pressure mounted. The more fearful he became about what the evidence seemed to suggest, the more he *used* fear as a dynamic to prevent himself from becoming what he feared most. "I must be afraid of being a homosexual or I will become one." These convictions were compounded and actually reinforced by another dynamic of his beliefs. He became aware of a growing displeasure and discomfort with women, that led to avoidance of the opposite sex. He could not possibly embrace what he feared most in himself (womanliness). But that belief created further unhappiness and self-defeating behavior. Ultimately, the discomfort became so intolerable, he decided to engage in a homosexual act as a way to relieve the "unbearable" strain of his fear. Then, he speculated, at least the constant anxiety would be over.

After his first encounter, he viewed the evidence as conclusive. He was now, by his own definition and standards, a homosexual. His fears were replaced by guilt. He wanted to hide the fact of his different sexual preference . . . for he, like the society in which he was rooted, believed "something was wrong with him." He had effectively utilized one incident as a binding confirmation of his fears. His beliefs about homosexuality and his own vulnerability to it had become a self-fulfilling prophecy.

He laughed as he quoted what he called the classic homosexual line: "Boy, was I drunk last night." His own first homosexual affair was clouded by alcohol. Yet, he knew even then, he had done what he had wanted, although his major preoccupation was responding to his fears.

After many years, he began to resent himself and the community at large for his predicament and for the secrecy. Based on these thoughts and the nagging concern of possible

216

exposure, he decided to confront the world, saying, "Yes, damn you, I am different (as if he was); I am a homosexual and it's beautiful to be a homosexual." His statement was made with anger and fury. In declaring his homosexuality, he relieved himself of the guilt and fear of being unmasked.

Although he might have tended toward homosexuality from unhappiness, he now felt generally comfortable and enthusiastic with his choice. To him, it was a moot point whether or not he would have been homosexual given a different set of circumstances. Perhaps, he contemplated, his vision of his parents, his fears and his frantic search for evidence were merely the tools by which he came to allow himself to express some of his desires. The question was not to judge his actions, but to explore why they were shrouded in fear and anxiety—why, even today, did he still feel a nagging discomfort?

One great contradiction did exist in his sexual declaration . . . Why did he "have to" announce it? Why is it that people who love people of the opposite sex don't go around announcing they're heterosexuals? Since they believe their inclinations are perfectly natural, they have no questions to ask or statements to make. In contrast, the affirmation, "I am a homosexual," is not merely a descriptive pronouncement . . . in our time, in our vocabulary, it is a judgment.

So when this student called himself a homosexual, he, too, was accepting the implicit and emphatic bias that he was "different" and, conceivably, "bad." Even though he insisted his sexuality was positive, he realized he still had many beliefs about his separateness and unacceptability . . . in essence, these were the very reasons for the declaration. He was angry, resentful, guilty and wanted to relieve himself. By his own admission, he knew his announcement, in part, was a disguised confession.

In addition, he had hoped to gain acceptance by exposing himself. "If I can convince them to accept me, to know I am not strange or perverse, then maybe I can more easily believe it myself." The more he explored his feelings, the more aware he was of his own continued prejudices. Beneath his assured and confident manner, he still harbored many notions about being special and less than normal. These were the beliefs he now chose to review and discard. As he became increasingly happier and more accepting of himself, his aversion to women completely dissolved. He also stopped identifying himself as a homosexual and started calling himself a human being.

This man's situation, his beliefs and his conclusions were his own . . . not an abstracted or easily generalized set of circumstances. We each create ourselves for our own reasons and in response to our own beliefs.

To varying degrees, *everyone is attracted to members of both sexes.* We can admire the body, skill and athletic movement of a major sports personality, irrespective of their sex. We can be fans of both male and female entertainers without creating an identity crisis in terms of our own sexuality. We can be male and be enthralled by the physical prowess of an actor. We can be female and be mesmerized by the sensuality of a female dancer. These attractions are at a distance and "safe." Yet even those involving acquaintances and close friends do not necessarily lead to questions and doubts about our own sexuality or "normalcy."

Nevertheless, *in order to suit the society in which we live, we focus on the acceptable attraction, which, in effect, presupposes an "unacceptable" attraction.* The effects of these beliefs can be traced through daily occurrences in which a man might freely embrace and kiss a female friend while only shaking hands with male friends . . . he keeps an appropriate distance, as if he did not trust himself. It is assumed we don't hug or kiss members of the same sex, unless, of course, we are strange and perverse. In other cultures, with different beliefs, physical expressions of friendship among those of the same sex are freely given and accepted without the undercurrent of judgments and disapproval.

In the context of our culture (and its constellation of generally accepted beliefs), the homosexual is a person, who through his fear and the judgment of others becomes something which does not exist . . . a fictitious character, i.e., one who is attracted solely to members of his own sex. He is no different from the staunch heterosexual, who often emphatically affirms his one-sided attraction and ridicules any deviations.

To be disgusted, afraid or "turned-off" to members of the opposite sex or those of our own sex is to be reacting to discomforts. In not allowing ourselves to be comfortable with one sexual group, we are functioning from our fears and from

218

unhappiness as well as from the beliefs which support them. The question to ask: Is our sexuality generated by our wants or is it a response to our not-wants?

If we are just people loving other people (be they of the same sex or the opposite sex), we then move with our own inclinations . . . coming from our happiness and wanting. We would not need to avoid members of one sex in order to justify or support our preference. This does not mean if we are happy, we would want to engage in sexual relations with members of the same sex or the reverse. Nor does it mean we will change our sexual preference or become bisexual. We would each do what seems to be natural to us.

In effect, if we were comfortable with ourselves, there would be no such judgmental label as homosexual . . . or heterosexual. There would be no homosexuals or heterosexuals. Those of us who use these terms participate, if only by default, in making implicit statements about the "differentness" and "unacceptability" of certain people and activities. Our culture, reflected in our language, creates separatism and disapproval with beliefs of "It's bad to be . . . homosexual, weak, poor, ugly, etc." Perhaps in our communal fears, we help create and reinforce the realities which we believe we "should" avert.

A sexual problem is again not sex alone. It is the fear of unhappiness working in the sexual arena.

Discard the beliefs behind the unhappiness and the problem disappears. The anxiety or fear or discomfort is in service to the superstitious belief that something bad is going to happen or is happening. Sexual behavior, like other behavior and its accompanying emotions, is infiltrated by judgments.

If I disconnect self-defeating beliefs, I then can allow myself to flow. If I find through these examples of others just one belief that I too uphold and I too want to change, then I have begun unloading some of the excess baggage collected in my head. It is not hard to choose to dump beliefs when I realize how destructive and unfounded some of them can be. And once I do that, I notice all sorts of exciting and beautiful changes. Ownership and responsiblity is not a burden, but, in fact, the wire cutters which help release

219

me from the bondage of all those beliefs I've been taught over all those years.

Sex is a beautiful and simple human procedure. It is a function of being and loving. It is communion and our stab at eternity. Sex is everything we want it to be by simply allowing it to be.

As in any other area of life, there is no right or wrong way, no good or bad, no should or should not. The tags and labels we put on sex are our way of remembering how to behave because we believe without the labels we would not know how to handle situations. Yet such beliefs, which originate from unhappiness (distrust and distaste), actually short-circuit the pleasure and freedom we could allow ourselves in our sexual relations.

If we always stay in touch with the awareness we are doing the best we can and so are our partners, that we are not responsible for their fears or enjoyments (only our own), that we can want our wants without worrying about not getting . . . then the possibilities of our sexual horizons will be more expansive and enjoyable. In addition, we would be significantly clearer in identifying the situations we would want to avoid.

Sex is from our nature. We don't require practice to do it.
The "how-to" uptightness and awkwardness usually is the direct result of moving away from ourselves (like the child, who comes not to know because he believes being himself is bad). In search for rules or cues, sex seems confusing and difficult. An appropriate example is the girl who believed she wasn't good in real life, but was superb in her fantasies. She was short-circuiting her natural flow with fears and unhappiness. In her daydreams, she knew exactly what to do to arouse and enjoy.

The books and movies of instruction are all manifestations of our self-doubt. Certainly, if we feel we could use them to be more sexually proficient, then we can do what we know to do. But perhaps a more direct way is to go with ourselves. Consult our own natural expertise. *Beneath any unhappiness, there is a knowing, natural expert.*

If I cannot be rejected, if what the other person sees and interprets is from his or her beliefs, if I am responsible for

220

only my own behavior and feelings, if nothing is wrong with me, if I am doing the best I can in accordance with my current beliefs, even when I stop myself—then, I can do anything I want, try anything I want. My happiness would no longer be hanging in the balance.

If I listen carefully and comfortably, I will learn to hear the voice within me. This doesn't mean that I would want to go out and have sex on every street corner. I'll know what I want. Allowing could mean a better sexual relationship with a boyfriend, a wife, a husband or an acquaintance. It could mean giving myself permission to explore and experiment.

If the Option attitude—to love is to be happy with—is adopted while engaging in sex, then there would be no judgments, no conditions and no expectations. And if that were so, whatever would happen would be okay. Each of us could then allow ourselves and our lovers the space in which to ask and try for what we wanted.

A note on the taboos of sex. Some of us were told masturbation would make us blind and crazy. Many were instructed that if we let a boy in our bedroom, we were bad, bad, bad. Still others heard that we could contract incurable diseases while indulging in sex. Many more were lectured that sex was "dirty" and we only do it out of sacrifice (grin and bear it). And there were those who informed us that we were not supposed to enjoy it. These are beliefs, given power by the people who act on them and transmit them.

Before I ever had the opportunity to explore and investigate my sexuality, I was bombarded by a truckload of self-defeating concepts. Sex became the garbage pail for many of my unhappy beliefs.

The first time I "dared" to touch, my arms almost collapsed under the tonnage of well-indoctrinated discomforts. But once I choose to discard my self-defeating beliefs about sex and decide to trust myself by going with my inclinations, I become more spontaneous and accepting . . . which doesn't mean I would be bad for myself. I could still know precisely how to take care of myself, to protect and check myself against disease, to practice contraception, to say no when it was not in my wanting. Originally, I was taught the fears and taboos in order to guide me to do what was "best." Un-

221

fortunately, they were couched in unhappiness (fears and distrust) and superstition which created liabilities and short-circuits. The lessons behind some of the beliefs remain. Yet, I can un-learn (choose to discard) what I know is no longer useful and wise.

Free to confront and change my beliefs, I am also as free to retain them. Each of us is the weathervane of our universe. As the wind is inseparable from the air and is part of the same movement, my sexuality is inseparable from me and is part of my movement. If I choose to consent to my own nature, then my body, my thoughts, my happiness and my sexuality become one.

We free the bird by dismantling the cage of beliefs that confines him.

THE "THINK" PAGE (SEX AND YOUR OWN NATURAL EXPERTISE)

QUESTIONS TO ASK YOURSELF:

How do you feel about your body? Are you comfortable with it?

Do you approach your sexuality and sexual relations with expectations?

Does the sex act have "shoulds" and "musts" in order to be considered good?

Are you great, good, average or poor at sex? How do you know? What are your beliefs about your skill?

Do you judge your partner's skill in sex? If so, why?

Do you say no when you mean yes? Or, the reverse?

OPTION CONCEPTS TO CONSIDER:

*HOW WE VIEW SEX IS HOW WE VIEW THE WORLD AND HOW WE VIEW THE WORLD IS HOW WE VIEW SEX.

*PEOPLE ENJOY SEX TO THE EXTENT THEY ARE HAPPY.

*POOR SEXUAL PERFORMANCE SAYS NOTHING ABOUT LOVING, BUT EVERYTHING ABOUT FEAR AND UNHAPPINESS.

*SEXUALLY, WE DO THE BEST WE CAN AND SO DOES OUR PARTNER.

*WE ARE ALL NATURALS AT SEX, IF WE ALLOW IT.

BELIEFS TO CONSIDER DISCARDING:

Sex is bad.

Sexual prowess is a sign of manliness.

Ineptitude at sex proves something is wrong with me.

Love and sex are the same thing.

If you loved me, you would desire me sexually.

The only thing that counts is orgasm.

NINTH DIALOGUE

Q. WHAT ARE YOU UNHAPPY ABOUT?
A. That I never reach a climax. God knows how I've tried.
Q. WHY DOES THAT MAKE YOU UNHAPPY?
A. A million reasons. First of all, I'm happily married . . . at least I think I am. But if I can't reach a climax, maybe it means something must be wrong with our relationship.
Q. WHY?

A. Because if we were compatible, I would have a climax.

Q. *WHY DO YOU BELIEVE THAT?*

A. Well, I don't know if I believe that . . . it's just such a damn problem. Each time we go to bed, I feel so tight inside. I always keep thinking, *Am I going to make it this time? Will it finally happen?* And it never does. Sometimes, when I'm just dressing in the morning, I start anticipating having sex that night or the night after. Even then, fourteen hours or a day before, I can feel my stomach tighten. When that happens, my mind goes blank.

Q. *WHY ARE YOU SO "TIGHT" ABOUT IT?*

A. Because I want it to happen. I'll do anything at this point.

Q. *Sure, but wanting it to happen and becoming upset about it not happening are two distinctly different things. I understand that you want to reach an orgasm. Why are you upset and unhappy about not reaching a climax?*

A. Wouldn't you be?

Q. *Maybe, but I have my own reasons, you would have yours. I'm not saying you shouldn't be unhappy, but merely asking for the reasons "why" you feel that way.*

A. Okay, I'm afraid it won't happen.

Q. *WHY WOULD YOU BE UNHAPPY IF IT DIDN'T?*

A. Because then I won't be a good lover and partner . . . maybe my husband will become dissatisfied. I don't know. Maybe I'll go someplace else for sex. That would really be awful!

Q. *If you decided to go someplace else, why would that be upsetting?*

A. Because I don't want to. I love my husband. Our marriage is not one of those made-in-heaven fantasies. We both worked at our relationship. There were many difficult years. We pulled through a lot. Now, we really enjoy each other and respect each other. This is my only big problem and I don't want it to ruin what we've worked so hard to achieve. I don't want to be unfaithful.

Q. *Then why would you be unfaithful?*

A. Because I want to reach a climax. It's like a completely

225

separate obsession. Although I love my husband, I feel I'm missing a lot!

Q. What do you mean?

A. If sex is good, then both partners should reach orgasm.

Q. WHY DO YOU BELIEVE THAT?

A. Isn't that true?

Q. What's true for one person is not necessarily true for another. Why do you believe that's true?

A. I don't know. When I really think about it, I sometimes lose all perspective on what sex is all about. Maybe someone told me climaxes were a must. Maybe it's from my past and I don't remember any more why I believe it.

Q. Sure, that's certainly possible. But since you're still believing it now, why?

A. I don't really have an answer.

Q. WHAT ARE YOU AFRAID WOULD HAPPEN IF YOU DIDN'T BELIEVE IT?

A. I wouldn't try to reach a climax. If it's not that important, not a must . . . then who would care. Oh, but that's silly, whether good sex is defined with or without orgasm, I'd still want it.

Q. If that's so, that you could still want it although it is not a "must," then do you still believe that "orgasm" is necessary for good sex?

A. No, I guess I really don't. And if I don't, maybe it's not such a crisis after all. At least, maybe it doesn't have all the implications I thought it did in terms of marriage. Maybe it is manageable. But I am still unhappy about it.

Q. WHY ARE YOU UNHAPPY ABOUT IT?

A. Because I still want it, even if my marriage would be great without it. My husband has been understanding and tries to be helpful, but that doesn't solve it.

Q. What about not having a climax makes you unhappy?

A. Maybe it means something is wrong with me; I'm not a complete woman or something. Maybe there is something strange about me.

Q. What do you mean?

A. Most of my friends don't have any trouble. We've talked. (laughing) Yet, sometimes, I wonder whether they told me the truth. It's really hard to face, no less admit it to someone else. But if they were honest about not having any trouble, why should I have such a problem?

Q. *Why do you think?*

A. Somehow, I always think if I just let myself go and I really want to, I'll become a nymphomaniac. Really, I'm not kidding. I know it sounds crazy. Every time that I have reached an orgasm, and that's been only several times in my whole life, I feel so high like I could just have sex day in and day out. And that really scares me.

Q. *WHY DOES IT SCARE YOU?*

A. Because I might exhaust my husband and ruin my marriage. And maybe I'd want it so much that I would start sleeping with anybody. That would be awful.

Q. *Why would you be unhappy if you decided to sleep with "anybody"?*

A. Because I don't want to.

Q. *Then, why do you believe you would?*

A. Because my sex drive will increase so much that it will be beyond my control.

Q. *How do you know that?*

A. I don't.

Q. *But, somehow, as you say, you act as if you do and become unhappy about it. If you wanted sex all the time, why would that be unpleasant?*

A. It wouldn't . . . but if I ruined my life, that's not what I want.

Q. *Okay, if that's not what you want, if you know that much to take care of yourself, WHY DO YOU BE-LIEVE YOU'D BE BAD FOR YOURSELF?*

A. I really wouldn't be bad for myself. I guess I'd just cut it off.

Q. *Cut what off?*

A. My sex drive.

Q. *Oh, if you ARE in control of your sex drive, then why are you afraid it would get out of hand?*

A. Oh (long pause).

Q. *What are you thinking?*

A. It really wouldn't get out of hand. There's nothing to be afraid of. I know, when I said I'd "cut it off" it was the first time I really knew that it was me in control.

If I could turn it off, then I could turn it on. Somehow, I had always wanted to believe this had nothing to do with me. Blame it on my organs. Blame it on my husband and my lovers before him. It seemed too "unapproachable" to be responsible for.

Q. *And now?*

A. It's really okay.

Q. *How do you feel?*

A. Better, but not finished.

Q. *What do you mean?*

A. I see now that I held myself back. If I wasn't afraid of becoming a "bad" person or nymphomaniac, then I could let myself go. My uptightness really was part of my holding back. Somehow, now it seems like I feel phobic about it. If I haven't allowed it to happen for so long, how can I do it now.

Q. *What do you want?*

A. To enjoy sex and allow myself to reach orgasms. But, I'm feeling uneasy.

Q. *What are you afraid is going to happen?*

A. That I'm still going to worry about it, not because of the other fears, but just simply worry that it's not going to happen now that I want it.

Q. *WHY WOULD YOU WORRY ABOUT IT?*

A. Because I want it to happen.

Q. *I know, but why does worry go along with wanting it to happen?*

A. I don't know.

Q. *What are you afraid would happen if you weren't worried?*

A. It wouldn't matter to me and then maybe I won't have it. Oh, but that doesn't make any sense. I really could want it without being worried. I guess my worrying, oddly enough, stops me from having it. Without the pressure, I'd be much looser and probably have it. Maybe the question for me is will it be okay for me not to have it since that's what I'm scared about?

Q. *Do you want to answer that?*

A. Yes. If I can't reach an orgasm now, after working through my beliefs and fears, then it will somehow say that it's beyond my control.

Q. *Why do you believe that?*

228

A. If I worked it out, then I should reach a climax.

Q. *WHY "SHOULD" YOU?*

A. There it is again. I'm putting pressure on myself. I'll end up in the same place for a different reason. It's crazy what I do to myself. As long as I "must" reach an orgasm, I tie myself up.

Q. *What do you mean?*

A. It's like a test. You tell yourself you have to get a good mark and usually become so upset and anxious, you can't even concentrate. You mess it all up, which is exactly the opposite of what you wanted.

Q. *Let's take your metaphor and bring it back to here and now. For you, right now, even though you think you've worked it out, DO YOU BELIEVE YOU "MUST" REACH A CLIMAX?*

A. No. Of course not. But if I say it's under my control, and all the doctors said I was physically perfect, then what does it mean if I still don't make it?

Q. *What do you think?*

A. I don't know.

Q. *If you guessed at it, what do you think?*

A. Well, maybe there are other beliefs that I haven't worked through or changed . . . maybe that's what would still be holding me back. Maybe I'd still have other reasons to hold myself back.

Q. *And how do you feel about that?*

A. It would be okay now. I know I rid myself of some really heavy beliefs. If there's more, I can work it out. I know that now. (smiling) I feel a whole lot better . . . much more accepting of me.

10

money: symbol of the easy life

His hair is jet black, the exact same color and shade of his shiny new Ferrari sports coupe. He sits in an office high above the city where the clouds kiss the window panes and leave their breathy moisture. His chair sinks into the thick pile rug. Three lights on his phone unit blink incessantly as he negotiates with a secretary and an assistant beside him. He shouts orders through the opened double doors of his office, which has been decorated with knickknacks from Tiffany's. In his world, he's king. This is *his* company, *his* furniture, *his* secretary, *his* assistant, *his* phone, *his* clients and *his* energy. In the hustle of wheeling and dealing, he has hardly had time for any other interests besides his financial endeavors. His children were born and literally grew old while he was on an extended business trip. They're strangers now. His wife lost the youth in her figure years ago, but he hasn't noticed . . . he never has time to look.

The house he lives in high on a hilltop is surrounded by twenty-two parklike waterfront acres of landscaped lawns and gardens . . . all of which forms its own peninsula jutting into a tranquil bay. A series of free-form patios create leveled areas in the hillside. They are made with pebbles from a coral island and shaded by trees imported from Japan. A knoll beside his home was converted into a man-made lake, edged in stone and stocked with fish. Sitting idle in the massive garage is the second car, an aging two-year-old Rolls Royce convertible. Ancient carvings from Kenya and Tanzania, a huge Miro, small pieces of sculpture by Rodin and an original Calder are elegantly placed amid his elite collection of Bauhaus furniture.

Rush hour. The traffic moves slowly as he finds himself trapped amid the cars in a vast slow-moving river. Years ago, he loved this time as a private period to contemplate his business, prepare for meetings or just review. Lately, these rides have been painful . . . as painful as his life. He watches an old beat-up powder-blue Chevy with a family of six people. Poverty glistens like sweat on their faces. A little girl in the back seat smiles at him. He doesn't smile back . . . not because he doesn't want to, but because he is distracted. He watches an old man trying to fix a flat tire on the side of the road, his face tight and strained with years of toil. These images scare him. He finds them difficult to comprehend. Old age would not be so troublesome if it were not for all those people he had seen grow old and poor. Loss of money is his question and his fear.

He's gone over it a thousand times. The figures never change, but as he reviews them, he uses the opportunity to reassure himself. But the reassurance lasts only a few minutes. The comfort is fleeting. He has accumulated four million in investments and savings. Figured at seven percent interest, it would amount to two hundred and eighty thousand a year in interest. Based on his current rent needs and projected expenses, he could support himself on just that money. Now, he considers the additional two hundred and fifty thousand he manages to make from his business. He carefully reexamines potential investments. The market is shaky. He's lost money on REIT's and his city bonds are greatly depressed. He is concerned that the total equity of his portfolio will diminish if the recession continues.

As he deliberates, he can feel the knot tightening in his stomach. His level of anxiety rises. He knows that it might

232

sound foolish to a stranger, but all he needs is two million more and he'll be poverty-proof. Yes, he does remember what he said before he made his first million dollars. "All I need is a million and I'll be untouchable." But as he became more successful and his life-style became more opulent, he noted that one million dollars is really not a lot of money. So he decided he needed two and then three and now six million.

He pulls out a small whiskey flask from the glove compartment in his classic car and slugs down two huge gulps. Memory flashes—words of the doctor telling him he was an alcoholic. "Rubbish," he assured himself. It was completely under his control. He just drank to calm his nerves. When that money-knot kept building, he could just wash it away with some spirits.

The panic kept increasing. He became diverted from driving and took out his midget electronic calculator. The number raced before him. He needed just two more million to make it. As he leaped through the figures again and again, he rammed his pretty jet black car into the rear of that beat-up powder-blue Chevy. Climbing out of his stalled automobile, he finally settled down to exchanging registration forms as waves of nausea washed over him.

Money can be a vehicle in which we sleigh-ride across the razor edge of our unhappy beliefs.

My ten dollars is another man's hundred. Your twenty dollars is another man's thousand. My apartment is another man's villa by the sea. Money is the symbol of the easy life and it, like everything else, is not cemented in absolutes. It is relative. The millionaire, when he is attending to his fears, believes four million is not enough to insulate him from potential unhappiness. He uses his discomforts to motivate him to continue to amass more money. His anxiety about money was never solved by money, because his beliefs of unhappiness made money a problem . . . getting it, giving it, retaining it.

Some of us believe money is a sign of dignity and self-worth. Others envision it as man's corrupter, cementing him to materialistic garbage. Some want money to buy food and shelter. Others want it to buy love, happiness and immortality. Money, like love, health, sex, is a multifaceted symbol to which we attach many fears and judgments.

What we feel abuot money, how we gather it, has little to do with an intrinsic characteristic of currency . . . but everything to do with our beliefs and wants.

No one is outside the circle of currency in a capitalistic economy unless he is a ward of the state confined to an institution or an infant whose association with the environment is very elemental.

Everyone else either directly pursues money or finds a caretaker to do it for them.

Whether I am overt in my approach to gather the fundamental tool of our barter system with my own labor (the direct method) or whether I find others (husbands, wives, parents, uncles, estates, religious orders, etc.) who do it for me (the caretaker system), I am involved . . . deeply involved.

Most of us spend a substantial segment of our waking hours working for it. The education of our children is dedicated to it.

Even if I were "poor" or "underprivileged," and by my own declaration or by apparent "victimization" of circumstances had no means of self-support, I might still pursue my piece of the nickel-dime pie by applying for aid and assistance from welfare agencies and charities. The waiting on endless lines in soiled gray corridors, the completing of intricate forms in duplicate and triplicate, the negotiating with faceless bureaucrats infatuated with rules and regulations, and finally the endorsing of checks delivered by social service agencies, is a very active method of pursuing and working for funds. As a welfare recipient, I would be using the state agency as the "caretaker" to gather and distribute funds to me . . . but not without a price.

Even as a radicalized progressive, who proclaims nonparticipation, my detachment would be suspect. Eventually, I, too, for certain select items would participate in the system of money and merchandise traders by deciding to be involved when it suits my personal concepts of acceptable effort and value. Thus, even the utopian communes I might elect to join, structured on an egalitarian and socialistic foundation, go outside their border for such staples as automobiles, tractors, and other equipment they cannot manufacture. The funds generated for such purchases are usually from the overflow of products made within the community . . . an overflow generated by a well-defined internal economic structure of trades and bartering.

By stripping away the beliefs of nonparticipation and accepting the awareness we all pursue money to varying degrees and in varying fashions, we begin to permit a journey through our related beliefs.

The preoccupation and focus on a monetary reality is merely an observation, not an indictment or criticism. Only when I complicate my fiscal activities with my fears or camouflage them with my discomforts do they become an expression of self-defeating beliefs and short circuits.

In unveiling any unhappiness that either fuels or infects my pursuits, I provide myself with an opportunity to clarify my financial concerns and employment endeavors so I may then gather money (as I choose and to the extent I choose) or not gather it, as a clear and comfortable response to my material wants rather than as a function of needing or fearing.

Money has its own vocabulary. Often wealth is equated with power, respect, and intelligence; middle income is envisioned as synonymous with steadiness, reliability, trustworthiness and honor; poverty is translated as deprivation or victimization.

Whether we advocate pride or embarrassment in wealth or poverty or in any economic level, we are attaching labels and making judgments about financial status. Such an activity is not without its disconcerting twists. For example, the respect and power money generates for us is usually based on fear or envy, both of which are hollow tributes.

And yet, the clichés abound, articulating the complex system of superstitions beneath the surface of our statements. "It's as easy to fall in love with a rich man as with a poor man." "It's difficult to hold onto a dollar." "Money makes the world go round." "Find the job that pays the most." "Money makes you happy." "Only the poor man suffers." "Money is power." "Money is evil."

To the degree we view money through the fog of illusion and unhappiness, our clarity is inhibited and our discomforts take precedence.

Oftentimes, just the fear of poverty and the pressure of maintaining my job can create short circuits that go against my apparent goals. Lack of understanding instructions, mistakes and forgetfulness, arriving late to work, the pain of unexpressed anger, colds, headaches and more serious illnesses are just a small sampling of the backfires. I do the best I can in accordance to all the beliefs I currently subscribe to. Thus, if I become fearful or anxious, I do so in an effort to take care of myself. But do I have to be unhappy in order to want money and work for it—or in order to decide *not* to work for it? The answer is clear: I "have to" become unhappy only if I want to or believe I have to!

Ultimately, in discarding the beliefs which are self-defeating and sources of unhappiness, I not only increase my effectiveness in generating money, but become more cognizant of my own inclinations and more concentrated on my wants as the primary concern of my efforts.

In flowing with our own propensities, money might just come as the natural by-product of our wants and energy.

On the surface, we each have our own money value system, manipulated by our own ingenuity, resources, efforts and time. But beneath those commitments, we are guided by a much more fundamental vision . . . the vision we develop as the result of our beliefs.

Pursuing money falls within two major motivational thrusts: To satisfy my material wants or as a function of fears and anxieties.

Material wants are those things I believe are worth pursuing as a trade for my talents. My time and energy are then converted into currency, which is, in turn, converted into merchandise. Whether I want food, housing, clothes, a radio, a tractor, satin sheets, jewelry, or medical services—these are all commodities to be purchased. But how do I know whether I am coming from my wants or attending to my fears? Again, I need only to return to the basic question: *Am I moving toward or away?*

Do I try to gather money to feed my children because I want them well-nourished or do I fear they will starve? Do I purchase an automobile for its utilitarian factors (whatever they may be) or do I use it to bolster my self-esteem? Do I work at my current job because I love the content and meaning of my labor or do I stay with it because I fear the repercussions and uncertainties of leaving?

In each case, although my labor may appear similar, the

input or motivation is dramatically different. The crucial variables materialize in the vision, the attitudes and the tone of my pursuits . . . all of which are intimately connected to my underlying beliefs.

Although money can buy many "things," can it buy a happy and loving life? There are those who BELIEVE it does. Unfortunately, it quite evidently does not. More often, it buys only the illusion of fantasies which tend to crumble under the pressure of fears and discomforts. The wealthy, the affluent, the modest and the poor all have their miseries, violence and suicides.

The expectation that money will bring happiness is a commonly held belief and a widespread cause of unhappiness.

If I am unhappy about not making enough money or discontented with the manner in which I pursue it, the questions to ask are: What am I unhappy about? Why am I unhappy about it?

Many of us have been taught we need money, that we must have money in order to be happy. Our parents and peer groups revered it. Television and Hollywood painted fantasy landscapes about it. And the classroom finally memorialized it . . . enshrining names like Rockefeller, Hearst, Getty and Hughes, celebrating their enormous, diverse and sometimes enigmatic impact on contemporary history.

By deifying money, we tagged unhappiness to it. In order to assure myself I would pursue money with the proper enthusiasm, I learned to assume my happiness depended on it. Otherwise, I once believed: "If I don't need it, I might not want it and that would be a catastrophe." The other axiomatic belief operating here was that I would always want more than I had. Thus, my quest for money immediately became pressurized. And since I must or have to go after it, I then felt pushed. The immediate inclination is to push against being pushed despite the fact I might really want money or not want it.

There are many of us who resent being "forced" to make a living, although we certainly want to enjoy the benefits of our labor—sometimes even the content of our labor. *Difficulties are not created by money, in itself, but by our beliefs and attitudes about it.*

One student noted quite emphatically that even before he

began his working career, he was plagued by mixed emotions about money. He wanted it for what it could buy, yet hated it because he saw the quest for money as an endless treadmill onto which he felt forced to step. This initial ambivalence was later amplified by the fear he might become a "bum," since he believed he genuinely did not want to work. Often, he would fantasize sitting alone on a beach, sunning himself and eating fresh strawberries as the world toiled through its work week. But then he would alter his vision as he realized those fresh strawberries would cost money. So he would resurrect his fear of poverty. He used his discomfort to give himself reasons to stay in touch with wanting to make more money. He believed if he did not push himself and remain constantly alert, he would do something bad for himself (like quit his job). He couldn't trust himself. He had to give the desired activity strong enforcement, otherwise he might not pursue what he considered to be in his own best interest. Thus, he, in fact, became afraid to be happy . . . "to let himself go."

The implications were dramatic. "There must be something wrong with me" was one of the global judgments at the base of his pyramid of unhappy beliefs. He envisioned himself without the innate propensity to take care of himself. His attention was therefore riveted on his discomforts—not his wants. The money issue had tapped his fears and their underlying beliefs. It was only after he disconnected the network of judgments giving life to his ambivalent feelings that he found himself altering his focus and finding new direction.

For many of us, money, like sex, has been a problematic pursuit because of the infiltration of superstitions, illusions and taboos which form a tightly woven web of self-defeating beliefs. The binds are innumerable. We say it is good to want money and in the same breath verbalize our beliefs (fears) that compulsion, obsessiveness, tension and anxiety are important factors in being a successful money-maker. Beneath such assessments are many common supporting beliefs: "If I am not unhappy, I won't pursue money—I'd be indifferent." "Tension and stress are needed for ingenuity and tenacity . . . happiness dulls the brain." "If I don't need it, I might not stay in touch with wanting it." All these judgments are further grounded in other basic and global beliefs. "I don't trust my wants." "Unhappiness is necessary to motivate me." And "there must be something wrong with me."

As a support system in a society which cheers its financially affluent and builds monuments to its rich, these beliefs seem valid. But since they are generated from unhappiness and create fears and stress which divert our attention from the projects at hand and precipitate disabilities like premature heart attacks and strokes, then such beliefs can only be blockages in our path.

If we fear becoming competitively impotent or motivationless without those beliefs, perhaps it is a sign for us to address not only those beliefs underlying our desire for money, but also the network of more global concepts that support them.

There is no suggestion here that we should or should not desire money nor is there any suggestion of what amount is viewed as necessary, sufficient, or appropriate. We each decide that for ourselves.

Perhaps one of the most compelling associations some of us make is "Money is power." On the face of it, the statement seems entirely accurate, if we translate power into ability to command goods and services. Certainly wealth has the *power* of purchase. But is that the question?

A lawyer, turned corporate entrepreneur, spent twenty-two years of his life building a construction and real estate firm. Yet, the submerged turmoil beneath the polished veneer of this obsessive power-money gatherer had taken its toll.

In his initial exploration of his beliefs, he often talked about his vision of the environment which was quite cryptic and fearful . . . "Either be the master of your segment of the world or be victimized by it." Money, for him, equaled power against the persistent threat of vulnerability and victimization. It became a buttress against attack. His industriousness and productivity was his frantic way of developing power so as *not to be powerless*—as if he was.

Ironically, in his consuming anxiety and tension, he did not fall victim to some mysterious external force, but to his own beliefs and unhappiness. Although he had survived a massive heart attack, he was still distracted by abdominal pains caused by tension. His second marriage had become brittle, marred by mutual criticism and unstated anger.

Twenty-two years of business had actually been twenty-two

years of undeclared warfare. He saw his daily existence as combat in a deadly serious power struggle in which he maintained apparent safety and security with the ever-increasing size of his bankroll. He had endured marvelously, considering the stress he had subjected himself to. In effect, he always moved emphatically away from his discomforts, never permitting himself to attend to or even consider his wants. He was always too busy pushing the antithesis of power (poverty) away from his door. But, unfortunately, the money only bought possessions and maneuverability, none of which soothed the pain, dispelled the unhappiness or altered the beliefs. It had been a hollow and painful journey.

The beguiling aspect of his personality was his single-minded direction and dedication, even as he maintained his constant vigil peering over his shoulder trying to avert potential disaster. Loss of money meant loss of power. Although there were many interconnecting and supporting beliefs, a global judgment of himself as impotent and imperfect (something must be wrong with me) was a major factor in his lifelong thrust. For him, his focus had never been directed toward being happy as much as toward keeping the lid on his unhappiness.

Becoming aware of his beliefs was an amazing process for him, like a little boy juggling with all he had previously accepted or fantasized as gospel. What he viewed as self-defeating, he discarded. What he continued to believe was pragmatic, he retained. Recreating himself as the result of discarding old beliefs and creating new ones was the first joyful involvement he had ever allowed himself.

At the opposite pole from the compulsive money-maker (the power seeker, the insatiable millionaire and other over-achievers) is the apparent nonpursuer. Yet, the same beliefs of unhappiness can operate in this arena as easily as in any other.

A woman, the wife of an unemployed electronics engineer and mother of two children, has lived for four years on welfare with her family. After working for eighteen years for one company, her husband lost his job as the result of his division's failure to win renewal of a government contract. Finding himself on the street at forty years of age and confronted with a business community that viewed him as an ancient "relic," he had extreme difficulty relocating. The opportunities available were meager, and required him to take substantial cuts in salary, position and responsibility. His self-image quickly deflated. He pounded the pavement, barely containing his unexpressed rage.

Rather than seek counseling, which both his wife and his friends had suggested, he decided literally to "drop out" and discard most of the values of his current social and economic system. His stated goal was to protest the inequities of the system by bleeding it in the same way he had been bled of his youth and talents for eighteen years. He would go from unemployment to welfare.

As he settled into this dependent, inactive life-style with the apparent dedication of a crusader, he became more phobic than ever about seeking employment. The resentment and anger grew. Meanwhile, his wife had grown weary of his negative attitudes. Four years had been quite enough. She considered maintaining involvement with welfare as difficult and even more humiliating than the endless interviews necessary to obtain other means of support. On numerous occasions, she suggested economic alternatives to her husband, who refused even to consider them.

For several weeks, she enthusiastically expressed her own desire to return to work, but suddenly became frightened. She believed her reentry into the mainstream would turn her growing ambivalence toward her husband into a concrete desire for separation . . . and then divorce. Rather than confront and explore her beliefs, she decided to suppress her inclination to seek financial independence. For dramatically different reasons, she too had created her own myths about money and what the production of it might do. In effect, both she and her husband were polarized by their own fears. Money was now intricately tied to their beliefs about victimization, self-worth and separation. In remaining poor, they were both achieving something quite specific . . . they were both choosing what they envisioned was the least threatening situation.

It was only after she laid bare and discarded her self-defeating beliefs about money, lack of self-worth, fear of separation, loneliness and her supposed power to create unhappiness in others, that she decided to alter her given environment and take the initiative in her marriage. After engaging in active employment while maintaining a nonjudgmental attitude toward her husband, she found her relationship did not disintegrate as she had once so emphatically predicted. In fact, her taking care of her wants precipitated her husband's rebirth. Feeling more comfortable about himself in light of his wife's loving perspective, he decided to follow her example by confronting his own fears and beliefs. Ultimately, he decided he wanted to rejoin the working community. After persistent applications and more than thirty interviews, he regained employment equal to the status and financial reward of his former position.

During those intervening years, he had allowed himself to be traumatized by his fears and his discomfort. His beliefs of unhappiness had been the guideposts for all his feelings and behavior. Money had been a function of fearing, not a tool in service to his wanting.

Why we do what we choose to do (the beliefs behind our actions) is the key to understanding the tone and texture of our commitments and our aversions.

There are many organizations and religious societies whose interest in money is minimal or nonexistent since their focus and pursuits lie in other directions. Their casual indifference to money comes as a *natural* result of their wanting . . . which, perhaps, has turned their attention toward spiritual or missionary ends. They are not reacting against fears or needs, not responding to any explicit or implicit taboos . . . they are just moving with themselves.

By contrast, there are other groups and religious cults, dedicated to lofty ideals, who focus obsessively on money as a negative fixation: "Money is the root of all evil." Here we have the intrusion of unhappiness. Fearing evil and its unknown complications, symbolized in this instance by money, might motivate some people to be financially celibate. But when we are driven by such judgments, even if we live the asceticism of a cloistered life, we are, in part, attending to our unhappiness and fears.

If money is labeled evil, then the person pointing his finger in an attempt to flee its mythological grasp trusts neither himself nor others. "There must be something wrong with me" is a basic belief of someone who thinks having money could "make" him do evil or terrible acts.

Evil is a belief based on the judgment that something is in-

242

herently "bad." Evidence in support of that premise is the product of other judgments made with the same prejudice as the original judgment.

There are no good and evil properties to money. Like fire, which can be used to heat our homes or as a deliberate weapon to destroy them, money is simply a tool in the hands of each individual. The person who sees it as "bad" or the genesis of hostile deeds, is acting out of the terror of his own distrust and fearful beliefs. Perhaps, rather than patronize or condemn such an attitude, we can see it as a cry for help from another who is plagued by his own unhappiness and fears.

If my feelings and behavior are a function of my personal set of beliefs, why is poverty and the fear of poverty such a universal concern? The answer is neither complex nor mysterious. As I share a common environment, I share common beliefs.

And since it is you and I who give beliefs their force, we might ask ourselves: Is poverty a cause of unhappiness? Being poor can never create anger or depression . . . it is only our *beliefs about it* which can cement us to pain and despair.

Even if we just consider our words, we can extract judgments which underlie our vision of poverty. A sampling of common dictionary definitions for poor and poverty reads like a catalog of judgments, rather than descriptions. Poor is classified as "lacking in material possession or in some quality." It is defined as "barren," "sterile," "insignificant," "inferior" and "inadequate." These beliefs about poverty spotlight how "bad" it is to be poor . . . how undesirable and, in essence, how humiliating. Beyond even the material and cultural questions, poverty becomes a celebrated and culturally accepted reason to be unhappy and miserable by our linguistic connotations alone.

Rather than describing poor in terms of having (no matter how small the quantity or quality), we create the "have-not" . . . deficient in what we need to be happy.

Moving one step further, we compound the judgment by using the expression "poverty-stricken." Like the plague, poverty now becomes an affliction, similar to a communicable disease (malaria-stricken). Poverty begins to sound like a condition beyond our control. We have colored our vision and loaded our judgmental assessments . . . all of which serve to polarize, to paralyze.

If I buy all the beliefs my culture assigns to being poor (and don't I do just that every time I use the word?), then I would have to see myself as bad, inadequate and inferior if I had little or no material wealth. My own beliefs would result in my being not only unhappily poor, but infuriated or humiliated by a society which labels me as such and attempts to limit my potential for wealth by seeing me as unequal. My response to my dilemma is either anger (in reaction to the judgment) or depression and hopelessness (seeing my inferiority or inadequacy as forever limiting my possibilities) . . . all of which does NOT reflect my reality or future, but speaks to the impact of my beliefs and those of my neighbors in molding both my current reality and my future.

In responding to my situation with unhappiness, I can hate you (the system) for judging me inferior (which I too believe) and strike out against you by acting the role of a poor person (victimized, out of control and incapable). Or, I can decide to "suck" the culture that "damns" me by using it as caretaker of my wants (welfare, charity, etc.).

There are many who are bitterly unhappy about living below subsistence levels (another judgment?). We can deduce from their discontent and anger that poverty taps many fearful and anxiety-producing beliefs. This does not mean if we were happy we would choose an impoverished condition for ourselves or want it for others . . . or that we would not want to see such situations remedied. *But wanting something is quite different from being unhappy about not having it.* There are those on welfare who are disenchanted and depressed, while others manage to create purpose and meaning in their lives.

Although we might want to buy a bigger home, drive a fancier car or wear more expensive clothes, how can we tolerate not having enough food or heat or living in unsanitary conditions? No one would suggest we should tolerate the continuance of such circumstances; but maybe in our misery and anger, we sap our energy and inhibit our ability to alter such conditions.

The question for each of us is distinctly personal: Why would I be unhappy if I couldn't buy what I want, even though I viewed those things as elemental? The underlying

244

beliefs might not only include fears of sickness and death, but also be married to the frustration and inertia caused by our judgments about self-worth, peer respect, victimization, impotency, loss of love and freedom.

The fear of poverty (fear of not having money) is often-times utilized as a tool of unhappiness to help motivate me to work harder and more conscientiously. "If I didn't fear it, I might not do anything to avert it." And then, "If I were 'poverty-stricken,' I might just stay there." But is that so . . . couldn't I want to live comfortably even if I did not fear being poor? Isn't it just another way I use unhappiness and dis-comfort to insure my staying in touch with taking care of myself? The implicit statement here is again one of distrust.

Even if I personally live above sustenance levels, what about the poverty of others? "Should" I be "cold" and "callous" about their problems? Since such a question is filled with judgments and prejudices, I might simply ask, "do I want to be concerned about others who have a limited quantity of funds for their support?" If I do, can I want to be responsive without first being unhappy? My unhappiness (empathy, guilt, depression) about their situation is used as a reinforcer for myself and others. More than just a motivator, it suggests I am a caring and concerned human being.

Yet, I could come from my comfort and my loving and still be just as concerned and committed. "But if I am not unhappy for them, maybe, in the end, I really won't do anything?" Well, we can ask ourselves, isn't it possible to be happy and still want to help and be involved? How many of us have shared the outrage of the poor and yet still have not been activated enough or clear enough to offer concrete assistance.

Even the benevolent hand, at times, has a reprimanding backlash. "Here, take the welfare checks, the food stamps and go away . . . your presence makes me uncomfortable and guilty about what I have. I'm not responsible!" Thus, our assistance is often clouded by the fears we too have of the very situation we are trying to remedy. We move away from our discomforts rather than toward our wants. The results can easily be self-defeating when neither the "giver" nor the "receiver" (can we really differentiate between them?) is attending to his desires. Ironically, while we are riveted to fears about money and its meaning, we are not reviewing our beliefs and creating an opportunity to change them. The input remains stifled and we perpetuate the circle of poverty.

Buddha once said . . . Give a man a fish and you feed him for a meal; teach a man how to fish and you feed him for a lifetime. But teaching and wanting to learn is extremely difficult in relationships couched in fear and embedded in judgments of sterility and inferiority.

If I come from my good feelings without all the judgments and expectations, I would certainly be as much a humanitarian as those coming from their fury and frustration. The ultimate wants might appear to be the same, but the beliefs about how to get there are very different. The comfortable person moves toward his wants with directed energy, while the angry person moves from his anger (fears and judgments) and away from his not-wants. In many ways, the happy person, who is not diverted by attending to his anger or outrage (and consuming energies in that direction) will be more focused and probably more effective in helping others help themselves. Here again . . . it is not simply a question of money or our response to the lack of money. Ultimately, it is a question of our beliefs.

Change the beliefs and you change the situation. If I had barely enough food, but did not believe my situation to be degrading and did not see myself as victimized, deprived or inadequate, then I would not act like a poor person (as if I was victimized, deprived or inadequate). I would not be responsive to my misery since there would be none. I would just function in accord with my wants and harness my power to help me get what I want.

This leads us back to an essential concern: Can we do what we want and trust that money (enough to fulfill our requirements) will come as the natural result of our activities? Do we have to worry about or even focus on money in order to get it?

Many of us graduated from academic wombs without ever considering what we truly wanted. Instead, we immediately searched for "realistic" money-making endeavors as we were supposed to ("you have to think ahead"). Many of us believed earning money would not be fun, but would instead probably be displeasing and difficult work ("you can't have your cake and eat it"). It was as if sweat and tears were necessary in order to live the decent, productive life. Think about all the beliefs we harbor which imply we could not earn a living at what we enjoy . . . perhaps such concepts resulted in our *never even trying*. "You can't look at life through rose-colored glasses," we were told.

Perhaps, instead of staying in touch with wanting money (a belief which we were taught was a necessary ingredient to achieve the "good" life), we could move beyond such preoccupations and concentrate on what we want to do and on the content and tone of the life-style we want to lead.

In trusting our inclination and pursuing our wants, we might find the money would come. "Well, that's absurd . . . suppose I decided to sit on the balcony of my apartment and contemplate the horizon—it would be silly to assume the money would just roll in." Perhaps, that's true. But would we want to sit all week or all year in one spot while contemplating the horizon? Remember, the consideration here is not to follow our fantasy or fear, but to go with our wants.

What we can consider is making our *wants* the primary concern and money the adjunct to that concern rather than the focus of our direction.

Perhaps, this very simple and mellow story of one "trusting" Option student would demonstrate the perspective. He was in his mid-thirties, a very successful stock analyst in a time when his associates in the market were having extreme difficulties just maintaining themselves. An honor graduate with a Ph.D. in economics and the owner of a massive colonial home on the outskirts of a major city, he was, nevertheless, unhappy with the nature of his job, the cool and impersonal tone of his working environment and the unenthusiastic quality of his own input.

By contrast, he would sit alone in his basement, thoroughly absorbed and elated when involved with his love: carpentry and the design of handcrafted wooden toys. But this interest had always been systematically dismissed by parents and friends as cute and frivolous, lacking in dignity and social relevance. Yet, from time to time, to his utter delight, someone would buy one of his wooden toys with great excitement or plead with him to hand-carve a chair or cabinet. The money generated was minimal, but the personal joy of combining his creative impulses with the use of his hands for just several hours each week was more than sufficient reward.

For several years, he quietly explored other professional endeavors, trying to find another application for his skills and credentials. Never once did he consider his "love," his "hobby," worthy of such a grand elevation as full-time involvement. In addition, he believed the amount of money he would make in handcrafted carpentry would be ridiculously limited compared to the lucrative aspects of his present occupation.

Finally, as his discomfort and resentment increased, he decided to explore his unhappiness and the beliefs which supported it. Like stripping away layers of an old shell, he began to shed his armor of old, but current, beliefs which were little more than a straitjacket of self-defeating concepts. After he unearthed and dispensed with his own fears about not being good for himself and his own confusions about his self-worth, he decided no longer to define his life by the judgments of others which he had so readily adopted and internalized. His choice of occupation had not caused his unhappiness, but his unhappiness had been influential in guiding him to choose his current occupation.

After several months of self-exploration, he began to shift his focus and seriously consider carpentry as a viable alternative. Several round-table discussions with his wife produced a quick and firm decision. He was dramatically to change his life-style. Without any foreknowledge of the future and without any guarantees, he defied thirty-five years of "drummed in" heritage and chose to follow his wants . . . now no longer encumbered by the fears and the beliefs which had glued him to an endeavor inconsistent with his developing interests and values.

He sold his home and purchased a combination workshop/barn/house. Using his minimal savings for immediate support, he worked at constructing more toys and designing individually hand-carved pieces of furniture. Little by little, with no specific sales effort of his own, a substantial audience became exposed to the masterful quality and unpredictable ingenuity of his creations (miniature steam engines, prehistoric animals with moving limbs, antique automobiles with faces, elongated characters from the old Flash Gordon series, rocking chairs with people-like arms and legs, and a vast array of cartoon commentaries on familiar items found in most households). He did what he loved to do and found people loved what he did. Old men, little girls, hard-nosed intellects and very conservative working people were mesmerized by this twentieth-century craftsman who translated his insight and humor into wooden mirrors of his mind.

By the end of the first year, he had literally sold every piece he had crafted and developed an endless crowd of admirers and potential buyers. Money had become the natural by-product of his labors, rather than its goal. Although he had not equaled his income as a financial analyst, he noted with surprise and infectious delight that he had generated a very handsome income doing what he loved, an income far exceeding the necessities of his newly acquired life-style.

The lesson is a beautiful one. Here is a man, who had once lived attending to fears and beliefs he never quesioned, now deciding to pursue his wants . . . to come from his good feelings and trust that they would generate their own fruitful results. From attending to his own inclinations, the money did come. Once he cleared himself of unhappiness, he KNEW what to do. The irony for him was the realization he had always KNOWN what to do, but had consistently chosen to ignore the voice within.

When I am unhappy about my economic circumstances, I inevitably divert my attention away from wanting, making and enjoying money. It even inhibits me from deciding to move in other directions. Tension and anxiety become more than just souring agents; they cloud my vision and veer me away from my wanting. Acting out of fear of losing or fear of not having is pushing against my *not-wants* (poverty, rejection and loneliness).

If I allowed myself, trusted myself, I could know anything I decided to do would be okay. Therefore, in permitting myself my wants, I might determine money is really a clear and important priority or decide to give it minimal significance.

There are no ground rules, except the ones we choose to live by.

Often, there are many more possibilities than we allow ourselves to perceive . . . for our vision of the world is taken in through the prejudices of our beliefs. *We create our own limits.* But in having that power, we can also expand and change them as we want. We can also dispense with them.

Then we would be free to move with our wants rather than

away from our not-wants . . . a movement in harmony with the flow of our nature.

Perhaps, like the stock analyst turned toymaker-lover, if we decided to allow ourselves to follow our natural propensities, we too might be witness to money becoming the natural and easy by-product of our efforts and energy. Or, perhaps, like the spiritualist or mystic or original thinker, in heeding the voice within, we might turn our eyes toward visions as yet unseen.

THE "THINK" PAGE (MONEY: SYMBOL OF THE EASY LIFE)

QUESTIONS TO ASK YOURSELF:

Are you afraid of not having enough money? If so, why?

Are you comfortable having the money you do have?

Do you want more money? If you don't get it, will you be unhappy?

Do you believe money buys happiness? Or freedom?

Are you comfortable doing what you do to earn money? If not, why not? Do you see yourself as having alternatives?

Is is hard for you to give money away? Why?

Do you envy those with more financial resources than you? If so, why?

OPTION CONCEPTS TO CONSIDER:

*WHAT WE FEEL ABOUT MONEY HAS EVERYTHING TO DO WITH OUR WANTS AND OUR BELIEFS.

*EVERYONE (WITH FEW EXCEPTIONS) EITHER DIRECTLY PURSUES MONEY OR FINDS A CARE-TAKER TO DO IT FOR THEM.

*MONEY IS GATHERED EITHER TO SATISFY WANTS OR AS A FUNCTION OF FEAR AND NEED-ING.

*MONEY CAN BE USEFUL IN BUYING A MATE-RIALLY EASIER LIFE, BUT NOT A HAPPY OR LOV-ING LIFE.

*THERE ARE NO GROUND RULES EXCEPT THE ONES WE CHOOSE TO LIVE BY.

*WE CREATE OUR OWN LIMITS.

BELIEFS TO CONSIDER DISCARDING:

Money buys happiness.

Money is evil.

The best job is the job that pays the most.

Only the poor man suffers.

Money makes the world go round.

If I don't NEED money, I might not stay in touch with wanting it.

TENTH DIALOGUE

Q. WHAT ARE YOU UNHAPPY ABOUT?
A. Not having enough money.
Q. What do you mean?
A. I have two children to support. My husband and I

split three years ago and he decided to live in Spain. He was an illustrator and I don't think it mattered where he lived. His last gracious gesture was to give me the house, both cars and all the furniture. Initially, I thought it was fair . . . after all, he had his life to lead. But, you know, after awhile, the money I received from the sale of the house and car finally ran out. At one time, it seemed like so much money, but now it's completely exhausted and here I am.

Q. *Which is where?*

A. Out of it . . . not enough to live on. I do free-lance work, writing and designing educational materials for secondary school children. But the jobs aren't frequent enough or well-paying enough to really support us. Oh, not that I'm not grateful. The work is super; it keeps my head alive and I'm glad for the money . . . but I don't know what to do (begins to cry). I'm sorry, I didn't mean to do that.

Q. *WHAT ARE YOU UNHAPPY ABOUT?*

A. I feel like such an ass. I mean there are so many people with more dramatic problems and here I am complaining. With Jackie and Tommy, two wonderful kids and a really decent place to live, who am I to complain?

Q. *WHY ARE YOU UNCOMFORTABLE ABOUT COMPLAINING?*

A. I guess because I feel like a money-grubber.

Q. *What do you mean?*

A. Like all I want is more money. But, it's true . . . that's all I want. I don't mean to sound simplistic or dense, but if I had just a bit more each month, it would make all the difference.

Q. *In what way?*

A. I have just about enough for the kids and the house . . . the food, bills, all those kinds of things. Let's say I can just about cover all the so-called necessities. But then I don't have a nickel left over for me and that's really a drag.

Q. *What do you mean?*

A. Well, it's the whole bit. Not to have enough money to buy clothes once in a while or go out for dinner or even go to a movie. That's all okay . . . until it becomes the scene month after month and finally, it's year after year. I can't stand being so trapped.

Q. *What do you mean "trapped"?*

A. Having no choices. If I just want a breather from the kids, I can't take one. Not that I don't love being with them. My children are really my joy. Yet, sometimes I just want a change of scenery, if only for a few hours. I don't even have enough money to spare for a baby-sitter. I feel condemned to some vague confinement. And what's really ironic is my prison has no bars ... its walls are invisible. It's just so damn frustrating.

Q. *What about it is so frustrating?*

A. I guess it's the feeling there is no way out.

Q. *DO YOU BELIEVE THAT?*

A. (long pause) Well, not quite like I said it. There's always a way out of everything, I guess. But what I would have to do, I don't want to do ... I don't even think I can do it.

Q. *Could you clarify that?*

A. Sure. I could apply for full-time work, but then I'd be away from the kids the entire day, leaving them in a day care center for working mothers. Not that it would be so bad for them, but it would be a disaster for me. I'd work all day and then get home every night to cook and handle all the other chores. It would be a worse grind than what I have now. You see, it's a bind ... no matter which way I move, I don't get the problem solved.

Q. *What do you want?*

A. Just a hundred dollars more each month ... that's all. It's not a lot of money, except when you don't have it. (loud sigh)

Q. *Why did you sigh?*

A. If I had the money ... believe me, if I could take a break just once a week, I'd be a better person, a better mother. I know I would! It's no picnic, I can tell you. It's like having a low grade infection ... not visible or obvious, but always there, always draining you.

Q. *WHAT ARE YOU AFRAID WOULD HAPPEN IF YOU WEREN'T UNHAPPY ABOUT YOUR SITUATION?*

A. How can I not be unhappy about it?

Q. *I'm not suggesting you should be. I'm only asking, what are you afraid would happen if you weren't?*

A. I don't know. Maybe, if I weren't unhappy, I'd just wallow in it, not knowing any better.

Q. *Are you saying by being unhappy you stay in touch with wanting more?*

A. Yes, I guess so. (long pause) You mean I stay unhappy about not having enough money so I will remember that I want more?

Q. *What do you think?*

A. Well, if that were true, then I would be purposely making myself unhappy about my money difficulties. (smiles) Stupid, really dumb. But as I talk about it, it sounds right. That's sad.

Q. *Why "sad"?*

A. Because I'd have to be a real idiot if I made money that important in my life.

Q. *Why would that make you an idiot?*

A. Listen, Jackie and Tommy and me, we're all fine. I'm not poor, just very, very tight. Who am I to complain?

Q. *What are you saying?*

A. I'm saying maybe I don't have the right to want more . . . and yet I do.

Q. *What do you mean by "right"?*

A. Like I'm not sure I'm deserving. I know this will sound silly, but sometimes I think if I get more money, maybe one of the kids will get sick.

Q. *DO YOU BELIEVE THAT?*

A. Yes and no.

Q. *Why don't we take the "yes" part of your answer. WHY DO YOU BELIEVE ONE OF YOUR CHILDREN MIGHT BECOME ILL?*

A. (long sigh) The first thing that pops into my head is . . . retribution for my selfishness. Maybe I want the wrong things, maybe in some weird way, I don't appreciate what I have. As if money is all important . . . more important than health. But, it isn't. I want my children to be healthy and I also want more money. It doesn't make much sense; the whole thing is just a superstition.

Q. *What do you mean?*

A. It's like an old wives' tale. You kind of hear a lot of people say it and somewhere underneath you buy it

255

without ever really talking about it or looking at it. But when you really unearth what you're afraid of, it dissolves. Like right now.

Q. *Are you saying you no longer believe it?*

A. Yes, that's over. I guess it was one of the thoughts I had that kept me going back and forth like a scared rabbit.

Q. *In what way?*

A. Every time I think of one of my babies getting sick, I would immediately stop thinking about money. It was a braking system. Like penance, I see myself as being deprived, feel terrible . . . all this as a trade for healthy children.

Q. *And now?*

A. (chuckling) Well, now that my superstition has lost its gravity, I think I can want money any time or more of the time . . . but then I'll just be aware of being unhappy more of the time.

Q. *WHY WOULD YOU BE UNHAPPY WANTING MORE MONEY?*

A. It's not wanting it that makes me unhappy; it is not getting it.

Q. *Okay. WHY WOULD YOU BE UNHAPPY IF YOU DON'T GET IT?*

A. Then my situation will remain the same.

Q. *And why would that be so disturbing?*

A. Because I don't want it to be the same, but what can I do?

Q. *What do you want to do?*

A. (looks away and smiles) I can write you a list as long as my arm.

Q. *Of your wants or your fantasies?*

A. Oh, those would be my fantasies . . . and yet, one day, I might really begin to want them.

Q. *What do you want now?*

A. Well, feeling freer to want more money, I'd like to maybe solicit for more free-lance work. I love the involvement, the research . . . it gets my juices going.

Q. *Can you do it if you want to?*

A. Sure, at least I can certainly solicit. I could try. (face cringes) Hey, I don't want to get up from all this and find I can't get more work. I'm just setting myself up for disaster.

Q. *What do you mean?*

A. Just what I said. I'm starting to feel much better, but for what? Suppose I can't get any more work. That would really be a downer.

Q. *In what way?*

A. Then I'd really be miserable.

Q. *Why?*

A. It's like having your heart set on something and then being disappointed.

Q. *Why would you be disappointed if you didn't get the jobs or the money?*

A. Wouldn't anybody?

Q. *Perhaps, but each person would have his own reasons. What are yours?*

A. I guess when I really want something and don't get it, that's my automatic response.

Q. *Why is that?*

A. It's like an up and then a down.

Q. *Could you explain what you mean?*

A. Sure. You picture the money in your mind and everything you're going to buy. You almost have it. So when reality doesn't match up, it's a real down.

Q. *What about not getting is a real down?*

A. Then I feel cheated. Lacking. I sort of begin to expect it will happen and when it doesn't, there's no place to go but down . . . I mean, become unhappy.

Q. *DO YOU BELIEVE THAT?*

A. That I have to be unhappy? (a sigh and then a huge grin) I guess not. There have been other things in my life which I didn't get and yet I didn't go berserk over it.

Q. *WHAT ARE YOU AFRAID WOULD HAPPEN IF YOU DIDN'T GET UNHAPPY ABOUT NOT GET-TING?*

A. Wow . . . the same thing pops into my head as before. Maybe I won't really go after it or maybe it'll prove it didn't matter.

Q. *Are you saying by being unhappy, you stay in touch with wanting money and proving to yourself it's important?*

A. Yes. I never realized how much that was part of the way I functioned. It's unbelievable, yet I see I do it all the time.

Q. *Do you think you could be happy and still want more money?*

A. Yes, yes of course I could. And proving things are important to me by being miserable doesn't make much sense anymore. I don't have to be unhappy to know I want something. Okay, that's a real change for me. Okay . . . now I'm not unhappy, but I still have my money problem.

Q. *What do you want to do about it?*

A. (broad smile) Find more free-lance work. Definitely! (drifts and begins to look agitated)

Q. *WHAT ARE YOU FEELING?*

A. Why is it so important to me?

Q. *Why is what so important?*

A. Money. It's been like this as long as I could remember. Even when I was married. There was always something else I felt I wanted that I didn't have. And then, when I would get it, there would be something else. And for each thing I decided I wanted, I always believed I had the best of reasons. I guess if I get more work, maybe I'll be unhappy because I'll decide it wasn't enough. That really scares me.

Q. *Why?*

A. Did you ever read the play NO EXIT, by Jean Paul Sartre?

Q. *Yes.*

A. Well, it would be like that. There would never be an end. Maybe that's why I haven't really tried to do anything these last couple of years. Oh God, it's such a vicious cycle. If I go to work and it isn't enough, that's terrible. If I don't, then this is an unsatisfactory condition, but there's still hope. I'm afraid it goes on forever.

Q. *DO YOU BELIEVE THAT?*

A. Sure. It would only end when I'm satisfied and you know, I've never before been satisfied with the money I've had.

Q. *Why not?*

A. Because I've always wanted more.

258

Q. *Wanting more and being dissatisfied are two very distinctly different movements. WHY DO YOU GET UNHAPPY if you see yourself as not having enough?*

A. I can't really answer that. It's the way I am.

Q. *I know you feel it's part of you . . . let's try to tackle it from another direction. WHAT ARE YOU AFRAID WOULD HAPPEN IF YOU WEREN'T DISSATISFIED WITH NOT HAVING ALL THE MONEY YOU WANTED?*

A. Then I wouldn't want more.

Q. *Are you saying being dissatisfied keys you into wanting more?*

A. Yes. I can't believe how this keeps coming up. It's incredible what I've been doing to myself. I get it both ways. Being dissatisfied motivates me, but then fear of being dissatisfied later stops me. In the end, neither gets me what I want. By seeing all this as "the way I am," I guess I would never believe I could change it, but now I see I can. I've had it and I'm different starting right now . . . and you know how I know I'm different?

Q. *How?*

A. I don't believe the same things any more.

Q. *What are you wanting?*

A. I was going to answer more money, but you know, I guess I'm really wanting to be happy . . . to feel the way I do right now. I don't have all the money I want, yet I don't feel deprived. I'll just find more work. Pure and simple. So beautifully simple. I'll try to make more money if I can . . . and that neither feels like a threatening nor unhappiness-producing situation. And if what I can generate is not enough . . . well, I can deal with it then. (long pause) Right now, I feel so good and for me, right now is all that counts.

11

possibilities of psychic experience

The little dot kept moving out of focus as the heavy drone of a radio seeped into the room and filled it like old cigarette smoke. My body felt almost weightless as if suspended just a fraction off the mattress. The floating was mellow and comfortable. There was nothing to do. The chores and obligations of my everyday existence were temporarily suspended during this siege with fever and flu.

Lying in bed for two days, trying to sweat it out by beating the temperature at its own game. My lips were parched and parted like the floor of an open field baked by the sun. I lingered in this soupy twilight where sleep borders on daylight, holding the very nodule of my consciousness in the balance. The howling wind whipped at the windows as a heavy blanket of snow powdered the world white.

Late evening. No work today or tomorrow. No important conference to consider, no complex problem requiring an immediate solution. Infatuated with the journey, I gave myself the freedom to float and concentrate on snow as it created the season's first blizzard . . . tapping its frozen melody on the window.

Then, just as peacefully and casually as any of my other perceptions and thoughts, a clear, yet foreign idea entered my mind. "My friend's Manor House is going to blow up." "Oh really," I answered myself, amused. My friend's house was a piece of real estate I had agreed to watch while he was on an extended business trip. It was a quaint old mini-estate house, with thirty-three rooms that had been divided into apartments.

Yet the unlikely concept recurred vividly in my mind's eye. "My friend's house is going to blow up." A soundless sentence never spoken, yet communicated. This time, I concentrated on the newly emerged thought. With no specific references or foreknowledge, I became aware that in the top-floor apartment a valve had been removed from one of the radiators. Remembering that the heating plant was one continuous closed-steam system, the result would be dangerous and a potentially explosive situation. Without water, the boiler would burst unless stopped by a back-up safety device. Somehow, I was also aware the safety valve was not operating. Yet, how could I know all this since I was barely familiar with the mechanics or even the physical layout of the house. Nevertheless, I sensed the danger was increasing during the very seconds in which I contemplated it.

Now! How clearly I could hear the urgency echo in my head. Now! Move rapidly! Avoid an unthinkable disaster!

With considerable effort, I rolled out of my bed and began to dress. I called my wife and casually informed her that my friend's house was going to blow up. I asked her to come with me. For several long seconds we both looked at each other; then she nodded. No hesitation. No resistance. Not even a question. In some bizarre way, her response was supportive of mine.

As I brushed the accumulating snow from the car window, I could feel the wobbly unsteadiness of my legs in response to a fever of over one hundred and three. During the drive, neither of us talked. All concentration was on the road, hardly visible beneath seven inches of soft and treacherous snow. Even later, when we reached the building, she never once asked me how I knew what I said I knew.

Her implicit and immediate trusting helped support my

impulse and direction. I believed what I was doing was absolutely wild . . . yet it felt absolutely right—moving without any questions or judgments.

It was eleven o'clock when we arrived. The snow had created small mountains and valleys against the side of the house. Graceful tunnels were formed under tightly-grouped trees. Trudging through the drifts, I fumbled with the unfamiliar keys in search of the one to the basement door. Reaching the rear of the house, I found the right key. On entering, I found the boiler room incredibly hot. For a moment, I hesitated and asked myself in a very sober tone, "What the hell am I doing here?" But just as I verbalized the question, it seemed answered and disappeared.

The boiler raced and belched out strange noises and groans. The gauge showed the pressure and heat to be well beyond the safety point—in fact, it was almost beyond being read. The safety valve, just as I had somehow known, had never functioned in closing down the unit.

Forty thousand thoughts ricocheted in the cradle of my brain. Nothing took root. "Should I evacuate the building?" "Should I add water through the hot water heating unit and replace the missing water?" "If I do that, will the boiler blow up in my face?"

The confusion grew. I could feel the energy speeding through me. Consciously, I focused my attention on my breathing in order to relax . . . to go back to the ease and the comfort of the float. Quietly, my mind ceased its internal rush. Slowly, my hands rose up from my sides and grabbed the feed valve. I turned the knob and let the water gush into the boiler. The hissing and gurgling were loud for several minutes, until the heat and pressure were restored to normal. A smile grew on my face.

After leaving the basement, I walked directly to the top floor apartment. I knocked on the door and asked the tenants if I could check a radiator. Out of thirty-three possible choices, I decided without any reason to go directly to the radiator at the rear of the kitchen. Lying on the floor, catching the glitter of a fluorescent light, was the valve. They had removed it and subsequently had forgotten to replace it. The vapor escaping from this single unit had exhausted the water supply of the entire system. I explained to the tenants the dangers of what they had done and left.

For weeks I searched myself for the meaning of what had happened. In a series of discussions I realized this very special experience occurred during a time *when happiness was no longer a question.* Whether it is for months, days, weeks or a lifetime, awareness and clarity increase significantly when we are not diverted by unhappiness or our efforts to escape from it. In this situation, I felt completely free, void of my usual daily concerns. The fever had also facilitated my drifting into a highly receptive and fluid state. I remembered feeling extremely peaceful, not as a function of premeditatedly making a decision to be happy, but simply by *allowing.* It was during this time that I seemed to know something for which I had no evidence.

Certainly, there are some who would want to classify this experience as ESP or psychic (an experience beyond known physical processes). Although my vocabulary propels me in that direction, those terms are tainted with a variety of mystical and bizarre connotations, including beliefs which suggest such experiences are uncontrollable and possibly dangerous. If there are any answers, perhaps they come not from our superstitions, but from understanding the nature of ourselves and our happiness.

If I am happy, coming from my own nature in which knowing and wanting are one, then what flows to me and from me would be anything and everything I am open to know, which would include receptivity to the "psychic experience." Where I have barriers (my fears), nothing will penetrate. I can always erect walls wherever I choose. The control of what I come to know and experience is always within my jurisdiction . . . as I monitor and mediate my thoughts and awareness.

In another mood, at another time, I might have thrown many spears at my apparent irrationality instead of preventing the catastrophe at my friend's house. "Logic" and "reason" might have prevailed, since I had no evidence or reason for believing my thoughts. Moreover, leaving my own house was reckless considering I was ill and accumulating snow made the roads dangerous. In effect I could have found many *good reasons not to go!* I could have "reasonably" handled the situation by ignoring it. Yet that would have served to

264

actually move me away from my awareness and wanting. It would have been *a statement of not trusting myself* ... unwilling to move implicitly with my own inclinations.

Often, we have had thoughts or feelings about people and things come to us for no apparent reason. Many parents have had "intuitive" feelings about danger to their children. Other people have reported hearing the voice of a friend or loved one in trouble although they're hundreds or thousands of miles away. Some of us know what others are going to say before the words leave their mouth. How often has a friend or acquaintance called us on the telephone at the very same moment we were thinking about them. And yet, the majority of these experiences are just dismissed as hunches, daydreams or coincidences.

Often unexplainable stories are either discarded, romanticized or cloaked in mysterious overtones. How many of us have said, "I don't want to know." Why not? The undercurrent is fear. It's my way of rippling the water and making the images disappear.

"I don't want to know because it might be bad; then I will be involved and responsible." "I might be deluded into believing my psychic intuitions and then what?" If I had said those fearful statements, I would be believing something which comes to me and through me could be "bad." And if I believed "bad" things come from me, then something must be bad or wrong with me ... otherwise, how would I come to know these "terrible" things. Ultimately, I might conclude: *trusting myself is a very precarious and dangerous activity.*

Conversely, if I trust myself, allow myself the happiness and wants, I would be in touch with knowing that nothing comes from me except what is of my nature. If I know beneath the fears and the doubts my nature is me experiencing my happiness and loving, then I could know all that I come to be aware of is also loving ... and useful to me.

In another instance, an associate of mine was working on a report for almost three consecutive hours when he decided to rest. His mind was drained by the concentrated effort. He was aware of feeling elated about the quality of the thesis. As relaxation filtered through his entire body, he piled his papers neatly beside his typewriter. Then, he described feeling a peculiar and definite inclination to look out the window.

At that very moment he saw his two-year-old daughter, who had been playing in the neighbor's yard, fall over the edge of their swimming pool. As his child's body broke the water, he bolted from the chair at a dead run.

The little girl's form went limp as it slowly descended to the bottom of the pool. Taking no more than thirty seconds, he crashed through the surface of the water and grabbed her from the deep end. He wrapped her small body in towels, amazed and joyful that she was perfectly at ease . . . almost unaware of what had just occurred. Her breathing was normal and it was obvious she had held her breath and not choked on the water.

Maybe the child knew her father was there . . . that she was okay. At the moment she fell over the edge, *father and daughter had become one*. It was as if the little girl moved WITHIN his consciousness and in some way, her falling body had triggered his first glance.

Perhaps, if we were unencumbered by unhappiness, the closeness and sensitivity that flows between us and those we love could bring us within a range of communication that defies logic and intellectual statement. It is not the product of specific effort as much as the natural result of free-flowing with our own nature. As the roar of a passing truck drowns out the music of a cricket or bird, so may the whirling frenzy of our fears and tensions drown out the messages of our inner voice. As we choose to detach ourselves from the stress and short circuits of unhappiness, we become more aware of our knowing and more allowing of our natural in-tuitions (whether we choose to view them as psychic or not). If what then surfaces exists outside a specific and documentable rationale, if our experiences become multidimensional, opening unique and penetrating connections with our environment, we can be glad for the specialness of ourselves and embrace the gift of our increasing awareness.

A frightened young woman once told of seeing a strange and unexplainable figure standing in her backyard. One morning, just before leaving for work, she glanced through a window at the rear of her house. To her amazement, she saw a strange man wearing a dark raincoat and rainhat. He looked absurd in the warm sunshine of the morning. The hot sun masked his face in shadow and the light broke around his body, softening the edges. She felt the adrenaline pumping into her system as she turned away frightened. She wanted to block the image from her mind, immediately sensing discomfort.

Then, with a great burst of determination, she swiftly turned back to the window. This time, there was no figure. She surveyed the entire area and asked herself whether or not she had really seen the man. After all, his presence and his dress seemed senseless. Her immediate impulse was to dismiss the incident, but somehow she couldn't. Each day she would look for the figure in her backyard. Each night she would peer uncomfortably from behind her bedroom curtains in search of the strange man.

Finally, after four days had elapsed, she saw the figure again. She inhaled deeply and decided to investigate. She would actually go to the back door and confront him. When she arrived, he was not there. Again, she had the queer feeling that her "apparition" was not a flesh-and-blood reality. Although the man did not appear aggressive or dangerous, her discomfort gripped her.

Opening the door, she walked to the very spot where he had stood. As she turned back to the house, she noticed that a giant old maple which literally hung over the house, had a massive vertical split. A huge portion of the tree seemed poised to fall. Remembering the intense thunder storms of the week before, she surmised it had been hit by lightning. A strong wind whipped across her face.

Immediately she decided to summon her father, who was working in his office at the rear of the house. As she and her father crossed through the living room, they heard an explosion. They both ran to the backyard, where they were aghast to find the large section of the tree had broken off and crashed through the wall of the house . . . demolishing the very office in which her father had just been working. They both looked at each other in amazement and horror. Neither of them chose to speak to the other about the incident.

Several days later, when she was consulting the sky for her own personal weather forecast, she saw the same raincoated figure standing in the yard. At first, her instinct was to alert her parents. Then, she stopped herself. Leaping down the stairs, she threw the back door open. But, again, the man had disappeared.

After surveying the broken tree she again became frightened and confused . . . wanting to erase the entire experience from her mind.

In recounting the story and allowing her memory and comfort to flow, several things became apparent to her. She had investigated the spot because of her image. In finding the broken tree and in alerting her father, she had saved his life, or at least precipitated his moving out of a situation in which he might have been seriously injured.

Previously, she had always considered herself "psychic," but tried to obliterate her thoughts and "reasonless" images believing they were bad. In effect, she thought what she might come to know would be "bad" for her . . . and she would also somehow then be responsible for things happening. Yet, in reviewing her strong attachment to her father and her good feelings for him, she realized her response to her "image" had actually helped her keep him safe.

Her multidimensional awareness and knowing was not cryptic or "bad," but beautiful and useful to her.

Sure, there are fears and anger which generate violent and vicious images. Those are very different from intuition and knowing. They come not from our good feelings, but from our unhappiness. Considering her mood and inclinations, she asserted her image did come from comfort. In allowing and acting on her awareness, rather than working against herself, she was able to actually help a loved one. Her "unexplainable" vision actually enabled her to get more of what she wanted.

As we talked, I could see the excitement capture her entire face. Before, she had been so very strained. I asked her to try to remember the image once again. The first time I suggested it, I could see her body tense. She said she couldn't remember it clearly.

Then, she relaxed and her face lit up. Yes, she could remember more now. The first time, the figure was inert with no particular expression. The second time, he almost appeared to be smiling. The third time, she distinctly remembered the figure made a gesture to her as if he was waving. She was amazed to realize her "image" actually was friendly. Her bout with the "unknown" changed as she allowed herself to remember and as she disconnected the fears surrounding the occurrence. As her beliefs changed, she reexperienced the event, had new thoughts and feelings and was in awe of her own understanding.

Whether her external "man" had real content (flesh and blood), was just a fiction of her imagination, or was of another dimension, his presence did result in a significant and life-supporting experience. Perhaps it was her way of getting in touch with her knowing . . . which comes without foundation, reasons or evidence.

Her experience was her experience. It need not be validated by another's substantiation. This again would be trying to use "evidence" to find truth. *Ultimately, she, like each of us, stands alone as the witness to truth and our own experience.* When we are not clouded by discomfort and inhibited by such self-defeating beliefs as "There must be something wrong with me," then our own personal clarity and trust become the only significant validator of all we come to know.

When we fear something, we give it horns and a tail. When we don't, we just see what there is to see.

If I knew whatever I see would be okay, I would be more permissive with my visions. If my happiness was not at stake, new awareness and information could only help me to be better equipped and more lucid as I make my way through the environment. Ideas and concepts that come from my discomforts could be filtered through my system of beliefs where they were born. Other awarenesses could simply be accepted or rejected as I come to know them.

Happiness could be my guide.

I could always ask myself the question, does this awareness move me away from my not-wants (fears) or move me toward my wants? If I am moving toward, then I can know I am coming from my own nature and not responding to discomforts and unhappiness. As a tool, the question can help me more clearly define my thoughts when I am in doubt, just as clarifying my not-wants often helps me know and move toward what I do want. There are no major decisions to make or rules to construct. I can decide what to do about my awareness when it comes to me . . . when I allow it.

These experiences are just part of a passing landscape; the flowers I pick are my own.

A major characteristic of the psychic experience is *psychic awareness either makes or could make a difference in someone's life (including our own).* The father's inclination to look at his daughter at the exact moment she fell in the pool facilitated his saving her life. My own effort to shut down a runaway boiler was infused with power and gravity because it involved others. The student with her raincoated phantom responded to an impulse that possibly saved her father's life

If we now had a "feeling" that somewhere in a forest a tree was going to fall, we'd probably ignore the fleeting image. But if our feeling or intuition seemed to indicate a little child would be crushed under the tree, the scope and significance of our experience would immediately be elevated. A casual thought would be converted into a psychic intuition.

If I were watching a horse race and suddenly saw the number five on my son's forehead, bet on number five and won, I would have called it a lucky hunch . . . an acceptable knowing. But if my son needed a very expensive operation I could not afford and winning this money enabled him to have the life-saving surgery, the experience would be shrouded in mystery and probably now classified as psychic. *The awareness and action made a difference in someone else's life.* Although, in kind, this experience is no different from what we call *knowing* . . . the accent is altered. When we speak of *knowing*, we speak of knowledge and information of ourselves and for ourselves. The *psychic experience* shifts us to a more externalized and cosmic focus . . . us in relation to others, us in relation to our environment.

At a gathering several months ago, we were discussing items about astrology and the possibility of seeing auras. Suddenly, the hostess called her three-year-old son into the room and quite casually asked him to tell us what colors he saw around each person in the room. With great ease and precision, her son said he saw yellow around me, red around someone else and a variety of other colors around the remaining people in the room. A psychic experience? Or just something within his vision to know? We later tried this experiment with several other children . . . four out of six

270

also reported seeing distinct colors around people. Somehow, the entire affair did not seem startling or mysterious. Although I had never had the experience of seeing auras when I was young (maybe that's a convenience of memory), I do not discount the awareness of these little people. Perhaps, "not seeing" auras is part of the same process by which, as a child, I came not to know.

I can run from my ideas and fears without dispelling them. I can fabricate consequences and inflate my designs. That's really okay, if I believe that would be best for me.

But somehow I notice I can never run far enough away. If I de-energize my discomforts surrounding an experience, I give myself the opportunity to remove the lid and explore the contents. The experiences cited in this chapter were not meant to amaze or even substantiate any ideas presented here. They were notations to be shared, either in the abstract or the particular. The quality or feasibility of what is said is for each of us alone to assess, not in vague terms or in the forum of debate, but in regard to the nature of our own experiences and awareness.

If something deep within us has been tickled or touched, perhaps it is a recognition and an invitation to allow more for ourselves.

If beauty is in the eyes of the beholder, so is meaning and value. I can make everything in the world beautiful by simply acknowledging it as such. It's as easy as that, *for beholding beauty is actually the experience of creating beauty.*

So it is or can be with what I decide about psychic experience. If I paint it purple with beliefs of fear, then I create my own unpleasant experience. If I color it black with concepts of doubt and distrust, then I create a confusing experience. But if I choose not to do either, but just be accepting and let it flow freely, then I might see the most I can see . . . and in the clarity of that white light, I can know or decide meaning and value.

The focus here has been on removing the barrier of unhappiness so that we might allow the flow of our own nature . . . and in that receptivity, allow a more multidimensional grasp of our environment and of those around us. For some, our inner voice has been permitted repeatedly to surface despite the distortion of unhappiness and the distractions of

271

fears. But for most of us, we have learned to turn a deaf ear, casually dismissing many of our "hunches," "feelings" and intuitions. And yet, without fanfare or specific reference, we all, at some time, have had the experience of moving with our inclinations—"I just *had an impulse* to turn at this corner," *"Something in me said* to relax and wait," *"I just knew* to go."

The Option Process of becoming happier sets the stage for increased psychic possibilities, but does it "make" me psychic?

Psychic reception is analogous to hearing. My ears and the supportive apparatus of audio perception are part of me . . . activated by sounds which occur internally and externally to my body. Before the sound, there was no hearing. Like the lute, which comes alive when someone plucks its strings, so my body and brain vibrate with the music of my world as it comes TO me. So it is with psychic perceptivity. I might discard much of my unhappiness and permit more of my nature to flower, yet I cannot create the impulse of psychic communication. How I interpret the data and what I do with it once I perceive it is, however, distinctly my choice.

The psychic experience does not originate in me, it comes to me and through me. There is nothing to do to precipitate it . . . I have only to wait, to allow.

And yet, such a description is a physical or material explanation of a multidimensional experience. Perhaps, from another vantage point, the psychic experience does originate in us . . . insofar as through our happiness and allowing, our consciousness expands beyond the walls of any physical container. Perhaps, in being more flowing, we merge more easily with people and the environment surrounding us. So when the cry for help is heard or a kiss is bestowed upon us from miles away, perhaps we have only noted what had actually occurred within.

One student described in vivid detail how he and several companions vacated a campsite in a ravine a full ten minutes before a giant boulder fell from an overhanging ledge. Without any material substantiation, he sensed the danger of a falling rock. Stone has its own life and energy (molecular activity) as does the ground beneath it. The air which encircles the rocks also responds to the stone's vibrations as its own movement. And so did this weekend explorer, who premeditatedly moved out of the rock's path—not because he had deduced the slide or seen indications of the fall, but because the rock and the ground and the air were no longer external to his awareness, but part of his ever-increasing and expanding grasp of the world. His energy was connected with his environment's energy. During the second night, he noted being aware of a mountain lion wading in the water several miles downstream. Again, beyond sight and hearing, he could describe the animal feeding on the side of the river (a fact substantiated the following morning). It was almost as if the cat moved within him or that his mind included the movement of the cat.

There are no rules to follow, no promises to adhere to, no judgments to make. In trusting our nature, we treat ourselves with a caring and loving embrace. Being open, like the child, with bristling ears, responsive eyes, receptive mouths, sensitive fingers and an alert curiosity is the beginning. Whether unexplained data, images or knowledge then comes to me or not is no reflection on who I am or what I am. When I have made it my time and for me to know, it will all come to me . . . not a moment sooner.

And the psychic experiences that might follow as the result of our personal Option evolution will be ours to confirm. We verify. We walk the path and take the journey. And "unexplained" images are just another way by which we are enriched.

THE "THINK" PAGE (POSSIBILITIES OF PSYCHIC EXPERIENCE)

QUESTIONS TO ASK YOURSELF:

Have you ever had visions or premonitions?

Are you afraid of having a psychic experience? If so, why?

Do you fear what you might allow yourself to know, really know? Why?

Do you believe in ESP types of experiences? If so, are you ready to have one? If not, why not?

Could you accept knowledge that comes from "nowhere"?

OPTION CONCEPTS TO CONSIDER:

*WHEN HAPPINESS IS NO LONGER A QUESTION, WE ALLOW OUR KNOWING, OPENING OURSELVES TO "PSYCHIC" TYPE EXPERIENCES.

*AWARENESS INCREASES SIGNIFICANTLY WHEN WE ARE NOT DIVERTED BY UNHAPPINESS.

*PSYCHIC AWARENESS DEFIES LOGIC OR INTEL-
LECTUAL STATEMENT.

*WE, ALONE, STAND WITNESS TO TRUTH AND
OUR OWN EXPERIENCE.

*WHAT COMES TO US AND THROUGH US CAN
ONLY BE BEAUTIFUL AND USEFUL.

*BEING HAPPY IS MY WAY OF ALLOWING MY-
SELF AND MY AWARENESS TO FLOW.

BELIEFS TO CONSIDER DISCARDING:

Knowing can be dangerous.

Psychic experience is reserved only for the very weird.

We are bad for ourselves.

We should fear what we don't know.

Normal, everyday people don't have ESP kinds of experiences.

If I can't explain it, it doesn't exist.

ELEVENTH DIALOGUE

Q. WHAT ARE YOU UNHAPPY ABOUT?
A. I'm not unhappy. I'm frightened.
Q. Okay; what is it that you're frightened about?
A. These uh . . . I don't know what you would call them
 . . . these premonitions I get.
Q. What do you mean?
A. Like a thought . . . no, a feeling. Not exactly a feeling
 or a thought. It's like my body tingles and I sense
 something. Every time it happens, I feel like I'm going
 to jump out of my skin.

275

Q. WHY?

A. Because it's usually something uncomfortable, to say the least. Like my sister is going to get hurt or a friend is going to lose her job. Always things like that.

Q. What is it about such awarenesses that makes you uncomfortable?

A. To know something terrible will happen.

Q. What do you mean "terrible"?

A. Well, if my "sense" tells me someone is going to have an accident, how could that be anything but terrible?

Q. But WHY is it terrible?

A. I don't want anyone to be hurt or suffer.

Q. Sure, I understand that, but why would you be unhappy that you sensed it coming?

A. Because then . . . Hey, wait a minute. How come you never asked me if my premonitions come true.

Q. Why is that a question for you?

A. Because it's important. Suppose this whole thing is just a game?

Q. Yes.

A. Then it would be pointless . . . meaningless. You know what I mean?

Q. If I saw this as meaningless or pointless, it would be because of my reasons and beliefs about what you're saying. But what are YOUR reasons? Why would you suppose it might be pointless?

A. I guess it really wouldn't be. If I made the whole thing up, it would still certainly be relevant to me. (begins to laugh)

Q. Why are you laughing?

A. I guess I was just testing you. (long pause, face contracts as if in pain) This is not a game. It's all true. I sense things and sometimes, without any logic, they happen. It's like having a weird, uncontrollable radar system.

Q. What do you mean?

A. I mean I get this premonition and suddenly three days later it happens. For example, one day, I'm walking on the street where I live and I can sense an accident . . . not mine, but someone else's. Later that week, a young man was hurt in a motorcycle accident on that very same section of the street. Another time, I was about

276

to go to classes, when I just decided not to go, feeling it would be a waste of time. But I never cut classes unless I'm really sick. When I realized what I was doing I couldn't believe it. Then, suddenly, I began to sense the instructor had died. God, sure enough, I get a call from my friend who tells me Professor Soren did die that morning. (She begins to cry.)

Q. WHAT ARE YOU UNHAPPY ABOUT?

A. About knowing. I don't want to know.

Q. WHY DOES THAT MAKE YOU UNHAPPY?

A. I have to sit and wait for it to happen. It makes me part of it.

Q. What do you mean when you say you're part of it?

A. Well, I know. I know in advance. Wouldn't that make me part of it?

Q. What do you think?

A. Yes. It would.

Q. DO YOU BELIEVE THAT?

A. Well . . . I think so, but I'm not sure why. It's awful being responsible.

Q. WHAT ARE YOU AFRAID WOULD HAPPEN IF YOU WEREN'T UPSET ABOUT BEING RESPONSIBLE?

A. If I wasn't upset, then I'd really be a monster!

Q. What do you mean?

A. I care about other people!

Q. Are you saying that being upset shows you care about people?

A. Yes.

Q. Why?

A. Why? (long pause) Well, if I didn't get upset, then I would be unfeeling. (long sigh) That's not necessarily true. Just yesterday, a dear friend was very troubled by a problem she had. I tried to help her with it, but I wasn't upset . . . yet, I really still cared.

Q. Okay then, DO YOU BELIEVE YOU HAVE TO BE UPSET TO BE A CARING PERSON?

A. No, I don't. And that really helps. I suddenly feel a little disconnected from all that misery. But, to tell the truth, I'm still unhappy about having premonitions.

Q. Why does that make you unhappy?

A. Because I still don't want them. I don't want to know

all those things that other people don't seem to be aware of.

Q. Sure, I understand you don't want to know, but why are you unhappy that you do know?

A. I guess it goes back again to responsibility.

Q. What do you mean?

A. Like I should stop certain things from occurring if I could . . . otherwise, why would I have the premonition?

Q. Why do you think?

A. God, I really don't know. It seems like I'm responsible.

Q. DO YOU BELIEVE THAT?

A. Yes and no.

Q. What's the part of your answer that is "yes"?

A. I'm not really sure. Part of me just believes it and that really makes me super uncomfortable.

Q. WHAT ARE YOU AFRAID WOULD HAPPEN IF YOU WEREN'T UNCOMFORTABLE ABOUT BEING RESPONSIBLE?

A. Wow . . . maybe then I'd be getting them all day. That would be horrible.

Q. WHY?

A. I don't want to have doomsday feelings all day long.

Q. WHY DO YOU BELIEVE if you weren't uncomfortable about your premonitions, they would occur all day?

A. I guess that sounds pretty irrational. It doesn't really make too much sense. I never realized that I believed being comfortable would mean having more. It doesn't mean that at all. I haven't solved it, but it feels like I've just let some of the misery go. A lot of times, my unhappiness is just an immediate reaction to my sixth sense.

Q. What do you mean?

A. I get angry . . . I didn't ask to be psychic.

Q. But why should you get unhappy if you were?

A. I feel like I'm going in circles. Maybe it's me. (pause) I'm sorry, I forgot the question. What was it?

Q. What do you remember?

A. You asked me something about being afraid? Wasn't that it?

Q. What do you think?

A. I don't know. What do I do now?

278

Q. What do you want to do?

A. I guess I got uncomfortable again. I want to answer the question. I'm really afraid if I allow myself to open to this thing, I'll become possessed.

Q. What do you mean by possessed?

A. I'll be sensing things all the time. I couldn't handle that.

Q. Why not?

A. It would be a trap.

Q. In what way?

A. (Her lips begin to quiver as she puts her hands between her thighs.)

Q. What are you feeling?

A. Cold . . . like a shiver just ran through me. Everytime I get into this, I always get this way. Even when I was in grade school. When I would get these feelings, I always got frightened.

Q. What is it about these feelings that frightens you?

A. They're horrid . . . it's like being with the devil (beginning to cry).

Q. What do you mean?

A. I see and sense bad things. That's awful. Sometimes I start to think I must be as horrid as my thoughts.

Q. DO YOU BELIEVE THAT?

A. Then why else would I know these things?

Q. Why do you think?

A. I can't find the answers. I don't know why.

Q. WHAT ARE YOU AFRAID WOULD HAPPEN IF YOU WEREN'T AFRAID OF BEING A "HORRID" PERSON?

A. Then, I would become one (long pause).

Q. Are you saying that by being afraid of becoming a bad person it prevents you from being that way?

A. Yes, that's what I did say and I guess it sounds ridiculous. I suppose I was thinking if I'm not afraid of it, then I might want it. Amazing! What a strange way to think. When I'm afraid, I get crazy. I mean I'm really heavy to be with when I'm anxious or scared (long sigh and closes her eyes).

Q. What are you feeling?

A. That I want to be finished with that whole scene. There's no way I want to keep frightening myself. None of that makes any sense to me anymore. (pause) Okay, if I was just calm about this whole thing, then I would get my next premonition and then . . . then, I might try to tell the other person or even try to change the situation. (seemingly jittery) Oh, that would be insane. The others would just laugh in my face, they wouldn't believe me . . . and worse, they would see me as some kind of freak.

Q. *And if they didn't listen or saw you as a freak, WHY WOULD THAT MAKE YOU UNCOMFORTABLE?*

A. That would hurt.

Q. *What do you mean?*

A. Maybe I'd end up alone. Everybody would avoid me.

Q. *And if your worst fears came to pass and everyone avoided you, WHY WOULD THAT MAKE YOU UNHAPPY?*

A. You know, I never heard that question before. I'll tell you, I never would allow myself to get close to dealing with such a thought. That's one fear I've had for a long, long time. I don't want people to push me away. Yet, right this minute . . . I don't know about tomorrow . . . it would be okay. (Smiling) I guess it's because I just know it wouldn't happen. Sure, some people might run away, but I know others won't. I think if I tried to help someone, I would feel really good about it. Up till now, I've always feared acting on my feelings, but that's changing.

Q. *WHAT DO YOU WANT?*

A. Well, to be comfortable with my premonitions.

Q. *And are you?*

A. Much more so than ever before. I understand more about what I was doing with all that fear. But I still have a sense that something bothers me. I don't know quite what it is.

Q. *If you guess at it, what do you suppose it would be?*

A. I think maybe it has to do with always seeing bad things.

Q. *What do you mean "bad?"*

A. Like knowing about negative events.

Q. *At the early part of our discussion, you referred to your premonitions as a radar system. Maybe an analogy made from your metaphor would help. If a radar system built to give advance warning of storms showed an*

*impending hurricane . . . which resulted in people being
safely evacuated from the area, would you be unhappy
about them knowing that or would you be grateful?*

A. Grateful . . . of course. Ah! (smiling) It starts to get
so clear. If my internal radar system enables me and
others to avoid problems and be safe, it's really just as
wonderful as any other radar system. Suddenly my
curse is beginning to look like a gift. Or maybe a talent.
I never thought of it like that before.

Q. WHAT DO YOU WANT?

A. To use my "radar" system. (She inhales a deep breath,
does ten turns of a Yoga neck exercise, stops gently and
smiles.) About responsibility . . . when weather stations
have radar systems, they don't create the storms, they're
just warning devices. I guess at that point, people have
the choice of listening or not listening. (She jumps from
the chair and begins to pace.) I'm so incredibly excited. What has haunted me all my life, what seemed
like a curse suddenly looks so different. Hey, I remember a situation when I was twelve. I had this feeling a
truck was going to come up on the sidewalk where I
was playing with a friend. So I told my friend to help
me bring my bike around to the back of my house.
Two minutes later, a huge truck, after being side-
swiped, ran up onto the sidewalk where we had been
playing. I was too scared to tell anyone about it. Too
scared to even remember. Yet, you know, I did use
it and what happened was really beautiful for us.

Q. How are you feeling?

A. Like I can see again. Maybe if I'm not afraid I will begin to see . . . and, ah ha! maybe enjoy my premonitions. If I could know when a truck will jump onto the
sidewalk, then I would know all the times it would
be perfectly safe to play there. And that's certainly a
happy knowing!

living option: an open letter

Our journey moves across the last pages of this book, yet the excursion we have begun to take through ourselves can continue. Together, we have accumulated the points of reference and created a blueprint which can always be reviewed and redigested. More than a text, this Option journal can be experienced and shared like the gift of a friend.

We have experienced change as we have come to perceive, understand and discard self-defeating beliefs. As *believing animals,* we have always set our own limits. But it is also within our power and providence to remove those limits or barriers which stifle us . . . for they remain only as living relics of a distrusting and fearful culture.

Our beliefs are judgments, freely made and maintained, yet alterable. *Each of us has the freedom to choose and change.*

It is within our grasp at this very moment. We can be happier and more effective in getting what we want NOW, for "now" is all we have. Perhaps, just reviewing Option concepts has precipitated the movement. For some, once tapped and stimulated, it is just a decision. For most of us, it is a considered evolution.

But for the skeptic, whose hesitancy illustrates a last unwillingness to let go and be done with all the unhappiness, there is a final question. "If I do discard my beliefs of unhappiness, if I come to trust myself and my own nature, if I allow my *knowing*, if I evolve the Option attitude of "to love is to be happy with," if the entire process transforms my perspective, feelings and behavior so that happiness becomes the predominant texture and tone of my life, how do I know I won't be acting alone, cutting myself off from those I love and, in fact, going against the values and wants of my peers?

We learned to be unhappy (acquired beliefs of unhappiness), which in scope and content taught us to move against our flow with self-defeating ramifications. If nothing is wrong with us and nothing ever was, then to listen to the truth of our own nature for guidance and direction is an affirmation of self . . . and an act of trusting our humanity. For some, this thrust might appear anarchistic, selfish and, perhaps, antisocial. Yet, in order to conceive moving in harmony with myself as an act against those around me, I would still have to be believing "something was wrong with me" . . . that in my wanting and moving from my good feelings, I would be acting in a manner harmful to others.

Such a notion is more a statement of fear and distrust, than one of observation. Reality would indicate the opposite is true, for *each of us is wanting the same thing*. Sure, we might use a different vocabulary to describe and express our wanting and pursue different immediate goals, but the essential wanting is the same. The desires for love, for health, for success, for comforts, are wants in service to a prime want . . . to be *happy*.

In my happiness, my movement would then necessarily be consistent and harmonious with others, if they, too, were happy.

It is only through the fog of unhappiness that we move in conflicting directions . . . as if the nature of each of us was radically different, disconnected, unloving and even hostile.

Violence is a product of people acting from their fears and discomforts.

As we become happier, we become more loving and accepting. This increased comfort results in a greater degree of clarity and ease with which we handle our affairs. Such input is beneficial to all involved. Thus, as a happier person, our self-serving efforts not only pay tribute to ourselves, but to those around us.

In our happiness, we move toward what everyone around us wants for us and for themselves.

When I am comfortable and clear, my awareness is that I would want people to be as happy as possible and know their happiness results in their being more loving and less self-defeating . . . which could only be beneficial to me. Even if my lover became alienated by my evolving happiness or my peers were off-balanced by my growing sense of comfort, they, too, if they were happy and non-judgmental, would want for me what I want for myself. And when I am happy, I too would want for them what they want for themselves.

Does that mean when I am happier, I would want for my lover or friends what they want for themselves, even if they are behaving with unhappiness and forming self-destructive involvements? By refraining from judging them or having conditions and expectations attached to my loving, I am in harmony with their wanting by my acceptance and respect for their unhappiness and self-defeating behavior. This does not mean I would still not want them to be happier or would not try to help them to become happier. If they function from discomfort, I can know they are believing it is the best way for them to take care of themselves based on their beliefs. For the moment, *they are doing the very best they can.*

The more loving, more lucid and more caring I become, the more I tend to give people around me the space and freedom to be all they want. It is only when I am encumbered by anxiety and fears that I see the confinement or restriction of others as advantageous to me. Motivating others through anger and threats reaps a self-defeating harvest.

If the universe is inscribed in the core of my nature, imprinted like an indelible mark, then for me to follow me is to follow the universe. Beneath the clouds of discomforts, there is an easy, direct flow. The Option Process is a way to hook into that flow . . . a way of becoming happier. Thus, Option is a path back to ourselves, not so much a rigid tool or learned technique as it is an attitude and a developing process of seeing. *The truths and revelations come through us, rather than to us.* What we confirm and affirm is on no one's authority but our own. We verify what is so based on our *knowing.* No one will stand at the crossroads directing us to the left or right, no one at the blackboard outlining the desired activities. It is for us to decide.

For some, the attitude of "to love is to be happy with" creates the method. For others, the method of the Option dialogues precipitates the attitude. In either case, Option provides a beautiful, loving and mellow route, which cuts through the ambivalence, complexity and judgments of many disciplines . . . giving each of us a blueprint into which we can breathe character and life.

The questions of the dialogue remain clear and simple. What are you unhappy about? Why are you unhappy? Why do you believe that?

Once we peel away the multilayered skin of beliefs which we have been systematically taught and which we have acquired (by acting on them and giving them power), we find our own equilibrium and learn to heed the direction of our inner currents. This expression of our individuality and creativity is an act of nature . . . in conformity with other acts of nature.

If I love by being "happy with" and I am happy by loving, then I take care of the potential of the whole human race while taking care of myself. In living Option, I create a vision and life-style with dramatic and diverse applications.

Each of us now stands on the threshold of endless possibilities. We do not need a hatchet to explore; we had only to give ourselves permission. This book has been but a guide in the journey across the landscape of our beliefs. Its meaning will change from hand to hand. It has been and will be as effective as we want it to be.

As it was for me initially, I suspect just an exposure to Option concepts generates real and lasting changes as we discard old beliefs. We can become our own "therapons" . . . gentle, prodding and accepting second voices for ourselves.

We have only to do it, only to choose to do it. This, then,

becomes *the gift of the Option Process . . . the opportunity for us to give ourselves back to ourselves.* With each new awareness, whether it be of our perfection or stumblings, we are enriched . . . and enriched . . . and enriched. The results of our acts are not indictments, but lessons on which we glide to greater happiness and effectiveness.

We can defrock unhappiness if we want. Significance, intelligence and caring is not measured by the "sensitivity" of discomfort and grief. Thinking and loving is neither dependent on nor enforced by misery. We can, here and now, choose to delight in our humanity not with a melancholy and skeptical indifference, but with a soft, gentle and loving embrace. The walls we have built around us are only monuments to fear. Allowing ourselves to be more loving is a joyful pursuit.

As we live the attitude "to love is to be happy with." as we change, the world around us begins to change . . . not only as a function of our perception, but as a response to our altered input and non-judgmental reaction to people and situations. Those who would fear us or find our happiness threatening might choose to create phantoms where none exist. They might even decide to walk away from us . . . turn in other directions. They, like us, would be doing the best to take care of themselves. But for many, despite the clouds of fear and discomfort, a loving individual ultimately stimulates a loving response.

As happy people, we will find ourselves getting more of what we want and wanting more of what we get. Being everything we ever wanted to be begins here.

Having begun to dispose of the burden of acquired beliefs and judgments which are self-defeating, and having learned to shift gears in perceiving our lives through using the Option Process dialogues, our newly enriched self-acceptance will liberate previously blocked energies and endow us with new power to move comfortably and lovingly with ourselves and our lives.

"I am you and you are me . . . and we are one together." If you are wanting, Option is now yours to live and to pass on.

287

*We are all on the same path
. . . trying to become happier.
The pages of this book
represent the best of who
I am . . . when I'm there.*